CW00944093

Family Law

Family Law

P J Pace

LLB(Lond), LLM(Manc),
Barrister, Principal Lecturer in Law,
Manchester Polytechnic

Fourth Edition

THE M & E HANDBOOK SERIES

Pitman Publishing
128 Long Acre, London WC2E 9AN

A Division of Longman Group UK Limited

First published 1981
Second edition 1984
Third edition 1986
Fourth edition 1992

© Longman Group UK Ltd 1986, 1992

A CIP catalogue record for this book is available from the British Library.

ISBN 0 7121 0748 7

All rights reserved; no part of this publication may be
reproduced, stored in a retrieval system, or transmitted in any
form or by any other means, electronic, mechanical, photocopying,
recording, or otherwise without either the prior written
permission of the Publishers or a licence permitting restricted
copying in the United Kingdom issued by the Copyright Licensing
Agency, 90 Tottenham Court Road, London W1P 9HE. This book may
not be lent, resold, hired out or otherwise disposed of by way of trade
in any form of binding or cover other than that in which it is
published, without the prior consent of the Publishers.

Typeset by FDS Ltd, Penarth
Printed and bound in Singapore

Contents

Part two   The economic aspects of marriage

Part three   Children

Preface

Family law, like so many areas of law, is predominantly concerned with the cataloguing of human failings, and it is difficult not to feel some sympathy with the seventeenth century poet and rake (not necessarily in that order), John Wilmot, the Second Earl of Rochester, when he wrote long before the days of sex equality:

'To all young men that live to woo,
To kiss and dance, and tumble too;
Draw near and counsel take of me,
Your faithful pilot I will be;
Kiss who you please, Joan, Kate or Mary,
But still this counsel with you carry,
    Never marry.'

It is to the conspicuous failure of both young men and young women to heed this advice that this book is dedicated.

It is intended that this book should provide a succinct and simplified introduction to the substantive part of most family law courses, whether degree or professional. This is not to say, however, that criticism of the existing law and proposals for reform are ignored.

To those familiar with the M & E Handbook series, it will come as no surprise to find that each chapter concludes with a progress test. For those unfamiliar with this device, it is strongly urged that, having worked through the text two or three times, the progress test should be attempted under examination conditions. This provides a useful method of checking that the relevant parts of the text have been assimilated.

I should like to record my thanks to the Senate of the University of London and to Manchester Polytechnic for their permission to reproduce the past examination questions set out in Appendix 3.

Since the publication of the 3rd edition (with Update) in 1987, the major event in Family Law has undoubtedly been the enactment of the Children Act 1989 (operative from 14 October 1991). Part three of this edition has been substantially re-written to take account of the sweeping changes made by this Act to so many aspects of the law relating to the upbringing of children. The opportunity has also been taken to update the rest of the contents from materials available to me in November 1991.

It is probable that the Law Commission's proposals in *Family Law: Ground for Divorce* (Law Com No. 192, 1990) will soon see the light of legislative day. Nonetheless, I have decided to retain the material relating to the 'facts' for divorce, if only to mark my reluctance to bid a fond farewell to such Family Law favourites as adultery and desertion.

November 1991   PJP

Table of cases

Table of statutes

Abbreviations

C.A.	Children Act.
C.E.A.	Civil Evidence Act.
C.Y.P.A.	Children and Young Persons Act.
D.M.P.A.	Domicile and Matrimonial Proceedings Act.
D.P.M.C.A.	Domestic Proceedings and Magistrates' Court Act.
D.V.M.P.A.	Domestic Violence and Matrimonial Proceedings Act.
F.L.R.A.	Family Law Reform Act.
M.C.A.	Matrimonial Causes Act.
M.F.P.A.	Matrimonial and Family Proceedings Act.
Mag. C.A.	Magistrates' Courts Act.
M.P.(M.C.)A.	Matrimonial Proceedings (Magistrates' Courts) Act.
M.P.P.A.	Matrimonial Proceedings and Property Act.
M.W.P.A.	Married Women's Property Act.
S.C.A.	Supreme Court Act.

Part one

Marriage and its breakdown

1
Introduction

The scope and development of family law

1. The scope of family law

The word 'family' may be variously defined but English family law is primarily concerned with the family unit which consists of a husband and wife and their children, if any. In other words, family law is essentially concerned with the rights and obligations which flow from marriage. The traditional importance to society of the institution of marriage is evidenced by the fact that a mass of legal rules has developed to govern not only its formation, functioning and dissolution, but also the personal and proprietary rights and obligations existing between the members of the family unit. A vivid example of the value society may place upon the family and the institution of marriage is provided by the provisions of Article 41 of the Irish Constitution of 1937, among which are the following:

> 'The State recognises the Family as the natural primary and fundamental unit group of Society, and as a moral institution possessing inalienable and imprescriptible rights, antecedent and superior to all positive law . . .
> The State pledges itself to guard with special care the institution of Marriage, on which the Family is founded, and to protect it against attack.
> No law shall be enacted providing for the grant of a dissolution of marriage.'

Family law is also concerned with the transfer of a child from one family to another by way of adoption, the assumption of parental rights by persons outside the family by way of, e.g. wardship or guardianship, and the one-parent family, whether this arises from the dissolution of the marriage, the death of one of the spouses or the care of a child by an unmarried parent.

A feature of modern society is the increasing number of people who choose to live together and have children outside the institution of marriage. To what extent legal recognition should be given to these *de facto* relationships is a matter of policy. Although English law has not gone as fas as, e.g. the South Australian Family Relationships Act 1975, which provides that in certain circumstances and for certain purposes a person living with another as *de facto* husband or wife will be regarded as the putative spouse of that other and be entitled to the same rights and benefits as a lawful spouse, there are instances where the law affords some measure of legal recognition to extra-marital relationships, but not as part of any consistent policy. Thus a party to a *de facto* marriage may seek protection from domestic violence under the Domestic Violence and Matrimonial Proceedings Act 1976, may claim an interest in property under the doctrine of the constructive trust as in *Cooke* v. *Head* (1972) C.A., may claim provision out of the estate of the deceased partner under the Inheritance (Provision for Family and Dependants) Act 1975 and, if the father of a child, may be given parental responsibility for it under the Children Act 1989.

It is clear, therefore, that as family law is concerned with the special legal relationship which arises between the parties to a marriage and their children, it is a part of 'private law'. Insofar as it is also concerned with the relationship between those persons and the state, as a result of the pervasive effect of the welfare state, it is a part of 'public law'.

2. The historical development of family law

In order to be able to obtain a proper perspective on the modern law and to gain a better understanding of some parts of it, it is helpful to have some idea of the factors which have shaped its evolution. These factors are considered in outline in **3–5** below.

3. The development of the law in relation to matrimonial causes

Before the Reformation the law of marriage was the canon

law of the Roman Catholic church as enforced by the ecclesiastical courts. As canon law adhered to the doctrine of the indissolubility of marriage, the ecclesiastical courts had no power to grant a decree of divorce *a vinculo matrimonii*, which would enable the parties to remarry. The decrees available were limited to those of:

(a) nullity, which were declaratory of the fact that there had never been a marriage;

(b) restitution of conjugal rights; and

(c) divorce *a mensa et thoro*, which did not dissolve the marriage but merely relieved the petitioner from the duty to cohabit with the respondent.

After the Reformation the authority of the Crown over the ecclesiastical courts replaced that of the Pope but the principles applied therein remained those of the canon law. The only way in which a divorce *a vinculo matrimonii* could be obtained was by a private Act of Parliament, which was prohibitively expensive and obtainable only in limited circumstances.

In 1857 jurisdiction in matrimonial causes was transferred from the ecclesiastical courts to the newly created Divorce Court by the Matrimonial Causes Act of that year. This Act abolished the doctrine of the indissolubility of marriage by giving the Divorce Court jurisdiction to grant decrees of divorce *a vinculo matrimonii*. Decrees *a mensa et thoro* became known as decrees of judicial separation. The Act specifically provided that in all proceedings, other than those for the dissolution of marriage, the Court should conform as far as possible to the canonical principles.

In 1875, as a result of the reforms of 1873 and 1875, the jurisdiction of the Divorce Court was transferred to the Probate, Divorce and Admiralty Division of the High Court, re-named the Family Division in 1970.

After the 1857 Act successive Matrimonial Causes Acts extended the grounds upon which decrees of nullity and divorce could be obtained and equalised the rights of the spouses in these matters.

As a result of growing dissatisfaction with the matrimonial offence as the basis of divorce and the desire to 'buttress, rather than undermine, the stability of marriage, and when, regrettably, a marriage has irretrievably broken down, to enable the empty legal shell to be destroyed with the maximum fairness and the minimum bitterness, distress and humiliation' (Law Commission, *Reform of the Grounds of Divorce, The Field of Choice*, Cmnd. 3123, 1966), the Divorce Reform Act 1969 introduced the concept of the irretrievable breakdown of marriage as the sole ground for divorce.

The present statutory basis for most of the modern law relating to matrimonial causes is the consolidating Matrimonial Causes Act of 1973 as amended by the Matrimonial and Family Proceedings Act 1984.

The next stage is likely to be the reform of divorce whereby the sole ground for divorce will continue to be the irretrievable breakdown of marriage but it will no longer be evidenced by one of five facts. Instead, such breakdown will be evidenced by the expiration of one year from the lodging at court of a formal statement that the marriage has irretrievably broken down. This was the recommendation of the Law Commission in *Family Law: The Grounds for Divorce* (1990) (Law Com No. 192).

4.   The development of family law in relation to property

The early law which applied to the property and finances of spouses was aptly characterised by the aphorism that in law 'husband and wife are one and that one is the husband'. Thus, at common law, during the subsistence of the marriage property rights vested in the husband to the exclusion of the wife, but he was given the corresponding duty to maintain her unless her conduct disentitled her.

Although equity ameliorated the strictness of the common law rule, it was not until the Married Women's Property Acts of the late nineteenth and early twentieth centuries that a wife was given the same legal capacity to hold and dispose of property as any other adult with full legal capacity. Thus the doctrine of separate property was introduced into matrimonial law.

This doctrine, coupled with the increasing tendency for a wife to be a wage-earner as well as her husband, rendered the husband's obligation to maintain his wife an anachronism. This is recognised in modern legislation concerned with financial provision for spouses, whereunder the rights and duties of spouses in this respect are equal.

The matrimonial home has played an important role in the

recent history of family law. As it will be most families' likeliest bulwark against rapidly rising inflation, the ownership of the matrimonial home is often a matter of dispute between spouses. Cases under s. 17 of the Married Women's Property Act 1882 have emphasised that ordinary rules of property law apply in determining this question. This has been seen to be inappropriate in the context of what may fairly be regarded as a family asset, and has led to proposals for reform along the lines of a system of community of property between spouses.

The right to occupy the matrimonial home, particularly in view of more widespread recognition of what has come to be known as the 'battered wife' syndrome, has received legislative attention in the form of the Matrimonial Homes Act 1967 (re-enacted in 1983), the Domestic Violence and Matrimonial Proceedings Act 1976 and exclusion orders under s. 16 of the Domestic Proceedings and Magistrates' Courts Act 1978.

5. The development of family law in relation to children

There are two major trends to be seen under this heading. First, just as the wife was gradually able to assert her independence from her husband in property matters, so too the law granted her equal recognition with him *vis-à-vis* their legitimate children. Secondly, there has been a move away from the enforcement of parental rights towards the advancement of the best interests of the child. This approach, which originated in the Court of Chancery, was first given legislative effect by the Guardianship of Infants Act 1925, s. 1 and re-enacted in the Guardianship of Minors Act 1971, s. 1. The Children Act of 1989 has put the welfare of children at the heart of the law relating to the upbringing of children. The Act has created new types of order relating to such upbringing, consolidated the previously fragmented powers of the courts to order financial relief for children, and reformed the law relating to local authority powers and duties in respect of children.

The general supervisory power of the Court of Chancery, which arose from its exercise of the duty of the Crown, as *parens patriae*, to protect children within the realm, was transferred to the Chancery Division of the High Court in 1875, and to this was added in 1926 the power to make adoption orders.

The courts administering family law

6. Magistrates' courts

These deal with a substantial number of family law matters as they provide a relatively cheap and speedy method of resolving such matters. It should be noted, however, that they do not have the power to dissolve a marriage.

The jurisdiction of magistrates' courts in matrimonial proceedings derives from their criminal jurisdiction. In 1878 magistrates' courts were empowered to make a husband convicted by them of aggravated assault on his wife pay her maintenance. Later Acts extended the grounds of application by a wife, provided grounds with no criminal connotation and allowed a husband a right, more limited than that of the wife, to apply for maintenance.

The grounds of application for a magistrates' order were generally based on the so-called matrimonial offence. After the Divorce Reform Act 1969 had replaced the matrimonial offence as the ground for divorce by the concept of irretrievable breakdown, there was a marked divergence between the law applied in the magistrates' courts under the Matrimonial Proceedings (Magistrates' Courts) Act 1960 and that applied in the divorce courts. In effect there were two different systems of family law operating side by side. This, and other criticisms, led to the enactment of the Domestic Proceedings and Magistrates' Courts Act 1978, almost wholly operative as from 1st February 1981, which brought the law applied by the magistrates in domestic proceedings more in line with divorce law. If the Law Commission's recommendations for the reform of divorce law are enacted, there will be corresponding alterations to the jurisdiction of the magistrates' courts.

7. County courts

County courts were first given jurisdiction in family matters in relation to children. They were later given jurisdiction over a wide range of family matters, e.g. property disputes, adoption and cases involving domestic violence, but a most important extension of jurisdiction was occasioned by the Matrimonial Causes Act 1967. This Act provided that *all* matrimonial causes should *begin* in a *divorce county court*, i.e. a county court so designated by the Lord Chancellor, but only those which were *undefended* should be *tried* there. If a case were to be defended, it had to be transferred to the High Court.

The 1967 Act has been replaced by the Matrimonial and Family Proceedings Act 1984. This restates that every matrimonial cause (i.e. actions for divorce, nullity and judicial separation) must begin in a divorce county court (s. 33 (3)). However, automatic transfer to the High Court should an action be defended has been replaced by a discretionary power to order transfer, at any stage, of the whole or part of the proceedings to the High Court (s. 39). A divorce county court also has jurisdiction to exercise powers under the M.C.A. 1973 in relation to financial relief and the protection of children, but it has no powers under ss. 32, 33, 36 and 38 of the 1973 Act (s. 34).

In 1977 the so-called 'special procedure' was extended to all undefended divorces. Under this procedure the district judge (formerly the county court registrar) registrar decides whether the petitioner is entitled to a decree and, if so, a judge grants a decree nisi in open court without the necessity for either the petitioner or respondent to attend. In such cases the role of the judge is purely formal and divorce partakes of the nature of an administrative act.

8. The High Court

As already mentioned in 3 and 5 above, the jurisdiction of the High Court in relation to matrimonial causes and children is derived from the ecclesiastical courts and the Court of Chancery respectively. In 1875 the former was transferred to the Probate, Divorce and Admiralty Division and the latter to the Chancery Division of the High Court.

In 1970, in order to avoid conflicts between these two Divisions which were possible, for example, if the custody of a child already made a ward of court in the Chancery Division was in question in the divorce proceedings, the Probate, Divorce and Admiralty Division was re-named the Family Division and the above jurisdiction transferred to it.

9. Proposals for reform

Several countries, notably America, Australia and Canada, have established a system of unified family courts. Although there are wide variations in the powers and procedures of these courts, there are several features which are the hallmark of the classic family court. There is an attempt to concentrate in one court the whole range of matters which may affect the family and this, in some instances, may include juvenile crime on the basis that this is seen as a symptom of family breakdown. There is an emphasis on conciliation rather than reconciliation, i.e. the counselling of the parties so that they are better able to deal with family breakdown and its consequences. Such courts also possess their own professional social workers and their proceedings are less adversarial and more inquisitorial, i.e. the court adopts a more positively investigative role instead of acting merely as the referee for the competing parties.

In 1974 the *Report of the Committee on One-Parent Families* (the Finer Report) recommended that a system of family courts should be adopted in England and Wales. However, successive governments have taken no positive steps to implement this proposal on the ground of the costs involved, although it seems that no estimate of the likely cost has ever been produced.

Jurisdiction in matrimonial suits

10. The meaning of jurisdiction
In the present context this term is used to mean the power of a court to hear and determine a particular issue. Thus if the court does not have jurisdiction it must refuse to deal with the matter.

As questions affecting a person's status generally depend upon the law of that person's domicile, it is necessary to explain the meaning of domicile before examining the grounds for the court assuming jurisdiction in particular matrimonial suits.

11. Domicile in general
Domicile signifies the territory which is subject to a single system of law and in which a person has his permanent home. In the case of a federal system of government this territory is usually the state where a person is resident. Thus a person who lives in the U.S.A. will not be domiciled there but will be domiciled in the particular state in which he lives. This general rule may, of course, be altered by statute.

Particular note should be made of the following points:

(a) *Domicile must be distinguished from nationality* which signifies a person's political allegiance to a particular country. Thus a person may be domiciled in one country but be a national of another.
(b) *Everyone must have a domicile* but a person cannot have more than one domicile at any one time: *I.R.C.* v. *Bullock* (1976).
(c) *The English concept of domicile determines a person's domicile*, though this may be subject to statutory exceptions.

12. Domicile of origin

This is *the domicile which every person automatically acquires at birth*. A *legitimate* child takes the domicile of his *father*; an *illegitimate* child takes the domicile of his *mother*. Neither the child's place of birth nor his nationality affect his domicile of origin. The domicile of children is more fully dealt with in **14** below.

13. Domicile of choice

Apart from an unmarried person under the age of sixteen, anyone can change his or her domicile and acquire a new one. This new domicile is known as the *domicile of choice*. The following two elements are necessary for the acquisition of such a domicile:

(a) *Residence.* Until this is established in the new country there can be no change of domicile.
(b) *Animus manendi*, i.e. the intention to reside in the new country for an unlimited period of time.

Though both of these elements must exist, it is not necessary that the *animus* should precede the establishment of the residence.

Animus is often difficult to prove and, whilst almost any incident which throws light on a person's intention may be of evidential value, it seems that greater weight is given to conduct than to mere declarations of intent.

The intention to change domicile must have been freely formed and once the domicile of choice has been acquired this will subsist until a further domicile of choice arises. However, if the domicile of choice is abandoned without a further domicile of choice arising, the domicile of origin automatically revives: *Udny* v. *Udny* (1869) H.L. Here U had a Scottish domicile of origin. He later settled in England and acquired an English domicile of choice. He left England with no intention of returning and went to live in France though he did not intend to settle there. HELD:

When he went to live in France U's English domicile lapsed and, in the absence of another domicile of choice, his Scottish domicile of origin revived.

14. The dependent domicile of children

(a) *Domicile of origin.* The domicile of a legitimate child is that of his father and the domicile of an illegitimate child is that of his mother.

In the case of an adopted child, treated from the date of adoption as if born in lawful wedlock, his domicile of origin is probably unaffected by his adoption.

An illegitimate child later legitimated by the marriage of his parents probably retains his mother's domicile as his domicile of origin.

(b) *Domicile of choice.* An unmarried child under the age of sixteen cannot acquire a domicile of choice. In such a case the child's domicile follows that of his father or mother, according to whether the child is legitimate or illegitimate. However, if both parents of a *legitimate* child are alive but living apart, the child will take his mother's domicile if he has his home with her and no home with his father: s. 4, Domicile and Matrimonial Proceedings Act 1973. Once the child has acquired his mother's domicile in this way, his domicile will follow hers provided he has not thereafter had a home with his father: *ibid*. This is so even after the mother's death unless and until he subsequently has a home with his father: *ibid*.

On the death of his father, a child's domicile follows that of his mother: *Potinger* v. *Wightman* (1817).

On adoption a child acquires the domicile of his adopter, or adoptive father in the case of an adoption by a married couple.

> NOTE: Once a child has attained the age of sixteen, or married before that age, he or she may acquire an *independent* domicile of choice: s. 3, Domicile and Matrimonial Proceedings Act 1973. Sections 3 and 4 of the 1973 Act apply only as from 1st January, 1974. In determining the domicile of a child before that date the common law rules will apply, as to which note that (*a*) a child cannot acquire an independent domicile until his or her majority, and (*b*) a married female child takes her husband's domicile, but if she is widowed her domicile reverts to her father's until her majority.

15. The domicile of married women

The Domicile and Matrimonial Proceedings Act 1973 abolished the common law rule that on marriage a woman automatically acquired her husband's domicile. By s. 1(1) of the Act a married woman may acquire her husband's domicile of choice like anyone else of full capacity. Where a married woman acquired a domicile of dependence before 1st January, 1974, she is to be regarded as retaining it as a domicile of choice (if different from her domicile of origin) until she acquires another one: s. 1(2). Such acquisition requires a change of residence plus *animus*: *I.R.C.* v. *The Duchess of Portland* (1981).

Jurisdiction in particular suits

16. Nullity

By s. 5(3) of the D.M.P.A. 1973 an English court will have jurisdiction in a nullity suit only in the following circumstances:

(a) if either party to the marriage is domiciled in England and Wales on the date the proceedings are begun; or
(b) if either party was habitually resident there for one year ending with that date; or
(c) if either party died before that date and the deceased was either domiciled at death in England and Wales, or had been habitually resident there for one year ending with the date of death. As a voidable marriage can be challenged only by the parties during their joint lives, this ground is applicable only to void marriages (which may be challenged by any interested person (*see* 3:**22**)).

If none of the above applies because the jurisdictional basis no longer exists, but proceedings for divorce, nullity or judicial separation are pending in respect of the same marriage, the court has jurisdiction to entertain later nullity proceedings under s. 5(5).

NOTE: 'Habitual residence' is difficult to define. The Law Commission (*Jurisdiction in Matrimonial Causes*, Law Com. No. 48, 1972) thought the term meant a residence that was more than transient or casual but, once established, it was not necessarily broken by a temporary absence. In *R* v. *Barnet*

London Borough, ex p. Shah (1983) H.L. 'habitual residence' was regarded as synonymous with 'ordinary residence'.

17. Divorce and judicial separation

The court has jurisdiction in the same circumstances as above, except for the provision regarding the death of one of the spouses which obviously has no relevance to either divorce or judicial separation: s. 5(2).

18. Decrees of presumption of death and dissolution of marriage

The court has jurisdiction in the same circumstances as for divorce and judicial separation, provided that the domiciliary and residential requirements are satisfied by the *petitioner*: s. 5(4).

19. Failure to provide reasonable maintenance

If proceedings are brought in the High Court or divorce county court under s. 27 of the Matrimonial Causes Act 1973, the grounds of jurisdiction are as in **17** above plus the respondent's residence in England and Wales on the date of the application (*see* 8:**6, 30**).

If the application is to a magistrates' court under the Domestic Proceedings and Magistrates' Courts Act 1978, the general jurisdictional rule applies, i.e. the court has jurisdiction if at the date of the application either the applicant or the respondent ordinarily resides within the commission area for which the court is appointed: s. 30(1). It is specifically provided in s. 30(5) that jurisdiction is exercisable notwithstanding that any party to the proceedings is not domiciled in England.

Progress test 1

1. What meaning may be attributed to the term 'family law'? **(1)**

2. Trace the development of the law relating to matrimonial causes. **(3)**

3. Trace the development of the law relating to matrimonial property. **(4)**

4. What role did the Court of Chancery play in the development of the law relating to children? **(5)**

5. Outline the development and powers of the courts which have jurisdiction in family law matters. **(6–8)**

6. What is the significance of the term 'family court'? **(9)**

7. Define domicile. Explain the meaning of (*a*) domicile of origin, and (*b*) domicile of choice. **(11–13)**

8. How is the domicile of a child determined? **(14)**

9. How is the domicile of a married woman determined? **(15)**

10. On what basis will English courts exercise jurisdiction in suits for the dissolution of marriage? **(16–18)**

11. When will an English court assume jurisdiction in a case of failure to provide reasonable maintenance? **(19)**

12. H, who was born in Scotland, settled in England where he married W, an Irish girl, in 1973. In 1975 they adopted a Vietnamese baby, X, and the following year they had a child, Y. In 1978 W gave birth to an illegitimate child, Z. On discovering Z was not his child, H went to Canada and took Y with him. H intended not to return to England but did not wish to settle in Canada. W and the two children, X and Z, have recently gone to live in Ireland where W intends to remain. Trace the domicile of H, W, X, Y and Z.

2
Marriage

Definition

1. Marriage defined

Though stated as long ago as 1866, the definition of marriage
for the purposes of English law is still that of Lord Penzance in
Hyde v. *Hyde* (1866), i.e., '*the voluntary union for life of one man and
one woman to the exclusion of all others*'. This definition involves four
elements and requires that the union must be:

(a) *Voluntary*. Though this implies that an involuntary union will
not produce a valid marriage, this is not so as s. 11, M.C.A. 1973
provides that lack of valid consent renders a marriage merely
voidable (*see* Chapter 3). Thus a marriage voidable because of lack
of consent may subsequently be ratified or proceedings to nullify
it may become time-barred, in both of which cases the marriage
will be as valid as any marriage contracted with true consent.

(b) *Capable of lasting for the parties' joint lives*. This seems to be the
meaning of the requirement that the union must be 'for life'. In
Nachimson v. *Nachimson* (1930) C.A. it was said that for the
definition in *Hyde* to be satisfied the parties must intend their
marriage to last for life. This is clearly erroneous since the validity
of a marriage entered into solely for the purpose of being able to
enter this country (*Silver* v. *Silver* (1955)) is not *thereby* called into
question.

(c) *Between persons of the opposite sex*. This is as true today as it was
in 1866. In *Corbett* v. *Corbett* (1970) it was held that sex was
biologically determined once and for all at birth (*see* Chapter 3).
As *Hyde* was a reflection of mid-nineteenth century morality, it
may be questioned whether, and if so why, public policy should

prevent post-operational transsexuals from contracting a valid marriage.

(d) *Monogamous.* English law will not allow a person domiciled in England to contract a valid polygamous marriage here. To attempt to do this may amount to the crime of bigamy. This does not mean, however, that English law does not recognise polygamous marriages for certain purposes (*see* **28** below) or that such a marriage may not be contracted abroad.

The agreement to marry

2. The abolition of breach of promise actions

At one time the breach of an agreement to marry (an 'engagement') gave rise to an action for damages. Probably as a result of changed social values this right of action was abolished by the Law Reform (Miscellaneous Provisions) Act 1970, s. 1(1), which provides that an agreement to marry shall not have contractual effect under English law.

3. Property disputes between engaged couples

(a) *As regards beneficial interests in property.* On the termination of an engagement the law which is used to determine spouses' rights to property in which each or both has or have a beneficial interest (*see* Chapter 7), shall apply equally to any property in which each or both parties to the engagement had a beneficial interest during the currency of the engagement: Law Reform (Miscellaneous Provisions Act 1970, s. 2(1). However, the powers of the court in relation to spouses which arise only on the granting of a decree, e.g. property adjustment under s. 24, M.C.A. 1973, do *not* apply: *Mossop* v. *Mossop* (1988) C.A.

Section 2(2) provides that an action to resolve such a matter may be brought under s. 17 of the Married Women's Property Act 1882 (*see* Chapter 7) within three years of the termination of the engagement.

(b) *As regards gifts between them.* Any gift between engaged persons made on the express or implied condition that it be returned if the engagement is terminated shall be recoverable notwithstanding that the donor terminated the engagement: s. 3(1) of the 1970 Act.

An engagement ring is, somewhat surprisingly, presumed to be an absolute gift. This presumption may be rebutted by proof that the ring was given on the express or implied condition that it was to be returned if the marriage, for whatever reason, did not take place: s. 3(2).

Capacity and formal validity

4.   The contract of marriage
In order to contract a valid marriage the parties must have the capacity to marry (*see* **5** below) and their marriage ceremony must comply with the proper formalities (*see* **6–19** below).

5.   Capacity to marry
Capacity is generally governed by the law of the country in which the parties are domiciled at the time of their marriage, i.e. the *lex domicilii*. This is the so-called *dual domicile theory*. The other theory is that capacity is governed by the law of the country where the parties intended to, and within a reasonable time did, establish their home. This is the law of the *intended matrimonial home theory* and was applied in *Radwan* v. *Radwan (No. 2)* (1972) in relation to capacity to contract a polygamous marriage. This decision has been criticised on various grounds, e.g. its somewhat selective treatment of the authorities, the inherent uncertainty of the theory and the fact that it conflicts with the assumption underlying s. 11(*d*) of the M.C.A. 1973 (*see* 3:4), and, although it was expressly limited to capacity to contract a polygamous marriage, it is questionable whether the law should differ according to which aspect of capacity is under consideration. In *Lawrence* v. *Lawrence* (1985) C.A. the court was divided over the validity of the test in *Radwan* but did not have to reach a conclusion on the matter.

If one party is domiciled in England, the marriage will be regarded as valid by the English courts only if both parties had capacity by English law, even if the marriage was valid by the laws of the country where it was celebrated (the *lex loci celebrationis*): *Sussex Peerage Case* (1844) H.L. (*see Radwan*, above).

If both parties are domiciled abroad and lack capacity to marry by their *lex domicilii*, English courts will treat their marriage as void, even if the parties had capacity by English law: *Sottomayor* v. *De Barros* (1877) C.A.

If one party is domiciled in England and the other party lacks capacity by his or her *lex domicilii*, their marriage will still be regarded as valid in England if both parties have capacity by English law: *Ogden* v. *Ogden* (1908) C.A.

To have capacity by English law the following must be satisfied:

(a) The parties must not be within the prohibited degrees of relationship as set out in the Marriage Acts 1949–86.
(b) Both parties must be aged 16 or over.
(c) Both must be single.
(d) The parties must be of the opposite sex.
(e) The marriage, if celebrated abroad, must not be actually or potentially polygamous.

6. Formal validity

The formalities which must be observed are those prescribed by the law of the country where the marriage is celebrated (the *lex loci celebrationis*), although there are exceptions to this rule.

7. Exception to the *lex loci*

In the following three cases a marriage will be regarded as formally valid in England even though its formalities did not comply with the *lex loci celebrationis*.

(a) If the foreign marriage is formally valid at common law it will be recognised here. The common law formalities require that the parties declare that they take each other as husband and wife (*per verba de praesenti*) and, if the marriage was celebrated in England or Ireland, that the ceremony be performed by an episcopally ordained priest.

A foreign marriage *per verba de praesenti* will be regarded as valid if the circumstances prevented the presence of an episcopally ordained priest as in *Wolfenden* v. *Wolfenden* (1946) where the marriage was celebrated in a provincial mission in China by a minister who was not episcopally ordained. Furthermore, if the parties, usually in the presence of an episcopally ordained priest, married *per verba de praesenti* but did not submit themselves to the local law regarding formalities, the marriage will be regarded as valid here. This principle of submission has been confined to marriages celebrated between members of an occupying force in occupied territory: *Preston* v. *Preston* (1963) C.A.

(b) The Foreign Marriage Acts 1892 to 1947 allow 'a marriage officer' (e.g. a British ambassador, consul or High Commissioner) to solemnise at his official residence a marriage between persons, at least one of whom must be a British subject. Provided the statutory requirements are fulfilled, such 'consular marriages' will be formally valid in England even if formally void where solemnised.

(c) The above Acts also permit a naval, military or air force chaplain, or person authorised by the commanding officer, to solemnise a marriage in any foreign territory, provided that at least one of the parties thereto is a member of Her Majesty's forces serving there.

8.   The formalities for marriages celebrated in England
The Marriage Act 1949 consolidated, but did not reform, the law relating to the formalities of marriage. Though this Act has been supplemented by various enactments, the Law Commission has concluded that the law requires reform and has made proposals to that end (*see* **19** below). The formalities required by law differ according to whether the marriage is an ecclesiastical or civil marriage.

9.   Church of England marriages
By s. 5 of the 1949 Act a Church of England marriage can be solemnised only:

(a) after the publication of banns (*see* **10**),
(b) by authority of a common licence (*see* **11**),
(c) by authority of a special licence (*see* **12**), or
(d) by authority of a superintendent registrar's certificate (*see* **13**).

10. Publication of banns
Publication should be in the parish church or authorised chapel of the parish(es) where the parties reside or which is the usual place of worship of one or both of them.
The publication must be by a Church of England clergyman during morning service on three Sundays preceding the marriage.

The names to be used in the banns are those by which the parties are generally known: *Dancer* v. *Dancer* (1948). If a party's identity is fraudulently concealed, the banns will not have been duly published: *Chipchase* v. *Chipchase* (1941).

> *Dancer* v. *Dancer* (1948): the wife was the legitimate child of Mr and Mrs Knight but after her birth her mother went to live with Mr Roberts and took his name. When the wife, who had discovered her true name was Knight, came to be married the vicar advised her to use the name Roberts in the banns, as she had always used, and was known by, that name. HELD: the banns had been duly published. The wife had used the name Roberts to identify herself correctly not to conceal her true identity.

> *Chipchase* v. *Chipchase* (1941): the banns were published in a name by which the wife had been known for some two years. HELD: as this name had been used mainly to conceal the fact that she had been married before, the banns were not duly published.

> NOTE: the use of a false name does not affect the validity of a marriage by licence in a register office (*see* **15**): *Puttick* v. *Attorney-General and Puttick* (1979).

11. Common licence

This allows the parties to marry without waiting for banns to be published. It is issued by the diocesan registrar or his surrogate and is granted only for the marriage in a church or chapel in the parish where a party has resided for at least 15 days before the grant of the licence, or in a church or chapel which is the usual place of worship of either party. Anyone who wishes to oppose the grant of the licence can do so only by entering a caveat.

12. Special licence

This can be granted only by the Archbishop of Canterbury. Its grant is discretionary and it enables a Church of England marriage to be solemnised at any time, in any place.

13. Superintendent registrar's certificate

This authorises marriage in any church or chapel where banns may be published and which is in the registration district where either party resides or which is the usual place of worship of either.

The Marriage Act 1983 amended the 1949 Act by extending the solemnisation of marriages on the authority of a superintendent registrar's certificate to the marriages of persons who are house-bound, or detained either as a patient in a hospital or as a prisoner, which take place where such persons are for the time being, such place being specified in the notice of marriage and certificate as the place of solemnisation.

14. The marriage ceremony

The following should be noted:

(a) The ceremony must be performed by a clerk in holy orders of the Church of England. Two witnesses must be present and, by implication from the tenor of the 1949 Act, so must both parties.
(b) Unless by special licence, the marriage must be solemnised between 8 a.m. and 6 p.m.
(c) The marriage must be solemnised within three months of the publication of the banns, grant of the licence or notice to the registrar, as the case may be.
(d) The marriage must be solemnised in the church where the banns were published, or the church or chapel specified in the licence or certificate, or other place specified in the certificate.

15. Marriages other than according to the rites of the Church of England

All such marriages may be solemnised only on the authority of a superintendent registrar's certificate, either with or without a licence, or a Registrar General's licence.

(a) *Superintendent registrar's certificate.*
   (*i*) The superintendent registrar of the district where the parties have resided for at least the seven preceding days must be given written notice of the proposed marriage. If the parties reside in different districts, notice must be given to both superintendent registrars.

(*ii*) The notice must be accompanied by a solemn declaration that there is believed to be no impediment to the marriage, that the residential conditions are satisfied and that any necessary consents have been given or dispensed with.

(*iii*) The superintendent registrar must then enter the notice in his marriage notice book and display a copy of the notice, or the notice itself, in a prominent place in his office for 21 successive days, after which the certificate may be issued.

(*iv*) The issue of the certificate may be resisted by the entering of a caveat or by a person whose consent is required to a minor's marriage writing 'forbidden' by the entry. In the latter case a certificate cannot be issued; in the former, issue cannot take place until either the caveat is withdrawn or found to be invalid.

(b) *Superintendent registrar's certificate and licence.* This procedure avoids both the 21-day waiting period and the publicity involved in **(a)**. The position is the same as in **(a)** except that:

(*i*) Notice should be given to the superintendent registrar of the district where *either* party has resided for at least the 15 preceding days, provided the other party is resident in England or Wales.

(*ii*) Neither the notice nor a copy of it need be displayed by the superintendent registrar.

(c) *Registrar General's licence.* Where a person is seriously ill and not expected to recover the Marriage (Registrar General's Licence) Act 1970 confers on the Registrar General a power similar to that possessed by the Archbishop of Canterbury to license a marriage to be solemnised at any convenient time and place. The Registrar General must be satisfied as to the following:

(*i*) Serious illness and no expectation of recovery,

(*ii*) No lawful impediment to the marriage,

(*iii*) Requisite consents have been given,

(*iv*) The party understands the nature and purport of the marriage ceremony,

(*v*) The impossibility of moving the ill person to a place where a normal marriage could be solemnised,

(*vi*) The proposed ceremony must not be according to the rites of the Church of England.

16. Marriage ceremonies on the authority of the superintendent registrar's certificate
The marriage may be solemnised in the following ways:

(a) By a civil ceremony in a superintendent registrar's office.
(b) In a registered building according to such form and ceremony as the parties to the marriage see fit to adopt.
(c) According to the usages of the Society of Friends (Quakers) at any place.
(d) Between two persons professing the Jewish religion, according to the usages of the Jews at any place.
(e) In the place where a house-bound or detained person usually resides.

17. Marriages in naval, military or air force chapels
These marriages are dealt with in Part V of the Marriage Act 1949. At least one of the parties to the marriage has to be a serving member or former regular of one of the services, or a serving member of one of the women's services, or a daughter of any such person.

18. Parental consent to marriage
If a party to a marriage, not being a widow or widower, is under 18, the consent to that marriage of the parent or other persons specified in Schedule 2 of the Marriage Act 1949 must be given unless the court consents or the superintendent registrar or the Registrar General dispenses with consent on the ground that it cannot be obtained because of absence, inaccessibility or disability. If the marriage is celebrated despite non-compliance with this requirement, the marriage is not thereby rendered invalid.

This formal requirement applies to marriages authorised by a common licence, superintendent registrar's certificate with or without a licence and a Registrar General's licence.

19. Proposals for the reform of the law of formalities
The Law Commission (Law Com. No. 53, *Report on Solemnisation of Marriage in England and Wales*, 1973) has made many detailed proposals for the reform of the law of formalities

so as to achieve the maximum simplicity and intelligibility. Some of its more important recommendations are as follows:

(a) There should be uniform civil preliminaries for all marriages wherever celebrated.

(b) The publication of banns before Church of England marriages should no longer be a legal requirement.

(c) Marriage by common licence should be abolished.

(d) Superintendent registrars should be expressly empowered to demand evidence of the termination of any previous marriage.

(e) Parents who consent to a minor's marriage should be required either to attend the register office or to have the signature to their consent witnessed by a person of standing.

(f) The statutory provisions defining the consents required on a minor's marriage should be clarified.

(g) The prescribed words used during the ceremony should emphasise that the marriage is monogamous and should be spoken in English (or Welsh where allowed) or repeated in a language the parties understand.

(h) The offences and penalties should be rationalised and it should be a serious offence to perform, or issue a certificate in respect of, a bogus ceremony.

(i) The reforms should be implemented in a new, comprehensive Marriage Act.

In 1990 the Government published a White Paper setting out proposed reforms relating to formalities. These include the proposal that people should be free to marry wherever they choose in England and Wales in a wide range of building.

The presumption of marriage

20. Introduction

There are three aspects to the presumption of marriage. If there is evidence of a marriage ceremony, this raises a rebuttable presumption, first, that the marriage was formally valid and, secondly, that the parties had capacity to marry. The third aspect of this matter is that if the parties merely cohabit, and hold themselves out, as husband and wife, this raises a rebuttable presumption that they are validly married. It is important to distinguish between these situations as the basic fact in the first two differs from that in the third and the standard of proof required to rebut the presumption may differ in each case.

21. Presumption of formal validity

On proof of the celebration of a marriage which, on proper compliance with the necessary formalities, would produce a marriage valid according to the law where it was celebrated, there arises a presumption that those formalities were complied with. Although it has been suggested that the presumption can be rebutted only by proof beyond reasonable doubt (*Mahadervan* v. *Mahadervan* (1962)), this view has probably not survived *dicta* in *Blyth* v. *Blyth* (1966) H.L. which lends support to the contention that the standard of proof in matrimonial cases is the ordinary civil standard of proof on a balance of probabilities (*see* 4:**7**).

22. Presumption of capacity to marry

Proof of a ceremony of marriage raises a presumption that the parties had capacity to marry and also gave true consent. It seems that the presumption may be rebutted by less weighty evidence than that necessary to rebut the presumption of formal validity.

The presumption of capacity is very often linked with the presumption of death and most commonly concerns the second marriage of a person whose first spouse disappeared some time ago but where there is no conclusive evidence of that spouse's death. If the person marries again in the erroneous belief that his first spouse is dead, the question of his capacity so to marry arises. According to *Chard* v. *Chard* (1956) the common law presumption of death operates if three conditions are satisfied:

(a) the person whose death is in question must not have been heard of for a continuous period of seven years or more,

(b) there are persons who would be likely to have heard of him during that period, and

(c) all due enquiries appropriate to the circumstances have been made.

NOTES: (1) The period of absence must be at least seven years, not, e.g. four, as in *Re Peete* (1952).

(2) Even if the period of absence is greater than seven years, a failure to make enquiries appropriate to the circumstances

will prove fatal, as in *Bradshaw* v. *Bradshaw* (1956) where a wife failed to enquire of the military authorities as to the whereabouts of her husband who, when she last saw him, was a soldier.

23. Presumption from cohabitation and repute

If the parties have lived together as husband and wife, there is a presumption that they did so in consequence of a valid marriage. This presumption may be rebutted if the contrary is 'clearly proved', though whether this means the same standard of proof as is required to rebut the presumption of formal validity is not clear. This type of common law marriage is the only type of irregular marriage recognised in Scotland.

Recognition of polygamous marriages

24. The need for recognition

With the increased influx into this country of persons who may have contracted a valid polygamous marriage abroad, circumstances may arise in which an English court finds it necessary to decide the extent of the effect of that marriage in this country. Thus, for example, the court may have to determine to what extent a polygamously married wife can claim social security, or whether such a wife can conspire with her husband to commit a crime, or whether a polygamously married widow may claim under the Fatal Accidents Act 1976.

25. Potentially polygamous marriages

If the law which determines the nature of the marriage allows a person to have more than one spouse at any one time, this marriage is regarded as polygamous notwithstanding that at the time the issue is raised that person has neither exercised the right nor intends to.

26. Which law determines the nature of a marriage?

Though there is some judicial authority for the view that it is the law of the matrimonial domicile which determines whether a marriage is monogamous or polygamous (*see*, e.g. *Warrender* v. *Warrender* (1835) H.L.; *Russ* v. *Russ* (1962)), the better view is that it is determined by the *lex loci celebrationis*. Thus in *Re Bethell* (1888) the husband had married his wife, a member of an African tribe which recognised only polygamy, in Bechuanaland according to tribal rites. After the husband's death a child was born to his widow and the question arose whether, for the purpose of inheritance under an English will, this child was legitimate. HELD: although the husband had an English domicile at the date of his marriage, that marriage was polygamous and void, and the child was consequently illegitimate.

27. Mutability of the nature of a marriage
    The nature of a marriage is not immutably fixed at its inception. A *potentially* polygamous marriage (i.e. where a polygamously married spouse has not yet taken a second spouse) will become monogamous in certain circumstances and the reverse may be possible.
    A potentially polygamous marriage will become monogamous if an event occurs which precludes the practice of polygamy. Examples of such an event are:

(a) *The birth of a child. Cheni* v. *Cheni* (1962): Jews domiciled in Egypt were married there under a law which allowed the husband a second wife if his wife did not give birth within ten years. On the birth of a child two years later the marriage became monogamous.
(b) *A change of religion. Sinha Peerage Case* (1939) H.L.: The question for the House of Lords' Committee of Privileges was whether the claimant could succeed to his father's hereditary peerage. His parents, Hindus domiciled in India, had married in polygamous form. Shortly before the claimant's birth, his parents joined a Hindu sect which practised monogamy and his father belonged to this sect until his death. The Committee found that it was the father's intention to contract a monogamous marriage and, accordingly, the claimant could succeed to his father's peerage.
(c) *A change in the lex loci celebrationis forbidding polygamy. Parkasho* v. *Singh* (1967): the Hindu Marriage Act 1955 converted polygamous Sikh marriages into monogamous marriages thereby allowing the English court to have matrimonial jurisdiction in respect of a marriage affected by the Act.
(d) *A change of domicile to a country which does not allow polygamy. Ali*

v. *Ali* (1966): the spouses were domiciled in India and contracted a valid polygamous marriage there. They later came to England and the wife left her husband. He later acquired an English domicile and the parties instituted divorce proceedings. Whether the court had jurisdiction depended upon whether the marriage, at the time of the proceedings, was polygamous or monogamous. HELD: the husband's acquisition of an English domicile had converted the marriage into a monogamous one.

NOTE: as a wife can now acquire a domicile separate from that of her husband (*see* 1:15), the question may arise whether *Ali* v. *Ali* applies if only one spouse acquires a domicile in a country which does not allow polygamy.

(e) *Apparently, a second marriage ceremony in monogamous form.* *Ohochuku* v. *Ohochuku* (1960): the spouses, who had contracted a potentially polygamous marriage in Nigeria, had later gone through a marriage ceremony in monogamous form in England, whilst still retaining their Nigerian domicile. The court did not then have the power to dissolve the first marriage, it being polygamous, but did grant a decree of divorce in respect of the second.

NOTE: insofar as a decree dissolves a status and not a particular ceremony (*Thynne* v. *Thynne* (1955) C.A.), the court seems to have regarded the monogamous ceremony as effecting a conversion of the parties' polygamous status. Though this was not a case involving bigamy or perpetuating polygamy, it is arguable that as the parties were already validly married they could not validly marry again, in which case the second ceremony was a nullity and they were still validly polygamously married.

It should be noted that a potentially polygamous marriage will not be converted into a monogamous one merely by a promise to convert it at a later date: *Sowa* v. *Sowa* (1961) C.A.; there must actually be an event or occurrence as above.

Logically the above methods of changing the character of a marriage should apply so as to effect a change from monogamy to polygamy and there is some slight authority for this view, *see Cheni* v. *Cheni* (1962) (*obiter*) and *A-G of Ceylon* v. *Reid* (1965) P.C.; *cf. Drammeh* v. *Drammeh* (1970) P.C. in which a husband's change of

religion to one practising polygamy was said by the Privy Council
not to have changed the character of his monogamous marriage.

28. The effect in English law of a polygamous marriage

In view of the widespread recognition afforded to polygamous
marriages, the position was well summed up by Lord Parker C J
in *Mohamed* v. *Knott* (1968) when he said that polygamous
marriages are recognised here 'unless there is some strong reason
to the contrary'. Some examples of such recognition are as follows:

(a) The parties to the marriage, whether actually or potentially
polygamous, are entitled to all the forms of matrimonial relief
available under English law: s. 47(1), M.C.A. 1973. This includes:

  (*i*)   divorce, nullity and judicial separation;
  (*ii*) a decree of presumption of death and dissolution;
  (*iii*) orders for financial provision in cases of failure to
          maintain under s. 27 of the Act;
  (*iv*) all the powers exercisable by the High Court or divorce
          county court in connection with the above;
  (*v*)   orders of a magistrates' court under Part 1 of the Domestic
          Proceedings and Magistrates' Courts Act 1978; and
  (*vi*) declarations as to the validity of a marriage.

NOTE: where a marriage is *actually* polygamous, the taking of
another spouse or sexual intercourse with such spouse would,
respectively, probably not amount to behaviour such that the
petitioner cannot reasonably be expected to live with the
respondent, and will not be adultery: *Onobrauche* v. *Onobrauche*
(1978) (*see* 4:4), though it may provide just cause for leaving:
Quoraishi v. *Quoraishi* (1985) C.A.

(b) A valid polygamous marriage constitutes a bar to the
subsequent contracting of a monogamous marriage here:

  Baindail v. *Baindail* (1946) C.A.: the husband, who was
  domiciled in India and polygamously married to an Indian
  woman, married an English woman in England during the
  subsistence of his polygamous marriage. HELD: as the
  polygamous marriage was recognised as valid, the second
  ceremony was void.

NOTE: (1) Though this did not involve a later marriage between the same parties, this decision casts doubt on the correctness of the first instance decision in *Ohochuku* v. *Ohochuku* (1960) (**27** above).

(2) For the purposes of the criminal law, a charge of bigamy cannot be based on a first marriage which is polygamous, unless it has become monogamous before the second ceremony: *R.* v. *Sagoo* (1975) C.A. Somewhat inconsistently, it seems that polygamously married spouses are 'married' for the purpose of the crime of conspiracy and cannot, therefore, conspire together: *Mawji* v. *R* (1957) P.C., and s. 2(2)(*a*), Criminal Law Act 1977.

(c) The children of a potentially (*Sinha Peerage Case* (1939) H.L.) and actually (*Hashmi* v. *Hashmi* (1972)) polygamous marriage are regarded as legitimate under English law. However, children of an actually polygamous marriage will not be able to succeed to an entailed interest in English land, or an English title of honour.
(d) Social security benefits are available in respect of a polygamous marriage for as long as it is *de facto* monogamous.
(e) A polygamous marriage will be recognised for the purposes of s. 17, Married Women's Property Act 1882 (*Chaudhry* v. *Chaudhry* (1976) C.A.) and for the purposes of the Matrimonial Homes Act 1983 (s. 10(2)).

Progress test 2

1. What criticisms may be advanced against the definition of marriage for the purposes of English law? To what extent do you think such criticisms are valid? **(1)**

2. What effect has an engagement on the proprietary interests of the parties thereto? **(2–3)**

3. What are the basic requirements for a valid marriage under English law? **(4–6)**

4. What determines whether a party has capacity to marry under English law? **(5)**

5.   What law determines whether a marriage is formally valid? **(6–7)**

6.   Outline briefly the formalities necessary for a marriage celebrated in accordance with the rites of the Church of England.   **(8–14)**

7.   Outline briefly the other forms of marriage open to intending spouses under English law other than according to the rites of the Church of England.   **(15–17)**

8.   What consents are required to the marriage of a minor?   **(18)**

9.   What reforms do you think are necessary to the law relating to the formalities required of marriages celebrated in England?   **(19)**

10. What do you understand by the 'presumption of marriage'? **(20–23)**

11. Why is it important to decide whether a foreign marriage may be recognised as valid under English law?   **(24)**

12. What do you understand by the term 'polygamous marriage'? What law determines the nature of a marriage? **(25–26)**

13. In what circumstances is it possible for a polygamous marriage to become monogamous? Is the reverse possible? **(27)**

14. To what extent may a polygamous marriage be recognised in England?   **(28)**

15. W went out to Redland as a nurse to help a relief agency operating there in the civil war. She met and fell in love with H, an English doctor, and in the presence of the director of the agency she and H exchanged vows to become husband and wife. Shortly afterwards W was captured by Government forces and disappeared. H returned to England and later married Miss Y. W has now reappeared and H wishes to know what his marital status is. Advise him.

16. W, a Newlandian, married H, an Englishman, in the Newlandian embassy in London. By Newlandian law a woman is allowed to have up to two husbands at any one time. The parties intended to live in Newlandia and they established their matrimonial home there. W later went through a ceremony of marriage with A. H was unable to accept this situation and returned to England where he met Miss B. He now wishes to marry Miss B. Can he do so?

3
Nullity suits

Introduction

1. Introduction
Although the parties may have gone through a ceremony of marriage and cohabited as husband and wife, certain defects may exist which render that marriage void *ab initio* or merely voidable.

(a) *Marriages void ab initio*. These are marriages in which the defect is such that the law regards the marriage as never having taken place. The parties may, therefore, treat the marriage as void without having recourse to the court though, as we shall see later, this course of action has its disadvantages. If a marriage is void, a decree of nullity is declaratory and effects no change of status.

(b) *Voidable marriages*. These exist as valid marriages unless and until a decree absolute of nullity is granted in respect of them. If a marriage is voidable, a decree of nullity does operate to change the parties' status.

(c) *Importance of the distinction*. The consequences arising from the distinction between void and voidable marriages are important and are dealt with more fully below (*see* **21–22**).

(d) *Nullity of Marriage Act 1971*. This Act, repealed and re-enacted in the Matrimonial Causes Act 1973, applied to marriages which took place *after* July 31, 1971, i.e. the date on which the 1971 Act took effect, hence the significance of this date in the 1973 Act.

2. Is the marriage void or voidable?
Deciding whether a marriage is void or voidable depends upon whether the marriage was celebrated before August 1, 1971 or

after July 31, 1971. If the former, the old law applies. If the latter, the provisions of the M.C.A. 1973 apply.

Void marriages

3. Grounds rendering a marriage void

As noted above the grounds which will render a marriage void *ab initio* depend upon when the marriage was celebrated, though in some cases the 1971 Act did not change the then existing law. Thus:

(a) *whenever the marriage was celebrated,* lack of capacity and formal defects make a marriage void;

(b) if the marriage was *celebrated before August 1, 1971,* lack of consent and polygamy based upon capacity as determined by the law of the intended matrimonial home will automatically invalidate the marriage;

(c) if the marriage was *celebrated after July 31, 1971,* polygamy based upon capacity as determined by the law of a party's antenuptial domicile will invalidate the marriage.

4. Lack of capacity

This may arise in the following ways:

(a) Where the marriage is between parties within the prohibited degrees of relationship: Marriage Act 1949, s. 1(1) and M.C.A. 1973, s. 11(*a*).

These relationships may arise either from consanguinity (blood) or affinity (marriage). The Marriage (Enabling) Act 1960 continued the relaxation of these prohibitions, first begun in 1907, by providing that a spouse might marry into the family of his former spouse, e.g. his sister-in-law, whether the previous marriage ended by death, divorce or nullity. The Marriage (Prohibited Degrees of Relationship) Act 1986 permits marriages between a man and his step-daughter, step-granddaughter, mother-in-law and his son's former wife if certain conditions are fulfilled.

NOTE: a marriage will be void if the provisions of the Royal Marriages Act 1772 (which applies to descendants of King George II) are not observed.

(b) Where *either* party is under the age of sixteen: Marriage Act 1949, s. 2 and M.C.A. 1973, s. 11(*a*).

In *Pugh* v. *Pugh* (1951) an adult man domiciled in England married a 15-year-old Hungarian girl in Austria. Though the marriage was valid by both Hungarian and Austrian law, it was void by English law since the man had no capacity to marry a girl under sixteen.

(c) Where one of the parties is already validly married, i.e. a 'bigamous marriage': M.C.A. 1973, s. 11(*b*).

(d) Where the parties are not respectively male and female: M.C.A. 1973, s. 11(*c*).

That this was also a ground rendering a marriage void before the Nullity of Marriage Act 1971 was operative is shown by the judgments of Ormrod J in *Talbot* v. *Talbot* (1967) (two women) and *Corbett* v. *Corbett* (1970) (two men).

> *Corbett* v. *Corbett* (1970): the respondent, who had been registered at birth as male, took the female sex hormone, oestrogen, and developed breasts and a feminine appearance. He later underwent a so-called 'sex-change' operation which involved the removal of his male sex organs and the construction of an artificial vagina. He thereafter lived and dressed as a woman. Knowing these facts the male petitioner went through a ceremony of marriage with the respondent. Soon after the marriage the petitioner sought a decree of nullity on the ground that, *inter alia*, the respondent was a male. HELD: as marriage is essentially heterosexual in character, the criteria for determining an individual's sex must be biological. As the respondent had male chromosomes, gonads and genitals he was a male, notwithstanding that he was psychologically a transsexual. As the parties to the marriage were both male, the marriage was void. It was said that if the biological criteria did not all point to the same conclusion, greater weight would probably be given to the genital criterion.

> NOTE: (1) This decision has been criticised because, it has been argued, too little weight was given to the psychological aspects. *Corbett* has not been followed in some American States because of this view. In New Jersey, for example, it has been held that, for marital purposes, sexual identity is to be

determined by the congruence of anatomical and psychological sex: *M.T.* v. *J.T.* (1976).

(2) *Corbett* stresses that the capacity for heterosexual intercourse is an essential element of marriage and the lack of such capacity was a reason for rendering the marriage void in that case. On this view the marriage of a person who has no such capacity because of, e.g. age or injury, would be void. However, this is not one of the grounds which renders a marriage void. Furthermore, if, after a valid marriage, a person discovers he is a transsexual and has his anatomy adapted to conform with his chosen sex, does the marriage then automatically become void notwithstanding that the parties are biologically of the opposite sex?

(3) The principle in *Corbett* has been applied in criminal law (*R* v. *Tan* (1983) C.A.) and accepted as valid by the European Court of Human Rights in *Rees* v. *U.K.* (1967) and *Cossey* v. *U.K.* (1990).

(e) Where a party domiciled in England and Wales contracts an actual or potentially polygamous marriage outside England and Wales: M.C.A. 1973, s. 11(*d*).

In *Hussain* v. *Hussain* (1982) C.A. the husband, domiciled in England, married, in Pakistan, his wife who was domiciled there, under a law which allowed only a husband to marry a second spouse. As the parties' personal laws prevented them from contracting an actually polygamous marriage, their marriage was monogamous and fell outside s. 11(*d*).

This ground clearly envisages that capacity in relation to contracting a polygamous marriage is to be determined by the dual domicile test (*see* 2:5). However, at common law the test to be applied in such cases has been held to be that of the intended matrimonial home. In *Radwan* v. *Radwan (No. 2)* (1972) a woman domiciled in England went through a ceremony of marriage in the Egyptian Consulate General in Paris with a domiciled Egyptian. The man already had a wife in Egypt where the parties intended to establish their matrimonial home. HELD: as the parties intended to live in Egypt where polygamy was permitted, the marriage was valid.

NOTE: the test of the intended matrimonial home has been criticised because, where questions of status are concerned, certainty is important and the test is less certain than the dual domicile test.

The Law Commission (Working Paper No. 83, 1982) provisionally recommended that s. 11(*d*) should be amended so that it will apply only to actually polygamous marriages. This reform was thought necessary because of the difficulties caused by the decision in *Hussain*, i.e.:

(a) *Hussain* does not apply to Scotland and it is undesirable that there should be a difference of approach where issues are dealt with on a United Kingdom basis, e.g. immigration, nationality and social security;

(b) the practical effect of *Hussain* is to restrict s. 11(*d*) to certain marriages entered into by men, but not women;

(c) *Hussain* might cause difficulties as regards the rights of the first wife where the husband later abandons his English domicile and validly marries a second wife;

(d) if *Radwan*, which was not cited in *Hussain*, is correct, an actually polygamous marriage contracted abroad between spouses intending to live in England will be void under s. 11(*b*) wherever the spouses are domiciled, whereas it will be void under s. 11(*d*) only if one spouse is domiciled in England. The Law Commission thought this interrelation 'not entirely felicitous'.

In 1985 the Law Commission (Law Com. No. 146, Scot. Law Com. No. 96) recommended the reform of s. 11(a) and its replacement by the rule that persons domiciled in England and Wales should have the capacity to enter a potentially polygamous marriage outside the U.K. Marriages which had been declared void as contravening s. 11(a) would not be retrospectively validated.

5. Formal defects

It is not every formal defect which invalidates a marriage. The formalities required for an English ceremony of marriage have already been considered in Chapter 2. The defects which, according to M.C.A. 1973, s. 11(*a*)(*iii*), render a marriage void are examined in 6 below; those which do not are examined in 7.

6. Formal defects which render a marriage void

A marriage will be void for the following reasons only if both parties 'knowingly and wilfully' marry in any of the following circumstances:

(a) *By s. 25 of the Marriage Act 1949, in ceremonies according to the rites of the Church of England.*

(*i*) Except in the case of the marriage of a house-bound or detained person, where they marry in any place other than a church or other building in which banns may be published;

(*ii*) Where they marry without banns having been duly published, a common licence having been obtained or a certificate having been duly issued by a superintendent registrar;

(*iii*) Where a minor, not being a widower or widow, is married and any person so entitled has dissented in public from the marriage at the time of the publication of the banns;

(*iv*) Where, since the publication of the banns, the granting of a common licence or the giving of notice to the superintendent registrar, more than three months have elapsed;

(*v*) Where the marriage is on the authority of a superintendent registrar's certificate and the marriage takes place in any place other than the church, building or other place specified in the notice of marriage and certificate as the place where the marriage is to be solemnised;

(*vi*) Where the marriage is solemnised by a person not in Holy Orders.

NOTE: none of the above applies when the marriage is by special licence.

(b) *By s. 49 of the Marriage Act 1949, in the case of other marriages.*

(*i*) Where due notice of the marriage has not been given to the superintendent registrar;

(*ii*) Where a certificate for marriage and, where necessary, a licence, have not been issued;

(*iii*) Where, since the giving of notice of the marriage, more than three months have elapsed;

(*iv*) Where the marriage was not solemnised in the specified building;

(*v*) Where the registrar, authorised person or superintendent registrar, as the case may be, was absent from the solemnisation of the marriage:

(*vi*) Where the superintendent registrar or registrar was absent from the solemnisation of the marriage of a house-bound or detained person.

7. Formal defects which never render a marriage void

By ss. 24 and 48 of the Marriage Act 1949 it is specifically provided that the following defects shall not render a marriage void.

(a) Where the residential requirements have not been satisfied;

(b) Where, in the case of a minor's marriage, the necessary consents have not been obtained;

(c) Where the registered building in which the marriage was solemnised was not certified as a place of worship or was not the usual place of worship of either of the parties;

(d) Where an incorrect declaration has been made in order to obtain permission to be married in a registered building in another registration district because there was no such building in the registration district of either party where marriages were solemnised according to the rites of the declarant's faith.

These are the only formal defects which are rendered harmless by the Act as regards the validity of a marriage. However, it is the general rule that, unless the formal defect is one which the Act expressly says may invalidate a marriage, it will not render the marriage void. Thus a marriage will be perfectly formally valid notwithstanding it was celebrated without witnesses and both parties were aware of this: *Campbell* v. *Corley* (1856) P.C. On the other hand it seems that a total failure to exchange vows would invalidate a marriage: *Hill* v. *Hill* (1959) P.C.

8. Lack of consent

Lack of valid consent, which will be considered in detail below (*see* **13**), will make a marriage void only if the marriage was celebrated *before* August 1, 1971; otherwise it will render it voidable. This distinction is of no practical importance as a petition based upon lack of consent must be presented within three years of the marriage: M.C.A. 1973, s. 13(2) (*see* **26**).

Voidable marriages

9. Introduction

If the marriage was celebrated *after* July 31, 1971, it will be voidable for any of the reasons set out in s. 12 of the M.C.A. 1973 and discussed in paragraphs **10–20** below. These reasons are essentially the same as for marriages celebrated before August 1, 1971, the only significant exception being in relation to a lack of consent.

10. Non-consummation

Both of the grounds contained in M.C.A. 1973, s. 12(*a*) and (*b*) are based upon the fact that the marriage has not been consummated. It is important to remember that the non-consummation must arise from a spouse's incapacity or wilful refusal to consummate; non-consummation *per se* is insufficient.

Consummation connotes ordinary and complete post-marital intercourse between the parties. Whether such intercourse must be consensual was left open in *Baxter* v. *Baxter* (1948) H.L.

It, therefore, follows from this definition that there is *no* consummation:

(a) If the only sexual intercourse took place *before* the marriage: *Dredge* v. *Dredge* (1947);
(b) If penetration by the male of the female organ was merely transient: *W* v. *W* (1967);
(c) Merely because a child is born to the wife after the marriage. This may have resulted from pre-marital intercourse, artificial insemination, adultery or fecundation *ab extra*.

Conversely, if the above definition is satisfied, the following matters *will not prevent* consummation:

(a) Sterility or infertility;
(b) Lack of sexual satisfaction;
(c) The husband's inability to ejaculate: *R* v. *R* (1952);
(d) The husband's refusal to ejaculate after penetration (*coitus interruptus*) will probably not prevent consummation, despite the decision to the contrary in *Cowen* v. *Cowen* (1945) C.A. The question of the effect of *coitus interruptus* was expressly left open by the House of Lords in *Baxter* v. *Baxter* (1948) and subsequent first

instance decisions conflict: *Grimes* v. *Grimes* (1948) (no consummation); *cf. White* v. *White* (1948) and *Cackett* v. *Cackett* (1950) (consummation);

(e) The use of contraceptives: *Baxter* v. *Baxter* (1948) H.L.;

(f) The fact that the woman's vagina is artificial or has been artificially enlarged: *S* v. *S (No. 2)* (1962). An artificial vagina constructed in a biological male would not allow consummation to take place: *Corbett* v. *Corbett* (1970) (*see* **4** above).

11. Incapacity to consummate

Section 12(*a*) of the M.C.A. 1973 allows either party to the marriage to petition on the ground of his or her own or the other's incapacity.

The incapacity must be incurable in the sense that there is no practical possibility of consummation at the date of the hearing of the petition: *S* v. *S* (1954). Thus incapacity will be regarded as incurable if a party refuses to undergo an operation to cure the defect or it can be cured only by a dangerous operation.

The incapacity, which may have either a physical or psychological origin, need not be general provided it exists in relation to the other spouse.

12. Wilful refusal to consummate

A petition on this ground can be based only on the *respondent's* wilful refusal to consummate: M.C.A. 1973, s. 12(*b*).

There must have been a request for intercourse and such a request may be implied, as in *Jodla* v. *Jodla* (1960) where the parties, who were Roman Catholics, went through a civil ceremony of marriage on the basis that they would not have sexual relations until after a religious ceremony. The wife's request to her husband for him to arrange such a ceremony was held to be an implied request for intercourse and his refusal to accede to her request amounted to wilful refusal to consummate.

There must have been a 'settled and definite decision come to without just excuse', *per* Lord Jowitt LC in *Horton* v. *Horton* (1947) H.L. It follows that there will be no wilful refusal if the failure to consummate is because of the respondent's indecision or there is a good reason for refusal, such as health. In *Ford* v. *Ford* (1987) a prisoner's refusal to have sexual intercourse with his wife during her prison visits, such intercourse being a breach of prison

3. Nullity suits 43

regulations, did not in itself amount to wilful refusal. This plus other behaviour by the prisoner whilst serving his sentence *did* amount to wilful refusal.

Section 12(*b*) requires that the non-consummation must be 'owing to' the respondent's wilful refusal. This requirement will not, therefore, be satisfied if the non-consummation was owing to a pre-marital agreement not to have sexual intercourse, as in *Scott* v. *Scott* (1959).

The refusal must have continued up to the presentation of the petition: *S* v. *S* (1954).

NOTE: once the marriage has been consummated any remedy for a subsequent refusal of marital intercourse must be by way of proceedings other than nullity proceedings, e.g. judicial separation or divorce.

13. Lack of valid consent

This may arise either from 'duress, mistake, unsoundness of mind or otherwise': M.C.A. 1973, s. 12(*c*). These grounds will be examined in **14–17** below, but it can be seen from the phrase 'or otherwise' that the section is not intended to be exhaustive.

14. Duress

The probable effect of duress on a marriage contracted before August 1, 1971 was to make the marriage void, not voidable.

Duress was defined in *Szechter* v. *Szechter* (1970), though it may be doubted whether this case will be followed in the light of the more flexible approach in *Hirani* v. *Hirani* (1983) C.A., below. In *Szechter* the petitioner, who had been a political prisoner in Poland, had married the respondent solely in order to be allowed to leave the country. HELD: the marriage was a nullity because of the duress emanating from the Polish authorities. For duress to vitiate a marriage it must be proved that *'the will of one of the parties thereto has been overborne by genuine and reasonably held fear caused by threat of immediate danger (for which the party is not himself responsible), to life, limb or liberty, so that the constraint destroys the reality of consent to ordinary wedlock'* per Simon P. This view of duress was adopted by Bagnall J in *In re Meyer* (1971) and applied so as to refuse recognition to a Nazi divorce decree obtained under duress. He amplified the test by holding that 'danger to limb' means a serious danger to physical or mental health and 'danger' includes danger to at least a party's parent or child. Moreover, penury or social degradation cannot be disregarded if they form an essential element in the danger to life, limb or liberty.

(a) *The party must not be responsible for the basis of the threat.*

> *Buckland* v. *Buckland* (1967): the petitioner, who was falsely alleged to have had unlawful sexual intercourse with a Maltese girl, married her because, in view of anti-British feeling at that time, he was advised that he was likely to be convicted and sent to prison for some two years if he did not. HELD: as he had not committed the act alleged and there was a threat to his liberty, he was entitled to a nullity decree.

In this case Scarman J purported to apply a *dictum* of Haugh J in the Irish case of *Griffith* v. *Griffith* (1944) to the effect that the fear must have been unjustly imposed in order to warrant a decree. It has been pointed out, however, that these two formulations do not necessarily mean the same thing. A person may be responsible for the basis of the threat, in which case *Buckland* would prevent a decree, yet the fear may have been unjustly imposed, in which case *Griffith* would allow a decree.

(b) *Life, limb or liberty must be threatened.* Earlier cases did not attempt to lay down any test as to the sufficiency or otherwise of the threat. In *Scott* v. *Sebright* (1886), although the respondent threatened to shoot the petitioner unless she married him, the court was apparently disposed to accept threats to ruin her socially and financially as sufficient for duress.

There seems no good reason for restricting duress to threats of physical force and excluding more subtle forms of threat. This view has been applied in *Hirani* v. *Hirani* (1983) C.A. There Ormrod LJ held that, whatever form it took, duress was a coercion of the will so as to vitiate consent. Surprisingly, he failed to refer to his earlier decision in *Singh* v. *Kaur* (1981) C.A. where he applied *Szechter*.

(c) *The threat must have caused fear. Szechter* holds that pressure falling short of fear will not suffice, though in *Ford* v. *Stier* (1896) the mother's influence on her seventeen-year-old daughter was held to be so great as to amount to duress. However, in *Singh* v.

Singh (1971) C.A. it was emphasised that duress has to be based on fear. There a Sikh girl went through an arranged marriage out of a sense of duty towards and respect for her parents' wishes. HELD: in the absence of fear there could be no duress.

(d) *The fear must have been reasonably entertained.* In *Scott* v. *Sebright* (1886) the court held that it did not matter whether fear was reasonably entertained or not. Furthermore, the subjective approach was favoured by the Law Commission (Law Com. No. 33), though it has not been applied in cases thereafter.

It has been noted that the cases fall into two classes. Where the threat emanates from a party unconnected with the respondent, the objective test has been applied, e.g. *H* v. *H* (1953) (Hungarian government), *Buckland* and *Szechter*. Where the threat emanates from the respondent, or his agent, a subjective test has been applied, e.g. *Scott* v. *Sebright*. The cases have not, however, been decided with this distinction in mind and there seems to be no valid reason why the test of the reasonable petitioner should be invoked.

NOTE: as 'either party' may petition on the ground of lack of consent, it seems that, by analogy with M.C.A. 1973, s. 12(*a*), a party to the marriage who imposed the duress may himself plead it as a ground.

15. Mistake
For a mistake to be operative it must be a mistake either as to the *nature* of the ceremony or the *identity* of the other party.

Valier v. *Valier* (1925): the petitioner, an Italian with little understanding of English, went through a marriage ceremony, arranged by the respondent, in a register office in the belief it was a ceremony of betrothal. HELD: the mistake as to the nature of the ceremony negatived the petitioner's consent.

C v. *C* (1942): in this New Zealand case it was said *obiter* that there would be an operative mistake if an engagement had been conducted by correspondence and a third party successfully impersonated the other spouse at the wedding.

A mistake as to the effect of the marriage or the status or quality of the other spouse will have no effect.

Moss v. *Moss* (1897): the husband's mistaken belief that he had married a virgin, when in fact she was pregnant by another man, was held to be of no effect.

16. Unsoundness of mind
The test to be applied to this ground was laid down in *In the Estate of Park, Park* v. *Park* (1953) as follows:

> 'Was the [person] capable of understanding the nature of the contract into which he was entering, or was his mental condition such that he was incapable of understanding it? In order to ascertain the nature of the contract of marriage a man must be mentally capable of appreciating that it involves the responsibilities normally attaching to marriage. Without that degree of mentality it cannot be said that he understands the nature of the contract.'

In *Re Roberts* (1978) C.A. (*see* **21** below) senile dementia rendered a marriage voidable.

17. 'Or otherwise'
This will cover situations where true consent is lacking owing to such matters as drunkenness, drugs, amnesia, hypnotism and, possibly, undue influence.

18. Mental disorder
A petition on this ground may be brought by either party. It is not necessary to show that the party subject to the disorder did not understand the nature of the contract provided he was 'suffering (whether continuously or intermittently) from mental disorder within the meaning of the Mental Health Act 1983 of such a kind or to such an extent as to be unfitted for marriage': M.C.A. 1973, s. 12(*d*).

Section 1(2) of the Mental Health Act 1983 defines 'mental disorder' as mental illness, arrested or incomplete development of mind, psychopathic disorder, and any other disorder or disability of mind.

A 'psychopathic disorder' is a persistent disorder or disability of the mind (whether or not including significant impairment of intelligence) which results in abnormally aggressive or seriously irresponsible conduct on the part of the patient: s. 1(2).

'Unfitted for marriage' means that the party must be incapable of living in a married state and of carrying out the ordinary duties and obligations of marriage: *Bennett v. Bennett* (1969).

19. The respondent's venereal disease
This must exist at the time of the marriage and be in a communicable form: M.C.A. 1973, s. 12(*e*).

20. The respondent wife's pregnancy by another man
This pregnancy *per alium* must exist at the time of the marriage: M.C.A. 1973, s. 12(*f*):

Void and voidable marriages distinguished

21. The distinction between void and voidable marriages
Lord Greene M R in *De Reneville* v. *De Reneville* (1948) C.A. distinguished between void and voidable marriages as follows:

> 'A void marriage is one that will be regarded by every court in any case in which the existence of the marriage is in issue as never having taken place and can be so treated by both parties to it without the necessity of any decree annulling it: a voidable marriage is one that will be regarded by every court as a valid and subsisting marriage until a decree annulling it has been pronounced by a court of competent jurisdiction.'

The effect of a voidable marriage is illustrated by *Re Roberts* (1978) C.A.: shortly before his marriage the deceased testator had made a will in favour of his brother. The testator's widow argued that, because of s. 18 of the Wills Act 1837, her marriage to the testator had revoked his will. The brother contended that, as the testator was suffering from senile dementia at the time of his marriage, the resulting lack of consent meant that there was no marriage for the purpose of s. 18. HELD: lack of consent makes a marriage voidable and, since such a marriage is to be treated as valid until annulled (*see* s. 16, M.C.A. 1973), the marriage had revoked the testator's will. Similarly, in *Ward* v. *Secretary of State for Social Services* (1990) a widow's army pension which ended when she contracted a marriage voidable for non-consummation did not revive when she obtained a nullity decree.

22. Some results of the distinction

(a) As the parties to a void marriage are treated as never having been married, they may contract a valid marriage with someone else without first obtaining a decree of nullity. It is, however, desirable to obtain a decree in such a case in order to confirm a party's unmarried status and to obtain ancillary financial relief.

In the case of a voidable marriage a decree absolute of nullity is necessary before remarriage is possible.

(b) Only the spouses can challenge the validity of a voidable marriage, and then only during their joint lives.

In the case of void marriages the parties themselves and any interested third party, e.g. the remainderman after a life interest given to a 'widow', may question the validity of the marriage, even after the death of the parties themselves.

(c) As a voidable marriage is valid until decree absolute, children born or conceived during the subsistence of such a marriage are presumed to be legitimate.

In the case of a void marriage, s. 1 of the Legitimacy Act 1976 provides that a child of a void marriage, whenever born, shall be treated as legitimate if at the time of the intercourse resulting in his birth (or at the time of the celebration of the marriage if later) both or either of the parties reasonably believed the marriage valid. This applies only if the child's father was domiciled here at the time of the birth or, if he died before then, was so domiciled immediately before his death.

Bars to a nullity decree

23. Bars where the marriage is void

As the marriage is void *ab initio* there should, in principle, be no bar to obtaining a nullity decree in respect of such a marriage. Although this is so in the case of most of the grounds rendering a marriage void, there is some doubt in the case of bigamy where a party may be estopped by a judgment *in rem* from denying the validity of a bigamous marriage.

In *Wilkins* v. *Wilkins* (1896) a wife obtained a decree of judicial separation on the basis that her first husband had died before her second marriage. The first husband then reappeared and the second husband's nullity suit was unsuccessful because of the previous decree. He was, however, given leave to appeal to the Court of Appeal to have the decree of judicial separation set aside. This case was followed in *Woodland* v. *Woodland* (1928) where the facts were substantially the same, except that the nullity suit was estopped by an earlier decree of restitution of conjugal rights.

Although it was said in *Hayward* v. *Hayward* (1961) that estoppel *per rem judicatam* could not apply to a bigamous marriage, it should be noted that the contrary was not argued before the court, the judge appears not to have distinguished clearly between estoppel by record and estoppel by conduct and, since it was held that the decision of a magistrates' court could not create an estoppel in the High Court, the judge's view on estoppel by record appears to be *obiter*.

It therefore seems that estoppel by record may still operate as a bar to denying the validity of a bigamous marriage. Arguments against such a bar are as follows:

(a) It perpetuates bigamy;
(b) It seems anomalous that the parties themselves are prevented from denying the marriage's validity but third parties are not; and
(c) Even in nullity cases the court has a duty to inquire into the facts (*see* **25** below: *D* v. *D* (1979)) and, by analogy with divorce, estoppel should not bind the court (*see* **4:4**).

24. Bars where the marriage is voidable
The only bars to a decree of nullity in respect of a voidable marriage are those contained in s. 13 of the Matrimonial Causes Act 1973.

This section applies to all voidable marriages whenever performed, provided that nullity proceedings are commenced after July 31, 1971.

The bars, which may be summarised as follows, are dealt with in **25–27** below:

Ground	Bar
Non-consummation (s. 12(*a*),(*b*))	s. 13(1)
Lack of consent; mental disorder (s. 12(*c*),(*d*))	s. 13(1),(2)
Venereal disease; pregnancy *per alium* (s. 12(*e*),(*f*))	s. 13(1),(2),(3)

25. Respondent misled into believing the petitioner would not seek a decree

Where the petitioner, knowing he may avoid the marriage, behaves so as to lead the respondent reasonably to believe he will not do so, the court *must* refuse to grant a decree if it would be unjust to the respondent to grant one: M.C.A. 1973, s. 13(1).

> *D* v. *D* (1979): the marriage was not consummated owing to the wife's wilful refusal. The spouses adopted their two foster children at a time when the husband knew that he had a remedy in nullity proceedings. He later left his wife for another woman and petitioned for nullity because of his wife's wilful refusal to consummate the marriage. His wife defended the proceedings on the basis of the common law doctrine of approbation and/or s. 13(1) of the M.C.A. 1973. HELD: s. 3(4) of the Nullity of Marriage Act 1971 had expressly abolished the common law bars and, in the absence of express statutory revival, they remained abolished. Consequently the only bars were those contained in s. 13. If s. 13(1) were satisfied, the court had no option but to refuse a decree and considerations of public policy were irrelevant. The husband's conduct satisfied the first limb of s. 13(1) but, as it would not be unjust to the wife to grant him a decree, his petition succeeded. The court also made the point that although there was no statutory equivalent to s. 1(3) (*see* 4:4) in nullity proceedings, the same effect could be achieved by virtue of s. 15 of the 1973 Act which allows for the intervention of the Queen's Proctor.

Though the common law bars have disappeared, cases decided in relation to those bars may be helpful in showing the kind of conduct which may satisfy s. 13(1). Thus, unreasonable delay (*Scott* v. *Scott* (1959)) and a wife's application to a magistrates' court for a matrimonial order (*Tindall* v. *Tindall* (1953) C.A.) were held to be a bar to a nullity decree.

26. Time bar

By M.C.A. 1973, s. 13(2) a decree of nullity must not be granted on the grounds stated in s. 12(*c*) – (*f*) unless proceedings have been instituted within three years of the marriage, or leave

to institute proceedings after that time has been granted under
s. 13(4).

This time limit is generally absolute, so that there can be no
decree even if the time limit has been exceeded only because of
the respondent's fraud: *Chaplin* v. *Chaplin* (1948) C.A.

Under s. 13(4) (added by the Matrimonial and Family
Proceedings Act 1984) a petitioner may apply for leave to institute
proceedings outside the three-year period, such leave to be
granted if the judge is satisfied that (*a*) the petitioner suffered from
mental disorder at some time during that period, and (*b*) it is just
in all the circumstances of the case to grant leave.

27. Petitioner's knowledge

Where the petitioner relies on the grounds set out in M.C.A.
1973, s. 12(*e*) or (*f*) there can be no decree if the petitioner was
aware at the time of the marriage of the fact alleged: s. 13(3).

By analogy with the approach to a similar provision under the
M.C.A. 1965, it seems that whether a petitioner is aware is to be
decided objectively: *Stocker* v. *Stocker* (1966).

Recognition of foreign nullity decrees

28. Introduction

For the first time, the question of whether a foreign nullity
decree will be recognised by an English court is covered by statute.
The Family Law Act 1986 amends, *inter alia*, the law relating to the
recognition of foreign divorces, annulments and legal separations
(Part II of the Act).

Subject to statutory exceptions, any nullity decree obtained in
any part of the British Isles will be recognised throughout the
United Kingdom if granted by a court of civil jurisdiction: s. 44,
Family Law Act 1986.

> NOTE: (1) the Act applies to decrees obtained before the
> commencement of Part II: s. 52(1).
>
> (2) recognition may also be afforded by the Foreign
> Judgments (Reciprocal Enforcement) Act 1933: s. 45(G).

29. Conditions for the recognition of overseas annulments

An overseas annulment is one obtained in a country outside

the British Isles. The rules for recognition differ according to whether the annulment has been obtained 'by means of proceedings' or 'otherwise than by means of proceedings'. 'Proceedings' mean 'judicial or other proceedings': s. 54(1).

(a) *Annulments obtained by means of proceedings.* Under s. 46(1) such an overseas annulment will be recognised as valid in the U.K. if:
- (*i*) it is effective under the law of the country in which it was obtained, and
- (*ii*) at the date proceedings were commenced, either spouse was habitually resident there, domiciled there or was a national of that country.

(b) *Annulments obtained otherwise than by means of proceedings.* Under s. 46(2) such an overseas annulment will be recognised as valid in the U.K. if:
- (*i*) it is effective under the law of the country in which it was obtained, and
- (*ii*) on the date it was obtained, *either* each spouse was domiciled there *or* one spouse was domiciled there and the other was domiciled in a country whose law recognised the annulment as valid, *and* neither spouse was habitually resident in the U.K. throughout the period of one year immediately preceding that date.

NOTE: (1)   If the relevant dates mentioned above fell after a spouse's death, such a date of death replaces the relevant date (s. 46(4)).

(2)   A spouse's domicile is to be determined either by the law of the overseas country or that part of the U.K. where the question of recognition arises (s. 46(5)).

(3)   Where a country comprises territories having different systems of law, each territory shall be regarded as a separate country (s. 49). This also applies to divorces and legal separations.

30. Recognition excluded

Under s. 51 of the 1986 Act recognition of an overseas annulment or an annulment granted by a court of civil jurisdiction in any part of the British Isles *may* be refused in any part of the U.K. if granted or obtained at a time when it was irreconcilable with a previous decision relating to the marriage's subsistence or validity given by a civil court in that part of the U.K.: s. 51(1).

(a) *An overseas annulment obtained by means of proceedings.* Under s. 51(3) recognition of such an annulment may be refused if:

(*i*) it was obtained without such steps having been taken for giving notice of the proceedings to a party to the marriage as, having regard to the nature of the proceedings and all the circumstances, should reasonably have been taken; or

(*ii*) it was obtained without a party to the marriage having been given (other than for lack of notice) such opportunity to take part in the proceedings as, having regard to those matters, he should reasonably have been given; or

(*iii*) recognition would be manifestly contrary to public policy.

(b) *An overseas annulment obtained otherwise than by means of proceedings.* Under s. 51(3) recognition of such an annulment may be refused if:

(*i*) there is no official document certifying that the annulment is effective under the law of the country where it was obtained; or

(*ii*) where either spouse was domiciled in another country where the annulment was obtained, there is no official document certifying that the annulment is recognised as valid under the law of that other country; or

(*iii*) recognition would be manifestly contrary to public policy.

NOTE: (1) A document is not 'official' unless issued by a person or body appointed or recognised for the purpose of certifying the effectiveness or validity under the law of that country: s. 51(4).

(2) Findings of fault made in proceedings or any ancillary order thereto are not required to be recognised: s. 51(5).

31. Regarding remarriage

If an annulment has been granted by a civil court, or is recognised, in any part of the U.K., the parties are free to marry in that part of the U.K. despite the fact that the decree is not recognised elsewhere: s. 50.

32. Effect of recognition

The marriage will be regarded as ended and a party to such a marriage is entitled to apply for financial provision under s. 12, Matrimonial and Family Proceedings Act 1984.

Progress test 3

1. What is the difference between a void and a voidable marriage? What are the consequences of the difference? **(1, 21–22)**

2. In nullity proceedings what significance, if any, has the date July 31, 1971? **(2, 3, 8, 9, 14, 24)**

3. What grounds render a marriage void? Which formal defects do not render a marriage void? **(2–8)**

4. When will a marriage be voidable? **(9–20)**

5. Explain, with reference to decided cases, the circumstances in which a marriage will be voidable for non-consummation. **(10–12)**

6. What factors negative true consent to marriage? To what extent may these be criticised? **(13–17)**

7. What bars may prevent the obtaining of a nullity decree? Discuss the arguments for and against a bar in the case of a void marriage. **(23–27)**

8. When will an English court (*a*) recognise, and (*b*) refuse to recognise, a foreign nullity decree? **(28–30)**

9. On what grounds, if any, may a petition for nullity be presented in the following circumstances?

(a) W, who has a morbid fear of pregnancy, refuses H intercourse unless he uses a contraceptive. H's religion forbids the use of mechanical contraceptives but he has always been willing to practise *coitus interruptus*. The marriage remains unconsummated.

(b) Prior to his marriage H, a well-known international rugby player, used occasionally to dress as a woman. Though he was reluctant to marry, W, who was attracted by the glamour surrounding H, said that unless he married her she would disclose to the press his liking for women's clothes. After their marriage H underwent a 'sex-change' operation and now lives and dresses as a woman.

(c) W, mistakenly believing her husband, X, to be dead, married H. W later obtained a decree of judicial separation from H. H, who now wishes to marry Y, has recently discovered that X is alive.

10. Three years ago H, a coloured man, and W, a white woman, who were both domiciled in Redland, were married in Whiteland whilst there on a visit. H later left W to live in Blueland and W came to England to work on a fixed-term contract which ends next year. A few months ago H obtained a nullity decree in Whiteland on the ground that mixed marriages were voidable. This decree is recognised in Redland, but not Blueland. W now wishes to remarry in England. What steps should she take to ensure that she is free to do so?

4
Divorce suits

The one-year bar

1. An absolute bar

As a result of the recommendations of the Law Commission (Law Com. No. 116, 1982) the Matrimonial and Family Proceedings Act 1984 substituted for s. 3, M.C.A. 1973 an absolute bar on the presentation of petitions for divorce within one year of marriage.

As it is only the *presentation* of a petition within the one-year period which is prohibited, it follows that there is no bar to presenting a petition after one year based upon matters which occurred during that year: s. 3(2).

This may be regarded as a welcome change in that wounding allegations of exceptional hardship or depravity need no longer be made in cases where marriages have clearly broken down irretrievably within three years of their celebration. On the other hand, it may be doubted whether such a short ban acts as sufficient persuasion to spouses to try to overcome the difficult early days of married life.

The Law Commission (Law Com. No. 192, 1990) has proposed that there should be no divorce until parties have been married for at least *two* years.

2. Steps open to a spouse during the one-year period

During the one-year period:

(a) either spouse may petition for a decree of judicial separation (*see* Chapter 5);

(b) either spouse may apply for a magistrates' order under the

Domestic Proceedings and Magistrates' Courts Act 1978 (*see* Chapters **6** and **8**);
(c) either spouse may apply to the High Court or a divorce county court for an order on the ground of the other spouse's failure to maintain (*see* Chapter **8**);
(d) either spouse may seek protection from domestic violence under the Domestic Violence and Matrimonial Proceedings Act 1976 or the Matrimonial Homes Act 1983 (*see* Chapter **6**).

> NOTE: a spouse may subsequently petition for divorce on the same or similar facts upon which the decree or order in **(a)** or **(b)** above was granted: M.C.A. 1973, s. 4(1). In such cases the decree or order *may* be treated as sufficient proof of the ground upon which it was obtained: s. 4(2).

The ground for divorce

3. The irretrievable breakdown of the marriage
The *sole* ground for divorce, evidenced by proof of one or more of the five facts set out in s. 1(2), is that the marriage has broken down irretrievably; M.C.A. 1973, s. 1(1).

Notwithstanding that the petitioner can establish one or more of the facts in s. 1(2), the court cannot grant a decree nisi of divorce unless it is satisfied that the marriage has irretrievably broken down. Proof of one of these facts is presumptive evidence of such breakdown and, in the absence of evidence to the contrary and subject to s. 3(3) and s. 5, the court must grant a decree nisi of divorce: s. 1(4).

Since the marital breakdown must be irretrievable, a decree cannot be granted if there is a chance of reconciliation. In such a case the judge may adjourn the proceedings to enable a reconciliation to be attempted: s. 6(2). The failure of such an attempt would indicate the breakdown was irretrievable.

The Law Commission (Law Com. 192, 1990) has proposed the retention of irretrievable breakdown as the sole ground but has advocated the abolition of the five facts evidencing such breakdown (*see* below).

4. Evidence of irretrievable breakdown
Irretrievable marital breakdown can be established only if the

petitioner can first prove one or more of the following facts set out in M.C.A. 1973, s. 1(2):

(a) that the respondent has committed adultery and the petitioner finds it intolerable to live with the respondent;
(b) that the respondent's behaviour has been such that the petitioner cannot reasonably be expected to live with the respondent;
(c) that there has been desertion by the respondent for a continuous period of at least two years immediately prior to the presentation of the petition;
(d) that the respondent has consented to a divorce after the parties have lived apart for a continuous period of at least two years immediately prior to the presentation of the petition;
(e) that the parties have lived apart for a continuous period of at least five years immediately prior to the presentation of the petition.

> NOTE: provided that one of these facts is proved, the petitioner does not have to show that it was that fact which caused the irretrievable breakdown: *Buffery* v. *Buffery* (1988) C.A.

The court is specifically charged with a duty to inquire into the facts alleged by both parties: s. 1(3). This inquisitorial obligation means that 'once an issue of a matrimonial offence has been raised between the parties and decided by a competent court, neither party can claim as of right to reopen the issue and litigate it all over again if the other party objects (that is what is meant by saying that estoppels bind the parties): but the Divorce Court has the right, and indeed the duty in a proper case, to allow either party to reopen it, despite the objection of the other party (that is what is meant by saying that estoppels do not bind the court)' per Denning L J in *Thompson* v. *Thompson* (1957) C.A.

> NOTE: the 'special procedure', whereby in an undefended suit a judge grants a decree nisi of divorce on the basis of written evidence filed by the petitioner and without the need for either party to attend court, has reduced the *practical* importance of the law relating to the ground for divorce (*see* **1:7**, and Appendix 1A, 5). However, from the point of view of the

student of family law, it is important to understand the conceptual basis of divorce.

The Law Commission (Law Com. No. 192, 1990) has proposed that irretrievable breakdown should be evidenced by the expiry of one year from the lodging at court of a formal sworn statement by either or both of the spouses that the marital relationship has irrevocably broken down. The court should have power to direct spouses to attend a preliminary interview with a specified person or agency so that conciliation or mediation may be explained to them and they may be given an opportunity to participate if they agree. The person or agency should be required to report back to the court within a specified time. The court should also have the power to adjourn the proceedings to enable the parties to participate in conciliation or mediation or otherwise to seek to resolve their dispute amicably. Such adjournment should be for a specified time and one or both of the parties should be required to report back to the court.

The parties must have been married for at least two years before a divorce may be obtained.

Adultery and intolerability

5. General considerations

The petitioner must prove adultery by the respondent *and* that the petitioner finds it intolerable to live with the respondent: M.C.A. 1973, s. 1(2)(*a*).

'Intolerable' is to be given its ordinary meaning and, since the Act requires 'the petitioner' to find living with the respondent intolerable, the test is clearly subjective and not that of the reasonable petitioner. There must, however, be some explanation of why the petitioner finds it intolerable to live with the respondent: *Goodrich* v. *Goodrich* (1971).

It need not be the respondent's adultery which the petitioner finds makes it intolerable to live with the respondent: these two matters may exist quite independently of each other: *Cleary* v. *Cleary* (1974) C.A. *Cleary* was reluctantly followed by the Court of Appeal in *Carr* v. *Carr* (1974) C.A. where it was pointed out that s. 2(2) of the Act (*see* 10) clearly envisages the need for a link between the discovery by the petitioner of the respondent's adultery and the petitioner's feeling of intolerability.

Lord Denning M R in *Cleary* thought *obiter* that a petitioner could not base his assertion of intolerability on his own conduct; it had to be based on the respondent's conduct. This view should be treated with caution since it conflicts with the literal approach to s. 1(2)(*a*) adopted by the Court of Appeal in both *Cleary* and *Carr*.

Although the Act does not say that the respondent's adultery must have occurred *after* the marriage, it is unlikely that the court would allow pre-marital adultery to be pleaded under s. 1(2)(*a*) by analogy with the rule in *Sullivan* v. *Sullivan* (1970) C.A. that pre-marital conduct cannot be pleaded as a justification for desertion (*see* **32**).

6. The definition of adultery

Adultery is consensual sexual intercourse between a married person and a member of the opposite sex who is not the other spouse. One consequence of this definition is that the party to the intercourse who is not married nevertheless commits adultery.

As the intercourse must be voluntary, a wife who is raped does not commit adultery, although the rapist does because he voluntarily had intercourse. Consent may also be negatived by such matters as drink, drugs and insanity. The burden of disproving consent is placed upon the person denying the adultery: *Redpath* v. *Redpath* (1950) C.A.

For the purposes of adultery the sexual intercourse must involve some, but not necessarily full, penetration of the female organ by the male: *Dennis* v. *Dennis* (1955) C.A.

An extra-marital sexual relationship which falls short of adultery may be pleaded under M.C.A. 1973, s. 1(2)(*b*) (*see* **12**).

7. The standard of proof

The usual standard of proof in civil cases is proof on a balance of probabilities. Whether this standard, or the more demanding criminal standard of proof beyond reasonable doubt, applies to adultery and the other facts evidencing irretrievable marital breakdown is not free from doubt. This is because of judicial disagreement as to the standard to be applied and the fact that this disagreement occurred when divorce was based on the now outmoded concept of the matrimonial offence.

In *Preston-Jones* v. *Preston-Jones* (1951) the House of Lords assumed that adultery must be proved beyond reasonable doubt and the case contains *dicta* to the effect that the same standard applied to all the then grounds for divorce. However, in *Blyth* v. *Blyth* (1966) a majority of the House of Lords held that the then bars to divorce could be disproved on a balance of probabilities. Lord Denning said *obiter* that the grounds for divorce could be 'proved by a preponderance of probability but the degree of probability depends on the subject-matter. In proportion as the offence is grave, so ought the proof to be clear.' This view was approved by a majority of the Court of Appeal in *Bastable* v. *Bastable* (1968), a case concerned with proof of adultery.

Despite these divergent views, it is likely that today the standard of proof for adultery and, by analogy, the other facts evidencing breakdown, is proof on a balance of probabilities. Factors tending to support this conclusion are:

(a) the abolition of the concept of the matrimonial offence;
(b) the departure, in a Practice Direction of 1973, from the practice of requiring corroboration of adultery (*see* 9);
(c) the abolition of the rule against hearsay evidence of adultery as a consequence of s. 6 of the Civil Evidence Act 1968 (*see* 9); and
(d) the anomaly which would result if the presumption of legitimacy, now rebuttable by proof to the contrary on a balance of probabilities (Family Law Reform Act 1969, s. 26), were rebutted but the adultery which led to the illegitimacy could not be proved beyond reasonable doubt. Note that in Serio v. Serio (1983) C.A. it was said that the standard of proof required to rebut the presumption of legitimacy must be commensurate with the seriousness of the issue involved and a child's paternity is an issue of great gravity.

8. Evidence of adultery

Since direct evidence will usually be lacking, reliance may be placed on circumstantial evidence, i.e. evidence of *inclination and opportunity*. Thus adultery *may* be inferred from the fact that a couple spent the night together in the same bedroom: *Woolf* v. *Woolf* (1931). This inference would not be drawn if the co-respondent's impotence prevented any penetration of the female organ: *Dennis* v. *Dennis* (1955).

Adultery may also be inferred from the wife's conception of a child during a period of non-access by the husband, e.g. when the husband is abroad or when a decree of judicial separation is in force.

The fact that a child was born to the wife more than nine months after the husband last had intercourse with her does not necessarily lead to an inference of adultery. In *Preston-Jones* v. *Preston-Jones* (1951) H.L. the husband had been abroad from August 17, 1945 until February 9, 1946. On August 13, 1946 his wife gave birth to a full-term child. The husband's allegation of adultery was based on his contention that the child must have been conceived in adultery, since 360 days had elapsed from August 17, 1945 until the child's birth, whereas the normal period of gestation for a full-term child was about 280 days. HELD: the court *would* take judicial notice of the fact that the minimum period of human gestation is from 270 to 280 days, or about nine months. However, the court would *not* take judicial notice that a child born to a woman 360 days after she last had intercourse with her husband could not be his child. In view of the medical evidence that it was highly improbable that the child was the husband's, the court was satisfied that the wife had committed adultery and her husband was entitled to a divorce.

NOTE: the 280 days are reckoned from the date of the menstruation preceding the intercourse in question: *Burgess* v. *Burgess* (1958).

9.   Some ways of proving adultery
The following are some examples of how adultery may be proved:

(a) *Confessions.* This is a most frequently used method of proving adultery. Confessions are evidence against only the maker unless they
   (*i*)   are made on oath: *Rutherford* v. *Richardson* (1923) H.L.; or
   (*ii*) satisfy s. 2 of the Civil Evidence Act 1968 which makes an out-of-court admission of adultery with another person admissible evidence against that other. The weight to be attached to such an admission is a matter for the trial judge: C.E.A. 1968, s. 6.

In undefended divorce proceedings a written admission of adultery signed by the respondent may be put in at the hearing, the petitioner identifying the respondent's signature: Practice Direction of 1973.

Out-of-court admissions of adultery are often made to private enquiry agents. Although such agents should caution persons they wish to interview, the absence of such a caution does not render an admission inadmissible in evidence: *Hathaway* v. *Hathaway* (1970).

(b) *Previous convictions of the respondent.* By s. 11 of the C.E.A. 1968 a subsisting conviction by a U.K. court or a court martial of a person is admissible in evidence where it is relevant to the proceedings as proof that he committed that offence.

Once the conviction has been proved the respondent will be taken to have committed the offence unless he proves the contrary: s. 11(2). The standard of proof is proof on a balance of probabilities: *Stupple* v. *Royal Insurance Co. Ltd.* (1970) C.A.

There is judicial controversy over the weight to be attached to the conviction in the subsequent civil proceedings. In *Stupple* Lord Denning M R took the view that the conviction of itself was a weighty piece of evidence, whereas Buckley L J thought it had no weight. Lord Denning's view was approved by Davies L J in *Taylor* v. *Taylor* (1970) C.A., yet that of Buckley L J was preferred by Stirling J in *Wright* v. *Wright* (1971).

Section 11 allows a petitioner to prove adultery by proving a relevant conviction of the respondent for such crimes as rape, bigamy or incest, as in *Taylor* v. *Taylor* (1970) C.A.

(c) *Findings of adultery and paternity in earlier civil proceedings.* By s. 12(1) of the C.E.A. 1968 the fact that a person has been found guilty of adultery in any matrimonial proceedings, or (in the case of a man) has been adjudged to be the father of a child in proceedings before a U.K. court, shall be admissible in evidence for the purposes of proving the adultery or paternity to which the finding relates.

'Matrimonial proceedings' are so defined as to exclude proceedings in a magistrates' court.

The effect of the previous finding of adultery or paternity is that the respondent will be taken to have committed the adultery or to be the child's father unless he can prove the contrary: s. 12(2). The standard of proof required to rebut the finding of adultery is proof on a balance of probabilities: *Sutton* v. *Sutton* (1969). Presumably the same applies to a finding of paternity.

Section 12 will allow, e.g. a wife to rely in her divorce on a previous finding of adultery against her husband when he was the co-respondent in someone else's divorce.

(d) *The result of scientific tests to determine paternity.* The husband may seek to prove his wife's adultery by showing that he is not the father of her child. The tests include blood tests and DNA (genetic) finger-printing. DNA (deoxyribonucleic acid) is the main constituent of the body's chromosomes and is responsible for the transmission of hereditary characteristics. By s. 20(1) of the Family Law Reform Act 1969 any court in which the paternity of any person is in question in civil proceedings *may*, of its own motion or on application by a *party* to those proceedings, order bodily samples to be taken from the person whose paternity is in issue, his father or mother and any other *party* to the proceedings.

Persons aged 16 and over must consent before a blood sample may be taken and in the case of a person under that age the consent of the person having his care and control is required. Where a person fails to comply with the court's direction the court may draw such inferences as appear proper: s. 23.

> NOTE: the fact that a child is proved to be illegitimate is not automatic proof of adultery since the definition of adultery (*see* **6**) may not have been satisfied because, e.g. the intercourse may not have been consensual or the child may have been conceived as a result of artificial insemination by donor.

10. Evidence concerning marital intercourse

By s. 48(1) of the M.C.A. 1973 the evidence of a husband or wife is admissible in any proceedings to prove that marital intercourse did or did not take place between them during any period of time. Both parties must answer questions on this issue in civil proceedings but they are not compellable in criminal proceedings: s. 16(4), C.E.A. 1968.

Parties to and witnesses in proceedings instituted in consequence of adultery are competent and compellable to answer questions tending to show their adultery: s. 16(5).

11. Statutory defence to adultery

By s. 2(1) of the M.C.A. 1973 a petitioner will not be able to rely on the respondent's adultery if they live with each other for more than six months after the petitioner learnt of *that* adultery.

If, after the discovery of the adultery in question, the parties live together between decree nisi and decree absolute, this will prevent a decree absolute being made and cause the decree nisi to be rescinded: *Biggs* v. *Biggs* (1977).

The total period of living together must *exceed* six months. Anything less will be disregarded, even for the purposes of deciding whether the petitioner finds it intolerable to live with the respondent: s. 2(2).

'Living with each other' means that spouses are living with each other in the same household: s. 2(6). The parties must live with each other as husband and wife, so that where a husband lived with his wife as a lodger they were not 'living with each other': *Fuller* v. *Fuller* (1973) C.A. The mere cessation of marital intercourse does not prevent living together provided there is some communal life between the spouses, e.g. eating together as in *Mouncer* v. *Mouncer* (1972).

The period in excess of six months may be constituted by several shorter periods totalling more than six months: s. 2(1).

The respondent's 'unreasonable behaviour'

12. The fact to be proved

The petitioner must prove that the respondent has behaved in such a way that the petitioner cannot reasonably be expected to live with the respondent: M.C.A. 1973, s. 1(2)(*b*).

Although it is a common form of shorthand to refer to this fact as 'unreasonable behaviour', it is important to remember that it was stressed in *Carew-Hunt* v. *Carew-Hunt* (1972) that the word 'reasonably' qualifies 'expected', *not* the respondent's behaviour. Thus 'the question is not whether the respondent has behaved unreasonably and the court is no longer required, except marginally, to pass judgment on whether a person's behaviour is right or wrong, good or bad' per Ormrod J in *Carew-Hunt*.

'Expected' means 'required': *Pheasant* v. *Pheasant* (1972).

13. The test to be applied

The test involves two stages. The court must consider the conduct of the respondent and then decide whether, in view of that conduct, the petitioner can reasonably be expected to live with the respondent. Thus the question the court must ask itself comprises a mixture of subjective and objective elements and has been formulated thus: 'would any right-thinking person come to the conclusion that this husband has behaved in such a way that this wife cannot reasonably be expected to live with him, taking into account the whole of the circumstances and the characters and personalities of the parties?': *Livingstone-Stallard* v. *Livingstone-Stallard* (1974).

In considering the respondent's conduct it has been said that the test to be applied approximates to that used in relation to constructive desertion (*see* **16** and **30**) which is based upon the notion of conduct which is sufficiently 'grave and weighty'.

Once the respondent's conduct has been considered, the question of whether the petitioner can reasonably be expected to live with the respondent must be decided. This is to be decided by the court and involves a consideration of the character and personality of the petitioner and the interaction between him and the respondent. The test as formulated in *Ash* v. *Ash* (1972) is: 'can this petitioner with his or her character and personality, with his or her faults and other attributes, good and bad, and having regard to his or her behaviour during the marriage, reasonably be expected to live with this respondent?' As a consequence of this approach it was said in *Ash* that a petitioner who was violent, alcoholic or flirtatious could reasonably be expected to live with a respondent who was similarly violent, alcoholic or flirtatious. This view should be treated with caution since the similar conduct of each spouse, whether it be violence or alcoholism, may be so extreme that they cannot *reasonably* be expected to live together.

Some examples of the courts' approach are provided by the following cases:

Pheasant v. *Pheasant* (1972): the husband alleged that as his wife could not give him the demonstrative and spontaneous affection that his nature craved for he could not reasonably be expected to live with her. HELD: his wife had given him all the affection she could and as there was nothing in her behaviour which amounted to a breach of her marital obligations his petition must be dismissed.

Archard v. *Archard* (1972): when the parties married they were both devout Roman Catholics and did not believe in the use of mechanical contraceptives. Later the wife, who had ceased to be a practising Roman Catholic, was told by her doctor not to become pregnant for at least two years. She therefore insisted that contraceptives should be used when having sexual intercourse and her husband was consequently told by his priest to stop sleeping with her. The wife then petitioned on the basis of her husband's 'unreasonable behaviour'. HELD: the wife's petition failed because the irretrievable breakdown had been caused by a conflict between two reasonable attitudes.

Shears v. *Shears* (1972): the wife's obtaining of a court order to exclude her husband from the matrimonial home on grounds which later proved illusory and her persistent and unwarranted refusal to let him have access to their child was conduct as a result of which he could not reasonably be expected to live with her.

Livingstone-Stallard v. *Livingstone-Stallard* (1974): the husband's constant and unjustified criticism, disapproval and belittling of his wife was held to satisfy her petition based on M.C.A. 1973, s. 1(2)(*b*).

O'Neill v. *O'Neill* (1975) C.A.: the husband caused considerable inconvenience, embarrassment and disorder in the matrimonial home over a period of some two years by attempting to carry out 'do-it-yourself' alterations. The wife left and the husband wrote to her falsely alleging that their two children were not his. HELD: the wife's petition under s. 1(2)(*b*) succeeded. The husband's letter of itself might have sufficed since it was a calculated and unjustified attempt to hurt the wife in as cruel a way as possible. *Bannister* v. *Bannister* (1980) C.A.: the husband lived a completely independent life from his wife. HELD: s. 1(2)(*b*) was satisfied.

Carter-Fea v. *Carter-Fea* (1987) C.A.: the husband's financial irresponsibility which caused his wife and children to suffer stress was held to be sufficient for s. 1(2)(*b*).

14. The meaning of behaviour

Behaviour connotes more than a mere state of affairs or state of mind. It requires some act, omission or course of conduct by one spouse which affects the other spouse and has some reference to the marriage: *Katz* v. *Katz* (1972). Though this definition is straightforward enough, problems arise in the case of a respondent who is mentally ill, particularly where the illness is such that the respondent's conduct may be said to be involuntary.

In the case of a mentally ill respondent the test of breach of marital obligations laid down in *Pheasant* (*see* **13**) has no application. The test is whether, having made allowances for the illness and the temperaments of both parties, the character and gravity of the respondent's behaviour is such that the petitioner cannot reasonably be expected to live with the respondent: *Katz* v. *Katz* (1972). It will clearly be a question of fact and degree whether a mentally ill respondent's conduct is sufficiently grave to warrant the granting of a decree. In *Richards* v. *Richards* (1972) a wife failed to establish the gravity of conduct required where her mentally ill husband, who was moody and prowled about the house during his bouts of insomnia, had assaulted her on two occasions but caused no serious injury.

As regards the passive mentally ill respondent it is a vexed question whether such a person 'behaves' in any real sense at all. In *Smith* v. *Smith* (1973) the wife, who was suffering from pre-senile dementia, was virtually a human vegetable. Although her doctor had recommended that she should be put into a mental hospital, her husband continued to look after her for some five years until the strain became too much for him. HELD: his petition under M.C.A. 1973, s. 1(2)(*b*) failed since 'behaviour' required the respondent's mind to go with her physical acts and this was not so in the case of his wife's involuntary conduct. However, a contrary view was taken in *Thurlow* v. *Thurlow* (1975) where the wife, who suffered from epilepsy and a severe neurological disorder, became incapable of performing any household duties. She threw things and burnt objects in the house and the stress caused by looking after her became too much for her husband who petitioned under s. 1(2)(*b*). HELD: he was entitled to a divorce because 'behaviour' included not only positive conduct, but also negative conduct such as total inactivity and involuntary conduct arising from illness. The court expressly disagreed with the approach in *Smith* but, since its views regarding completely passive conduct were clearly *obiter* and the decisions are both at first instance, the problem of the meaning of 'behaviour' in this context remains unresolved.

It is submitted that the approach in *Thurlow* is to be preferred to that in *Smith* which seems unduly legalistic. There are many instances where the courts have been prepared to give effect to the spirit of the legislation rather than the letter of the law and *Smith* was surely deserving of that approach.

15. Defences to a petition based on s. 1(2)(b)

Apart from a denial of the petitioner's allegations or a counter-allegation that the petitioner has conducted himself or herself in a similar way (*see Ash* v. *Ash*, **13**), there is no statutory defence available to a respondent. Section 2(3) of the M.C.A. 1973 provides that if the parties live together for a period or periods of *six months or less* after the respondent's last act on which the petitioner relies, this must be *disregarded* in considering whether the petitioner cannot reasonably be expected to live with the respondent.

As there is no provision similar to that which applies to adultery (*see* **11** above), it seems that where the parties have lived together for *more* than six months the court has a discretion as to whether the petitioner can still argue that he cannot reasonably be expected to live with the respondent. In *Bradley* v. *Bradley* (1973) C.A. the wife had obtained a magistrates' order based on her husband's persistent cruelty. Because she was unable to find other accommodation she remained in the matrimonial home for more than six months. She slept in the same bed as her husband as there was nowhere else in the house for her to sleep and she cooked for him because she was frightened to do otherwise. HELD: as the wife had no alternative but to stay with her husband she was not prevented from alleging that she could not reasonably be expected to live with him notwithstanding that they had cohabited for more than six months.

The court may refuse to exercise its discretion in favour of a petitioner where there is no reasonable excuse for the cohabitation and the cohabitation is considerably longer than six months.

Two years' desertion

16. Simple and constructive desertion

The petitioner must prove that the respondent has deserted the petitioner for a continuous period of at least two years immediately preceding the presentation of the petition: M.C.A. 1973, s. 1(2)(*c*).

The deserter is the spouse who intends to bring marital cohabitation to an end and actually causes its termination. Thus if a husband, intending to end cohabitation permanently, leaves his wife for no just cause, he is the deserter since he caused the separation with the required intention. This type of desertion is called *simple* or *actual desertion*. However, if the wife leaves because of her husband's bad conduct this is *constructive desertion* by the husband, as his conduct caused the separation. Constructive desertion is, therefore, based on *expulsive* matrimonial misconduct (*see* 31–32).

Section 1(2)(*c*) covers both simple and constructive desertion but it should be noted that the expulsive conduct which led up to the desertion, but not the desertion itself, may be pleaded under s. 1(2)(*b*): *Stringfellow* v. *Stringfellow* (1976) C.A. If desertion itself could be pleaded under s. 1(2)(*b*), this would be a way of avoiding the minimum period of two years required by s. 1(2)(*c*) and this subsection would become redundant.

> NOTE: it may be possible for there to be *mutual desertion*, i.e., each spouse, independently and without just cause, leaves the other. In *Price* v. *Price* (1968) it was decided at first instance that mutual desertion was possible, though the actual decision was reversed on another ground by the Court of Appeal which expressly refused to discuss the point. Denning L J in earlier cases had expressed the *obiter* view that mutual desertion is legally possible: *Hosegood* v. *Hosegood* (1950) C.A.; *Beigan* v. *Beigan* (1956) C.A.

17. The period of desertion

The time limit varies according to whether a divorce petition or a magistrates' court order is involved.

(a) *Divorce petition.* Desertion must be for a period of *at least two years* immediately preceding the presentation of the petition. The desertion must still be continuing when proceedings are begun, except when it is immediately followed by a decree of judicial separation or a court order exempting one spouse from the obligation to cohabit with the other, e.g., an injunction or order excluding one spouse from the matrimonial home. In such cases, where a divorce petition is presented after such decree or order, the desertion will be regarded as immediately preceding the presentation of the petition, provided the parties have not resumed cohabitation and the decree or order has been continuously in force: M.C.A. 1973, s. 4, as amended by the Domestic Proceedings and Magistrates' Courts Act 1978, s. 62.

(b) *Magistrates' order.* For the purposes of an order under the Domestic Proceedings and Magistrates' Courts Act 1978 (*see* Chapter 8) there is *no minimum period* of desertion.

18. The four essentials for desertion

The following four elements are necessary before desertion can be established:

(a) The fact of separation (i.e., *factum*) (*see* **19**).
(b) The intention to live apart *permanently* (i.e., *animus deserendi*) (*see* **20**).
(c) Lack of consent by the other spouse to the separation (*see* **21–24**).
(d) Lack of just or reasonable cause for the separation (*see* **25–29**).

19. The fact of separation

Since 'desertion is not the withdrawal from a place, but from a state of things' (i.e. *all* the duties of married life), per Lord Merrivale P in *Pulford* v. *Pulford* (1923), it follows that:

(a) A refusal to carry out merely some, and not all, of the obligations of marriage is insufficient. Thus in *Weatherley* v. *Weatherley* (1947) H.L. an unreasonable refusal by the respondent to have sexual intercourse did not amount to a separation as the parties did eat together.
(b) There can be a sufficient separation even though the spouses have never had a matrimonial home.

> *Shaw* v. *Shaw* (1939): the spouses agreed at the time of their marriage that they should not cohabit until the husband had

found work and was in a position to provide a home. They each stayed at their parents' home and kept their marriage secret. The husband eventually obtained a job but persistently failed to set up a home despite his wife's requests to do so. HELD: the husband was in desertion from the moment he refused to establish a home.

(c) There can be a sufficient separation even though the spouses remain under the same roof, provided they live as two separate households and not as one.

Smith v. *Smith* (1939): the husband left his wife and went to live with his mother who occupied the basement of the matrimonial home. He and his son continued to sleep on the first floor of the house but he left his wife in sole possession of the ground floor. There was no communication between the spouses except for the fact that the husband left his wife money for her maintenance. HELD: since it was impossible in any real sense to regard the spouses as living toghther, there was a cessation of cohabitation sufficiently complete to amount to separation.

Hopes v. *Hopes* (1949): the spouses shared the whole of the matrimonial home but slept in separate bedrooms. There was no sexual intercourse and the wife refused to wash or mend her husband's clothes. The family did, however, eat together. HELD: since the spouses were not living lives separate and apart from each other, there was insufficient separation for desertion. See also *Weatherley*, above.

The period of desertion must be continuous. By s. 2(5) of the M.C.A. 1973 the period of desertion will still be regarded as continuous even if the spouses resume living with each other, provided they do not do so for one or more periods together exceeding six months.

Any such period(s) of living together must be excluded when calculating the total period of separation: s.2(5). Furthermore, the actual day on which the parties separate is to be excluded in calculating this total: *Warr* v. *Warr* (1975), and this applies to the period(s) of living apart under s. 1(2)(*d*) and (*e*) (*see* **35, 39**).

20. The intention to live apart permanently (*animus deserendi*)

This must *always* be proved in simple desertion, though this may not be so in cases of constructive desertion (*see* **31**). An intention to live apart for a limited period, e.g. for business or health reasons, is insufficient. The intention must be to end cohabitation *permanently*.

The following points on *animus deserendi* must be noted:

(a) *Animus* may be negatived by supervening events such as, e.g., the onset of insanity, in which case desertion will cease to run.

> *Perry* v. *Perry* (1963): the wife, who was mentally ill, left her husband because she was under the insane delusion that he was trying to kill her. HELD: her conduct should be judged as though her belief were true. Therefore she was not in desertion because her belief, if true, would give her just cause for leaving.

Conversely, an insane belief that marital intercourse was merely a grave sin and not a matrimonial offence did not negative *animus*, since such a belief on the part of the wife did not give her just cause for leaving: *Kaczmarz* v. *Kaczmarz* (1967).

> NOTE: section 2(4) of the M.C.A. 1973 provides that, for the purpose of that Act, desertion may be deemed to continue, despite supervening insanity, if the court can infer from the evidence that *animus* would have continued but for the insanity.
>
> There is no comparable rule in proceedings in magistrates' courts, where there is a rebuttable presumption that insanity negatives *animus*: *Crowther* v. *Crowther* (1951) H.L.

(b) Though *animus* may be lacking at the time of the original parting, it may subsequently supervene so that desertion may run from then.

> *Sifton* v. *Sifton* (1939): the spouses agreed to separate for six months. Towards the end of the six month period the husband asked his wife to return. She did not do so as she had decided never to live with him again. HELD: the wife was in desertion as she had no justification for not returning to her husband.

(c) *Animus* may exist even though the spouses are forced to live apart and could not live together even if they so wished.

> *Beeken* v. *Beeken* (1948) C.A.: the spouses were imprisoned by the Japanese and shared a room in the same prison camp. The wife became friendly with another internee and refused to perform any marital services for her husband. In 1943 the spouses were interned in separate camps and in 1944 the wife told her husband that she intended to marry the other man. After their release from prison the wife refused to return to her husband and he subsequently petitioned for divorce because of her desertion. HELD: the wife had *animus* and, at the latest, *factum* existed in 1944, at which time she was in desertion even though she could not have lived with her husband had she so wished.

21. Lack of consent to the separation by the deserted spouse

If the petitioner agrees to the other spouse leaving the matrimonial home or agrees to separate, the former cannot complain that he or she has been deserted. For there to be desertion the separation must *not* be consensual.

There are several aspects to consent which will be discussed further in **22**.

22. Consensual separation

Consent to separation, which necessarily precludes desertion, may be either express or implied.

(a) *Express consent.* Express consent usually takes the form of a separation agreement. A separation agreement, which binds the parties to live apart, must be distinguished from a maintenance agreement, which merely defines the duration of a spouse's financial liability towards the other and/or their children. The latter type of agreement does not involve consent to a separation.

(b) *Implied consent.* A spouse's conduct may indicate a desire not to have the other spouse back and, by implication, a consent to the separation. This may occur when a spouse obtains a judicial separation or a court order relieving him from the obligation to cohabit with the other spouse (this is the position at common law; for the position under the M.C.A. 1973, *see* **17** above).

Joseph v. *Joseph* (1953) C.A.: the husband deserted his wife who subsequently obtained a *get* which, by Jewish but not English law, terminated the marriage. HELD: by obtaining the *get* the wife had shown that she intended and consented to live apart from her husband and could not thereafter allege he was in desertion.

This case may be contrasted with

Corbett v. *Corbett* (1957): the facts were similar to those in *Joseph* except that the wife, after obtaining the *get*, asked her husband to return but he refused. HELD: on the facts the wife had not consented to the separation because of her request for a resumption of cohabitation. The husband's refusal of that request put him in desertion.

In all cases, for consent to be effective, it must have been freely given and not, as in *Holroyd* v. *Holroyd* (1920), given under what virtually amounted to duress.

23. The test for consent
Mere thankfulness at the other spouse's departure does not mean there is consent and consequently no desertion. Equally desertion does not require that the deserted spouse wants the other spouse to stay: *Harriman* v. *Harriman* (1909). If the law were otherwise, the worse the behaviour of the departing spouse, the less likely it is that he would be in desertion.

The test of whether there is consensual separation is based upon whether a causal link can be established between the separation and the other spouse's consent to that separation. If it can, there is no desertion. If it cannot, and the cause of the separation is the deserter's conduct in leaving, there is a sufficient non-consensual separation for desertion, notwithstanding relief at the spouse's departure.

24. Withdrawal of consent
As soon as consent to the separation is withdrawn desertion will begin to run, provided that the other three elements of desertion are present.

There are various types of consensual separation and the rules regarding the withdrawal of consent differ according to the particular type of agreement in question:

(a) The agreement may be for a *limited time* as in *Sifton* v. *Sifton* (1939) (*see* **20** above), or a *particular purpose* as in *Shaw* v. *Shaw* (1939) (*see* **19** above). In such cases consent to the separation ceases at the end of the time or on fulfilment of the purpose.

(b) If there is a consensual separation for a *particular time or purpose* and, *before* the end of the time or fulfilment of the purpose, a spouse unjustifiably refuses to return in any event, desertion will commence as soon as the other spouse learns of the *animus deserendi*. If he does not learn of the *animus* and neither the time has expired nor the purpose been fulfilled, there can be no desertion as the separation is still with his consent.

> *Nutley* v. *Nutley* (1970) C.A.: the husband agreed that his wife should go and look after her sick parents who were not expected to live for very long. In fact they survived for some five years. About a year after she left her husband, the wife decided she was never going to return but she did not tell her husband of her changed intention. HELD: in reality the husband had consented to his wife looking after her parents for the rest of their lifetime. Although she had decided not to return before the purpose of the agreement had been fulfilled, the lack of communication to the husband of her changed intent meant that she continued to be absent with his consent. Therefore she could not at that time be in desertion.

(c) If the consensual separation is for an *indefinite period*, as opposed to being for the spouses' joint lives, either party may withdraw consent at any time. The courts are, however, reluctant to construe a consensual separation as being other than for an indefinite period: *Bosley* v. *Bosley* (1958) C.A. If the court does construe the agreement as being for the *spouses' joint lives*, it may be terminated, and desertion will thereafter run, if *either*

　　(*i*)　both spouses agree to its termination, *or*

　　(*ii*)　there is a breach of a term going to the root of the agreement *a nd* this is accepted by the other party as discharging the agreement, as in *Pardy* v. *Pardy* (1939) C.A.

Pardy v. *Pardy* (1939) C.A.: the spouses entered into a separation agreement which was intended to last for their joint lives. Under this agreement the husband agreed to pay his wife 25 shillings (£1.25) per week maintenance. For a short time he paid regularly, but then irregularly paid smaller sums. For over three years before the wife petitioned for divorce on the grounds of her husband's desertion he had paid nothing and she had done nothing to enforce the agreement. HELD: as both parties had clearly regarded the agreement as dead for over three years it could not be said that during that time their separation was consensual. Desertion could therefore run.

This case may be contrasted with

Clark v. *Clark* (1939): the parties entered into a separation agreement which provided, *inter alia*, that the wife should receive 35 shillings (1.75) per week maintenance. When her husband defaulted in making the payments his wife sued in the county court to enforce the agreement. HELD: although non-payment did not of itself amount to a repudiation of the agreement, since for non-payment to have that effect it must be wilful, even if it were to be so regarded the wife's suing on the agreement showed she did not treat it as at an end. Desertion did not, therefore, run since the separation was still consensual.

25. Lack of just or reasonable cause for the separation
The final element in desertion is that the spouse who causes the separation must have done so without any just or reasonable excuse. Just cause may arise from the conduct of either the petitioner or the alleged deserter.

26. The petitioner's conduct as just cause
As the question of whether the petitioner's conduct is or is not sufficient just cause is a question of fact in each case, it is misleading and unhelpful to attempt to classify particular types of conduct as sufficient or not. Rather it is better to remember the general

principle to be applied that, whatever the particular conduct in any particular case, it must be '*so grave and weighty as to make married life quite impossible*', per Barnard J in *Dyson* v. *Dyson* (1953). Care must be taken to distinguish grave and weighty conduct from what has been termed '*the reasonable wear and tear of married life*' per Asquith L J in *Buchler* v. *Buchler* (1947) C.A., which does *not* suffice.

> NOTE: since grave and weighty expulsive conduct is also required for constructive desertion (*see* **30–32** below), the spouse who has given the departing spouse just cause for leaving will usually be in constructive desertion.

Conduct for which the petitioner is not responsible may provide just cause for separation:

> *G* v. *G* (1964): the husband, who was mentally ill, was given to uncontrollable outbursts of temper which so frightened his children that one of them was undergoing treatment for a serious nervous disorder. The husband went abroad to find a job but when this proved unsuccessful he returned to the matrimonial home in England. His wife refused him entry until he had recovered from his illness because of the effect of that illness on their children. HELD: the need to protect the children gave the wife just cause for living apart from her husband.

Even if conduct is found to be sufficiently grave and weighty, it will justify a spouse's separation only if it was the cause of that separation. Thus in *Day* v. *Day* (1957) it was held that a husband who had left his wife not knowing that she had committed adultery had no just cause for leaving.

27. An honest and reasonable belief in just cause

An honest and reasonable belief by a spouse that the other spouse's conduct is such as would entitle him to end cohabitation will provide just cause, even though the belief is mistaken. This usually applies to a mistaken belief in the other's adultery, although it has been held to apply to a belief in a spouse's unwillingness or inability to consummate the marriage: *Ousey* v. *Ousey* (1874).

> *Glenister* v. *Glenister* (1945): the husband, who was a member

of the armed forces, came home on leave one night to find
three men in the house with his wife. He was not allowed to
enter until the following day. His wife admitted that one of
the men had been in her bedroom but claimed they had
broken into the house against her wishes. The husband,
who on an earlier occasion had contracted venereal disease
and believed his wife to be the source of infection, left his
wife because he thought she had committed adultery.
HELD: as a matter of fact the wife had not committed
adultery. However, as the husband's mistaken belief in her
adultery was reasonable and based on her conduct, he had
just cause for leaving and was consequently not in desertion.

The following points under this heading should be noted:

(a) The belief must have been induced by the other spouse's
conduct and not by, e.g. the revelation by a third party of adultery
as in *Elliott* v. *Elliott* (1956) C.A. where a husband left his wife
because his mother had told him that his wife had committed
adultery.

(b) The belief must have been reasonably held and whether this
was so is decided objectively. Thus in *Cox* v. *Cox* (1958) the husband
honestly believed in his wife's adultery but he was held to have had
no just cause for leaving because the facts negatived opportunity
for adultery.

(c) Facts tending against reasonableness include:
- (*i*) failing to ask for an explanation within a reasonable time:
  Marsden v. *Marsden* (1967);
- (*ii*) failing to accept a reasonable explanation showing the
  conduct to be innocent: *Beer* v. *Beer* (1947);
- (*iii*) failing to bring proceedings based upon the suspected
  adultery: *Forbes* v. *Forbes* (1954);
- (*iv*) failing to accept a previous finding of no adultery: *Allen* v.
  Allen (1951) C.A.

(d) Presumably, and by analogy with *Perry* v. *Perry* (*see* **20** above),
a belief in grounds for separation would give just cause even
though the belief was induced by insanity. The requirement of
reasonableness would, however, be difficult to apply in such a case.

28. The respondent's health as just cause
If a spouse were to be advised, or his health were such, that in

the interests of his health he should remain apart from the other spouse, this would provide the spouse with just cause for a separation as long as the danger to health existed. If the ill-health were to be used as an excuse for a permanent separation there would be no just cause.

> *Lilley* v. *Lilley* (1959) C.A.: a mentally ill wife developed an apparently incurable repugnance to her husband and, on being discharged from a mental hospital, she said she would never return to him. HELD: as the wife's decision never to return was made rationally and at a time before any question of curability arose she was in desertion. At the time of her decision her illness justified only an intention to remain apart until such time as she was cured.

> NOTE: *G* v. *G* (1964) (*see* **26** above) was distinguished from *Lilley* v. *Lilley* since in the former case the wife intended cohabitation to end only for so long as her husband's illness rendered him a danger to their children.

29. Just cause and the location of the matrimonial home

Neither spouse in law has the right to have the last say on where their home is to be situated. This is a matter for compromise and reasonableness between the spouses, upon which such matters as the nature of the accommodation and its proximity to a spouse's (or the spouses') place of work will have a bearing.

Where spouses separate because they are unable to agree where the matrimonial home is to be, the spouse who has acted reasonably will not be in desertion since he will have just cause for the separation. As regards the question of reasonableness there are two situations to note:

(a) If *one* spouse only has been unreasonable that spouse will have no just cause and may be in desertion:

> *McGowan* v. *McGowan* (1948): on the husband's discharge from the Royal Navy the spouses lived at his parents' house. The wife stayed for three days and then returned to live with her mother. The wife refused to return to her husband because she was not prepared to live with his parents. HELD: in view of the circumstances the wife was acting

unreasonably and her refusal to return to her husband put her in desertion.

(b) If *both* spouses have been unreasonable neither is in desertion, because neither can say the separation is the other's fault as each has failed in the duty to compromise:

> *Crossley* v. *Crossley* (1962): the parties lived in India and after the husband lost his job there they came to England and agreed to acquire a public house. The husband's suggestion that they should run a boarding house was rejected by his wife. While the wife was in India winding up their affairs the husband bought a boarding house. On her return the wife refused to live with her husband because he had broken the agreement to acquire a pub. At first instance the husband was held to be in desertion but he appealed against this decision. HELD: since each spouse had acted unreasonably neither could show that the other's conduct was the cause of the separation. As each spouse was to some extent responsible for the separation there was no desertion.

> NOTE: there are *dicta* to the effect that in this type of case both spouses are in desertion, i.e. there is mutual desertion (*see* **16** above).

30. Constructive desertion
As pointed out earlier, there may be occasions when one spouse is justified in terminating cohabitation because of the grave and weighty expulsive conduct of the other spouse. In such cases the deserter is the spouse who intends to bring cohabitation to an end and who actually causes its termination, i.e. the spouse who remains behind is said to be in constructive desertion.

It should be remembered that grave and weighty expulsive conduct will probably satisfy s. 1(2)(*b*) of the M.C.A. 1973 (*see* **12**). This fact will be much more attractive to a potential petitioner than s. 1(2)(*c*) in that it will obviate the need to wait for the two year period of desertion to expire. It is, therefore, likely that for the purposes of divorce constructive desertion will be of little practical importance.

31. The test for constructive desertion

Prima facie constructive desertion, like simple or actual desertion, requires the four elements of *factum, animus deserendi,* lack of consent and lack of just cause. However, the formulation and interpretation of the test for constructive desertion as laid down in *Saunders* v. *Saunders* (1965) has posed a problem in relation to the need for *animus* on the part of the respondent.

In *Saunders* v. *Saunders* the test laid down was: '*Has the [respondent] been guilty of such grave and weighty misconduct that the only sensible inference is that he knew that the [petitioner] would in all probability withdraw permanently from cohabitation with him if she acted like any reasonable person in her position*' per Sir Jocelyn Simon P.

In order to prove *animus* the petitioner will usually have to rely on the presumption that the respondent intended the natural and probable consequences of his conduct. Though rebuttable (*Hosegood* v. *Hosegood* (1950) C.A.), it was the view of the Privy Council in *Lang* v. *Lang* (1954) that the presumption may be rebutted only on proof of a contrary *intent,* not a hope or desire that the other spouse would stay. Lord Reid thought *obiter* in *Gollins* v. *Gollins* (1963) H.L. that the effect of *Lang* was to abolish the need for *animus* in constructive desertion. If this view is correct, conduct for which the respondent is not responsible owing to illness may amount to constructive desertion. In support of this conclusion it may be noted that such conduct can amount to just cause for leaving (*see G* v. *G,* **26** above) and just cause and constructive desertion are complementary in the sense that if the spouse who leaves can show just cause for so doing, i.e. grave and weighty matrimonial misconduct by the other, the spouse who remains will usually be in constructive desertion.

On the other hand the courts may be attracted by the argument that, if the respondent's illness precludes the inference that he *knew* the probable effect of his conduct, the test laid down in *Saunders* is not satisfied and there is no constructive desertion.

32. 'Grave and weighty' expulsive conduct

The following are merely *some* examples of the various conduct which has been held to be sufficiently or insufficiently 'grave and weighty'.

Winnan v. *Winnan* (1948) C.A.: the husband left his wife

because of the filthy state of the matrimonial home which at one time housed 25 to 30 cats kept by his wife. When the husband complained, his wife told him she preferred the cats to him. HELD: the wife was in constructive desertion, particularly in view of her stated preference for the cats.

This case should be contrasted with:

Bartholomew v. *Bartholomew* (1952) C.A.: the wife had allowed the matrimonial home to become filthy and both she and the children were dirty. Her husband told her that, unless she cleaned up herself, the children and the home, he would leave. When she failed to heed this ultimatum he left. HELD: the husband was in desertion as the wife's conduct was insufficiently grave and weighty. The remedy was for the husband to help to keep his house and family clean.

Buchler v. *Buchler* (1947) C.A.: the wife left her husband because he had formed a non-sexual relationship with a male employee and paid her little attention. She had told her husband that if he persisted in this conduct she would leave and he retorted that if she did not like it she could go. HELD: the wife was in desertion because her husband's conduct was no more than the fair wear and tear of married life.

Patching v. *Patching* (1958): the husband became a Jehovah's Witness and in order that they might have a common interest so did the wife. However, the husband's pursuit of his religious beliefs involved almost total disregard of his wife, whom he left alone all week excepts on Mondays. HELD: the husband's conduct was an invasion of his wife's personal freedom which went beyond anything she might reasonably be expected to put up with in the ordinary course of married life. He was consequently in constructive desertion.

NOTE: the respondent's conduct which is alleged to amount to constructive desertion must have occurred *after* the marriage. In *Sullivan* v. *Sullivan* (1970) C.A. the wife married but did not tell her husband that, as she knew, she was pregnant by someone else. Immediately he discovered this fact her husband left and later petitioned for divorce on the ground of his wife's constructive desertion. HELD: the wife was not in constructive desertion because her pregnancy was not conduct during the marriage but a physiological condition which affected only the validity of that marriage.

33. The termination of desertion

Desertion must be continuing at the time of the presentation of a divorce petition (or magistrates' court hearing). If one or more of the four elements considered earlier is missing, desertion will cease to run. Thus desertion will terminate where:

(a) *There is a resumption of cohabitation.* This will negative *factum.* It requires a *bilateral* intention on the part of the spouses to resume married life. This is a question of fact, in respect of which the resumption of marital intercourse, though of great weight, is not conclusive.

> *Mummery* v. *Mummery* (1942): the husband deserted his wife in 1937 and in 1940 he spent the night with her and had sexual intercourse with her. The wife hoped this might help their reconciliation but the evidence showed that the husband had no intention of resuming cohabitation with her. HELD: the husband's desertion had not been terminated as there was no bilateral intention to resume married life.

> *Abercrombie* v. *Abercrombie* (1943): before the spouses separated they had no settled home. The husband, a doctor, worked as a *locum* in various towns and the wife lived with her mother. The spouses met from time to time in different places and sexual intercourse took place between them. HELD: the spouses' meetings during what the evidence showed to be negotiations for a reconciliation amounted to a resumption of cohabitation.

> NOTE: no account will be taken of a period or periods of living together not exceeding six months, though such period(s) will be excluded when calculating the total period of separation: M.C.A. 1973, s. 2(5) (*see* **19** above).

(b) *There is a loss of animus deserendi.* This must be evidenced by the deserting spouse making a bona fide offer to return. If the deserted spouse refuses to consider such an offer and to afford an opportunity to discuss its terms, the tables are turned and that spouse will thereafter be in desertion: *Pratt* v. *Pratt* (1939) H.L.

The offer to return must be genuine, in the sense that the offeror is prepared to carry out his offer if accepted, and free of unreasonable conditions. In *Hutchinson* v. *Hutchinson* (1963) the husband offered to return to his wife on condition there was no sexual intercourse, a condition he knew she would not accept. HELD: the husband remained in desertion as the condition imposed by him was unreasonable.

The offer must be such that in all the circumstances of the case it would be unreasonable for the deserted spouse to refuse it. In *Trevor* v. *Trevor* (1965) C.A. it was held that the wife was justified in refusing her husband's offer to return because he had previously deserted her on nine separate occasions.

In cases of constructive, but not simple, desertion, the deserter's offer must be accompanied by some words of repentance and he may have to give assurances of future good behaviour. Failing these the deserted spouse may reject the offer: *Price* v. *Price* (1951).

> NOTE: where a spouse is justified in refusing an offer to return this does not mean that the offeror ceases to be in desertion. Logically the offer shows a lack of *animus* but cases like *Trevor* v. *Trevor* show that the *continuation* of desertion, as opposed to its inception, requires no *animus*; it merely requires that the rejection of the offer is justified in the circumstances.

(c) *The deserted spouse has consented to the separation.* The most obvious way in which a separation may become consensual is by the parties entering into a separation agreement or by one party obtaining a decree of judicial separation or an order relieving him from the obligation to cohabit with the other spouse (*see* **22** above). However, consent may take less obvious forms. In *Fishburn* v. *Fishburn* (1955) the spouses slept in separate bedrooms because the husband suspected his wife of adultery. The wife later ceased to perform any wifely services for her husband who had assaulted her. Subsequently he kept his room locked against his wife and she fixed a lock to her door for the express purpose of keeping her husband out and preventing him from eating with her. HELD :

the wife's act of fitting a lock to her door showed a determination that her husband should not return to her and amounted to a consent to the separation.

(d) *Just cause arises subsequent to the desertion.* If, after one spouse deserts, the other commits an act so grave and weighty as to justify the former in remaining apart, desertion *may* be brought to an end. Desertion will be terminated only if it can be shown that this act was the reason for the spouse's continuing refusal to live with the deserted spouse.

> *Richards* v. *Richards* (1952) C.A.: two years after her husband had deserted her the wife committed adultery and became pregnant. She informed her husband of these facts through her solicitors. The wife later petitioned for divorce on the ground of her husband's desertion. HELD: as the wife was unable to prove that her husband was not aware of, or unaffected by, her adultery, her petition failed. The wife could not show that her conduct had not impeded the possibility of a future reconciliation.

> *Church* v. *Church* (1952): the wife deserted her husband in 1946. In 1949 the husband went to live with another woman and confessed his adultery to his wife. The husband petitioned for divorce on the ground of his wife's desertion but she argued she was not in desertion because his adultery had given her just cause for remaining apart. HELD: as the marriage had irrevocably broken down in 1946, the husband had satisfied the court that his adultery had in no way affected his wife's mind. She was, therefore, still in desertion.

Two years' living apart and consent to a decree

34. Divorce by consent

The petitioner must prove that the spouses have lived apart for a continuous period of at least two years immediately preceding the presentation of the petition and that the respondent consents to a decree being granted: M.C.A. 1973, s. 1(2)(*d*).

It should be noted that this subsection covers both consensual and non-consensual separations, provided that consent to the granting of a *decree* is obtained.

35. Living apart for at least two years

By s. 2(6) of the M.C.A. 1973 a husband and wife must be treated as living apart unless they are living with each other in the same household (*see* 11).

A literal interpretation of this subsection, with its emphasis on the '*same* household' and its deeming provision, i.e. 'shall be treated', suggests that, if the spouses are physically separated for whatever reason and with whatever motive, they are living apart for the purposes of the Act. However, this has not been the view of the court and the cases on the meaning of 'living apart' are to the following effect:

(a) If the parties live in different places but both of them regard the marriage relationship as still subsisting, this will not amount to living apart. In *Santos* v. *Santos* (1972) C.A. the spouses had at various times during their separation lived together, on one occasion for a month. HELD: in 'the vast generality of cases' under s. 1(2)(*d*), (*e*) mere physical separation is insufficient. Living apart will commence when at least one spouse recognises that the marriage is at an end. This need not, however, be communicated to the other spouse.

It has been suggested *obiter* in *Beales* v. *Beales* (1972) that the intention to regard the marriage as at an end must be that of the petitioner, though this limitation on *Santos* would seem to be unwarranted.

The fact that the principle in *Santos* was expressed to apply to the 'vast generality of cases' may be taken as suggesting that in some cases physical separation alone may suffice. Indeed the court in *Santos* declined to say how the 'wholly exceptional' case where both spouses are of unsound mind for the five-year period should be dealt with. Since the mental element must exist for the whole of the required period, and *Santos* leaves open the question of the effect of supervening insanity on the mental element, in the absence of a statutory equivalent to s. 2(4) of the M.C.A. 1973 (*see* **20** above) it seems that the rebuttable presumption that insanity negatives *animus* will apply.

(b) If the spouses live under the same roof but lead separate lives, this will constitute living apart. This is the same position as under *factum* in desertion (*see* **19** above).

Mouncer v. *Mouncer* (1972): the spouses slept in separate bedrooms for some two years although they ate together and shared the cleaning of the house. HELD: as a common life had not ceased the spouses had not been living apart.

Fuller v. *Fuller* (1973) C.A.: the wife left her husband for her lover but, on learning that her husband was seriously ill, she allowed him to come and live with her and her lover. The husband gave his wife money for his keep and she cooked and washed for him though she continued to sleep with her lover. HELD: the spouses were not living together because 'living with each other' in s. 2(6) required that the spouses live each other as husband and wife and not, as here, as lodger and landlady.

Although the period of living apart is required to be continuous, no account is to be taken of any period(s) during which the parties resumed living with each other, provided that the period(s) does not exceed six months. Any such period(s) must be deducted when calculating the total period of living apart: M.C.A. 1973, s. 2(5), as must the day on which living apart began: *Warr* v. *Warr* (1975). These rules apply equally to petitions based on s. 1(2)(*e*) (*see* **39** below).

36. The respondent's consent to a decree

It is not sufficient merely that the respondent does not object to the granting of a decree; there must be a positive consent by the respondent.

McG (formerly R) v. *R* (1972): the wife petitioned under what is now M.C.A. 1973, s. 1(2)(*d*) and her solicitors sent her husband an acknowledgement of service which did not mention the need for the husband's consent to a decree. There was no evidence that the husband was opposed to a decree. Indeed there was a letter from him to his solicitors to the effect that he wanted the matter to be finalised as soon as possible. HELD: consent is a positive requirement and, as the husband's letter was merely an indication that he did not object, the court was unable to imply consent by him. The court reserved its position on whether the Matrimonial Causes Rules in relation to consent are mandatory.

Matcham v. *Matcham* (1976): the wife petitioned under s. 1(2)(*d*) but the husband's whereabouts were unknown. He had written to his solicitors saying he did not object to a divorce provided he did not have to pay any costs and the wife's solicitor gave evidence that he had met the husband in the street when he had again said he had no objection to a divorce. It was submitted that the Matrimonial Causes Rules were not mandatory and did not provide a comprehensive code for the giving of consent, in which case the letter and other evidence was sufficient to show that the husband consented to a decree. HELD: since consent was a positive requirement, the court must be satisfied beyond reasonable doubt that the husband had consented. Here there was no evidence of positive consent, merely a passive, negative attitude on the part of the husband. The court inclined to the view, but did not decide, that the Matrimonial Causes Rules were not mandatory. These Rules provide that the respondent must give notice to the registrar, signed by him personally, that he consents to a decree.

The respondent's consent, which may be given and revoked at any time, must exist at the time of the decree nisi: *Beales* v. *Beales* (1972). The respondent must have been given sufficient information to enable him to understand the effect of his consenting to a decree: M.C.A. 1973, s. 2(7).

If a spouse whose consent is required is mentally ill, the test for a valid consent is the same as that required for capacity to contract a marriage, i.e. does the respondent understand the nature and effect of what he is doing, and the burden of proving this lies on the petitioner: *Mason* v. *Mason* (1972). In *Mason* the court left open the question of whether, where a mentally ill respondent was a patient under the Court of Protection, consent to a decree could be given by the Court on his behalf. As this would effect a change in status it may be doubted whether the Court could so act.

37. Where the respondent is misled into consenting to a decree

By s. 10(1) of the M.C.A. 1973, if the respondent has been misled (innocently or not) into consenting to a decree and the court has granted a decree solely on the basis of s. 1(2)(*d*), the respondent may apply to have the decree *nisi rescindet*. This power to rescind is discretionary and can be exercised only before the decree is made absolute.

The respondent must have been misled about any matter which he took into account in deciding to consent. This will usually cover such matters as arrangements covering financial provision and the living arrangements for the children of the family.

38. Financial protection for the respondent

Provided the decree nisi was based solely on either two or five years' living apart, plus consent to a decree in the case of the former, the respondent may apply for that decree not to be made absolute: M.C.A. 1973, s. 10(2).

In considering the application the court must take into account all the circumstances, including such matters as the age, health, conduct, earning capacity and financial resources of the parties: s. 10(3).

The general rule is that the court *must not* make the decree absolute unless it is satisfied either that the petitioner should not be required to make any financial provision for the respondent, or that the financial provision made by the petitioner for the respondent is reasonable and fair or the best that can be made in the circumstances: s. 10(3). In *Wilson* v. *Wilson* (1973) C.A. it was held that this subsection required financial provision actually to have been made; mere proposals for such provision are insufficient.

As an exception to the general rule, the decree *may* be made absolute if the court is satisfied that it should be made absolute without delay *and* the petitioner has given the court a satisfactory undertaking to make such financial provision for the respondent as the court may approve: s. 10(4). This subsection requires that the petitioner must put before the court an outline of what he proposes and an undertaking should then be taken from him on the basis of his proposal if this is approved by the court: *Grigson* v. *Grigson* (1974) C.A.

NOTE: by s. 7 of the M.C.A. 1973 provision may be made by rules of court to enable the parties, or either of them, to refer to the court agreements or proposed agreements relating to their divorce to enable the court, if it thinks desirable, to express an opinion as to the reasonableness of the agreement and to give such direction as it thinks fit. The Family Proceedings Rules 1991 contain no such provision.

Five years' living apart

39. The fact to be proved
The petitioner must prove that the parties to the marriage have lived apart for a continuous period of at least five years immediately preceding the presentation of the petition: M.C.A. 1973, s. 1(2)(*e*).

Apart from the fact that the period of living apart is five years and consent to the granting of a decree is not required, the meaning of this subsection is the same as for s. 1(2)(*d*). Thus 'living apart' and the calculation and continuity of the time apart are to be interpreted in the same way.

There is, however, a bar which is peculiar to a petition based on s. 1(2)(*e*) which is discussed in **40**.

40. Grave hardship to the respondent
Where the petitioner alleges five years' living apart, the respondent may oppose the granting of a decree by showing that the dissolution of the marriage will result in grave financial or other hardship to him and that it would in all the circumstances be wrong to dissolve the marriage: M.C.A. 1973, s. 5(1).

The respondent must be able to show that it is the *dissolution* and not the breakup of the marriage which will cause the grave hardship: *Talbot* v. *Talbot* (1971).

The court *must* enquire into all the circumstances of the marriage, including the parties' conduct, their interests and the interests of any children or other persons concerned, *only* if it finds that a five-year period of separation is the sole fact relied upon by the petitioner and that, but for the respondent's opposition under s. 5, a decree nisi would be granted: s. 5(2). 'Conduct' in this context is not confined to, but does include, matrimonial misconduct in the sense of the old matrimonial offence: *Brickell* v. *Brickell* (1973) C.A. 'Children' is not limited to children who are minors: *Allan* v. *Allan* (1974) (children aged 29 and 22).

The word 'grave', which is to be given its ordinary meaning (*Reiterbund* v. *Reiterbund* (1975) C.A.), qualifies not only 'financial hardship' but also 'other hardship'. 'Hardship' is expressed to include the loss of a chance of acquiring any benefit which the respondent might acquire if the marriage were not dissolved: s. 5(3). In practice this will usually mean pension rights.

Whether hardship, financial or otherwise, is 'grave' is to be determined objectively according to the standard of sensible people: *Rukat* v. *Rukat* (1975) C.A.

> NOTE: the Law Commission (Law Com. No. 192, 1990) proposed the retention of this bar on the application of one party where the other has made a sole application for a divorce. The court should have power to postpone a divorce if it is probable that the bar will be made out; there are exceptional circumstances making it impracticable to decide the case and postponement is desirable in the interests of a proper determination. An order imposing a bar may be revoked if the court is satisfied on an application by either or both the parties that grounds for continuing it no longer exist.

41. Grave financial hardship

> *Parker* v. *Parker* (1972): the wife, aged 47, argued, *inter alia*, that she would lose her police widow's pension if she were divorced. HELD: as the husband could provide her with a deferred annuity equal to the pension she would lose, and his obligation to make his annual premium payments was made feasible by virtue of a second mortgage, there was no grave financial hardship.

This case may be contrasted with:

> *Julian* v. *Julian* (1972): the husband's financial inability to provide his wife with an annuity allowed her to succeed on a plea of grave financial hardship.

> *Reiterbund* v. *Reiterbund* (1975) C.A.: the mentally ill wife, aged 52, was unable to obtain employment and lived on supplementary benefit. She would probably always be incapable of earning her own living. Her husband, aged 54, was himself poor and mostly dependent on state benefits.

The wife argued that if she were divorced she would lose her widow's pension and this would amount to grave financial hardship. HELD: if there were a divorce and the husband died within eight years, the wife would lose her widow's benefit but she would be entitled to a larger state contribution in the form of supplementary benefit. If there were no divorce and the husband died before she was 60, the wife would get the same amount from public funds, albeit from a different source. Therefore there would be no grave financial hardship if a divorce decree were granted. The case was not to be taken as deciding that in other cases the right to receive supplementary benefit would necessarily decide, or be relevant when deciding, whether the respondent would suffer grave financial hardship.

42. Other grave hardship

Parghi v. *Parghi* (1973): the wife, who was a Hindu still living in India, opposed a decree nisi by arguing that, as a divorcee, she would be socially ostracised by Indian Hindu society. HELD: the Hindu Marriage Act of 1955 had introduced into India the concept of divorce and the attitude of educated Hindus towards marriage and divorce was similar to that here. There was no evidence that a divorce decree would materially increase the hardship the wife had already suffered from the breakdown of her marriage and a decree was granted.

Lee v. *Lee* (1973): the husband's petition was dismissed because the proceeds available to the wife after the husband's intended sale of the matrimonial home would be insufficient to allow her to buy accommodation near to where her son lived. Such accommodation was necessary because her son was seriously ill and required constant attention and his home was not large enough to take his mother.

Bars to a divorce

43. Bars already considered
Although some of the matters preventing the granting of a

decree have already been considered in this chapter, it is useful to consider them together under the above heading as follows:

(a) The petitioner's failure to prove the irretrievable breakdown of the marriage (*see* **3**).
(b) The misleading of the respondent into consenting to a decree where the petitioner is relying on two years' living apart (*see* **37**).
(c) Grave financial or other hardship to the respondent where the petitioner is relying on five years' living apart (*see* **39**).
(d) The unsatisfactory nature of the financial provision proposed by the petitioner for the respondent in petitions based upon two or five years' living apart (*see* **38**).

44. Two further bars
In addition to the above there are two other matters which may prevent the obtaining of a decree:

(a) Intervention by the Queen's Proctor or other person to show why the decree should not be made absolute: M.C.A. 1973, ss. 8, 9.
(b) The court's direction that the decree should not be made absolute in the interests of any child of the family: M.C.A. 1973, s. 41 (*see* **9:22**).

Recognition of foreign divorce decrees

45. The Family Law Act 1986
This Act, which repealed the Recognition of Divorces and Legal Separations Act 1971, provides that the grounds for the recognition of overseas divorces are the same as those for nullity decrees (*see* **3:31–32**). The overseas divorce must have been obtained as a result of judicial or other proceedings. 'Other proceedings' includes extra-judicial divorces obtained by, for example, *talaq* (where the husband thrice states his intention to repudiate his marriage) (*see Quazi* v. *Quazi* (1979)). However, such proceedings will still exclude a 'bare' *talaq* (a *talaq* which does not require any further formality), *see Chaudhary* v. *Chaudhary* (1984). As regards extra-judicial divorces granted in the British Isles, these will *not* be recognised: s. 44(1).

46. Recognition where no 'proceedings'

Section 46(2) makes the same provision for decrees of divorce as for nullity decrees (*see* Chapter 3:**29**). Consequently, the *whole* of the divorce must take place overseas. In *R* v. *Secretary of State for the Home Department, ex p. Fatima* (1986) H.L. the husband wrote a *talaq* in England and sent notice of it to the appropriate Pakistani authorities, as required by Pakistani law, in order to divorce his wife there. He later wanted to marry Ghulam Fatima but she was not allowed to enter the country because it was doubted whether the *talaq* would be recognised here so as to allow the marriage to proceed. The court upheld the decision of the C.A. and concluded that the *talaq* had not been obtained wholly in Pakistan and would not be recognised here.

47. Recognition by virtue of s. 45(b)

This section allows for the recognition of divorces and annulments treated as valid under other statutory provisions. However, doubt has been expressed over the applicability of the Foreign Judgments (Reciprocal Enforcement) Act 1933, seemingly the most appropriate legislation in this situation. In *Maples* v. *Maples* (1987) the wife petitioned, *inter alia*, for a nullity decree on the ground that her marriage was void because she was already validly married. Her first husband had obtained a Jewish divorce (*get*) in London and this was later adjudged valid by the Rabbinical Court in Haifa, Israel. It was argued that the *get*, an extra-judicial decree, should be recognised because s. 8 of the 1933 Act provides that ' . . . a judgment . . . shall be recognised in any court in the United Kingdom as conclusive between the parties thereto in all proceedings founded on the same cause of action . . . ' HELD: s. 8(1) did not apply to judgments relating to marital status since they affected more than 'the parties thereto' and 'cause of action' did not aptly describe the Haifa judgment. Consequently, the *get* did not dissolve the first marriage and the second marriage to Mr Maples was void.

48. Recognition excluded

The grounds on which an overseas divorce will be refused recognition here are the same as in the case of nullity (*see* 3:**31–32**).

49. The effect of recognition

If recognised, a decree terminates the marriage and a party to such a marriage is entitled to apply for financial provision under s. 12 of the Matrimonial and Family Proceedings Act 1984 (this applies even where the relevant decree was obtained before the commencement date of the statute, i.e. 16 September, 1985 (*Chebaro* v. *Chebaro* (1987) C.A.).)

Where there has been an overseas divorce, nullity or legal separation, obtained by means of judicial or other proceedings and recognised in England and Wales, either party to the marriage may apply to an English court (i.e. the High Court or county court) for financial provision or property adjustment (s. 12), provided that leave to apply has first been granted (s. 13).

An English court will have jurisdiction in such cases if at the date of the application for leave under s. 13:

(a) either party was domiciled in England and Wales (or was so domiciled) when the overseas divorce, etc., took effect there); or
(b) either party had been habitually resident in England and Wales for one year ending with that date (or had been so resident for one year ending with the date on which the overseas divorce, etc., took effect there); or
(c) either or both of the parties had at that date a beneficial interest in possession in a dwelling-house situated in England and Wales which had at some time been a matrimonial home of the parties (s. 15).

Where the court has jurisdiction only by virtue of para. **(c)** it has restricted powers to give financial relief (s. 20).

Before making an order the court must have regard to whether, in all the circumstances of the case, an English court is the appropriate venue (s. 16). Once it has decided to make an order, the court must act in accordance with the provisions of s. 25, M.C.A. 1973 (*see* Chapter 9).

Progress test 4

1. How does the law seek to deter spouses from prematurely ending their marriage? **(1)**

2. What other forms of matrimonial relief are open to a spouse prevented from petitioning for divorce by the time bar? **(2)**

3. What is the ground for divorce and how may it be established? **(3–4)**

4. Explain the operation of s. 1(2)(a), M.C.A. 1973. **(5–7)**

5. How may adultery be proved and what standard of proof is required? **(7–10)**

6. What effect would it have on a petition for divorce based on M.C.A. 1973, s. 1(2)(a) that after the petitioner learnt of the respondent's adultery they lived together (a) for less than six months; (b) for six months, and (c) for more than six months? **(11)**

7. Explain with reference to decided cases the meaning of 'unreasonable behaviour' for the purposes of M.C.A. 1973, s. 1(2)(b). **(12–14)**

8. How may a respondent defend a petition based on s. 1(2)(b)? **(15)**

9. Explain the meaning of 'desertion' and the circumstances in which it provides a basis for a divorce petition. **(16–21)**

10. What is the significance of (a) a consensual separation and (b) just cause in relation to desertion? **(22–29)**

11. What is meant by constructive desertion? **(30–32)**

12. How may desertion be terminated? **(33)**

13. In what circumstances will the consensual separation of the spouses provide a basis for a divorce? **(34–42)**

14. How may a spouse oppose a petition based upon s. 1(2)(d) or s. 1(2)(e)? **(37–38, 40–42)**

15. Explain the factors which may prevent a petitioner from obtaining a divorce? **(43–44)**

16. In what circumstances will an 'overseas divorce' be recognised here? **(45–47)**

17. In what circumstances will an extra-judicial divorce be recognised here? **(45)**

18. When will the English courts refuse to recognise a foreign divorce decree? **(48)**

19. What are the effects of recognising a foreign divorce decree? **(46–48)**

20. H and W were married almost three years ago. W has recently given birth to a child with marked Oriental features. Nine months ago she went to a party with her Japanese judo instructor where she had intercourse with him. She alleges she was drunk at the time. Advise H who now wishes to divorce W. How would your answer differ if the Law Commission's recommendations on the reform of the ground of divorce were implemented?

21. Advise H in the following circumstances whether he has grounds for a divorce:

(a) W was injured in a road accident and suffered severe brain damage which has made her completely withdrawn and passive. H now finds that he can no longer stand the strain of looking after her.

(b) W has formed a sexual relationship with another woman. Would it make any difference if H were a homosexual?

(c) W has undergone artificial insemination by donor without her husband's knowledge.

22. Discuss whether the following circumstances disclose grounds for instituting divorce proceedings:

(a) Three years ago H began to suffer from depression and he and his wife, W, agreed he would receive better treatment if he entered a hospital on a long-term basis. Shortly after admission to hospital H told a doctor that he never wanted to return to W. W later overheard H telling another patient the same thing but she took no notice as she thought this to be a symptom of his illness. A few months later H became incurably insane. W now wishes to remarry.

(b) H left W because he wanted to be alone so that he could decide whether they had a future together. On deciding that they had he returned to the matrimonial home to find that W had changed the locks on the doors. W refused to see or speak to H.

(c) Two years ago W had a miscarriage and H erroneously believed that she had had an abortion. Consequently he subsequently refused to have anything whatsoever to do with her, although they still live under the same roof.

23. A year after his marriage to W some ten years ago, H obtained a job which required him to work abroad. It was agreed that W should remain here because the climate abroad did not suit her. Initially H spent his leave, of three months per year, with W in England. However, during his last five and a half years H, unknown to W, has been living with Miss X abroad and has consequently visited W on only six occasions, each lasting one month. H has now petitioned for divorce on the basis of five years' separation. W does not want a divorce because as a practising Roman Catholic she has conscientious objections to divorce. Furthermore, H's uncle has left her a large sum of money in his will provided she is H's wife or widow on the uncle's death. Advise W.

24. W left H while they were both living in Manchester. W later went to work in America on a three-year contract. W obtained a divorce from H in Nevada after she presented to the court there a letter written to her by H in which he agreed that they were incompatible. W then married X in Nevada and, after a few months, they both came to England. H, who has never forgiven W for leaving him, has threatened to bring proceedings based upon her adultery with X. Advise W whether H can successfully bring these proceedings.

5
Other decrees and declarations

Presumption of death

1. Decree of presumption of death and dissolution of marriage

If a spouse were to remarry after the other spouse has disappeared in circumstances suggesting that the other spouse had died, the discovery that the other spouse was still alive at the date of the remarriage would render that remarriage void (*see* 3:**4**). The possibility of a marriage being rendered void in this way posed a real problem for a spouse contemplating remarriage in the absence of conclusive evidence of the other spouse's death. Steps to solve this problem were first taken in the M.C.A. 1937, now re-enacted in s. 19, M.C.A. 1973. Section 19 allows a spouse, who alleges reasonable grounds for supposing the other party is dead, to petition the court to have it *presumed* that that party is dead *and* to have the marriage *dissolved*. The dissolution of the marriage is an obvious precaution in case the assumption of death subsequently proves to be wrong.

2. Reasonable grounds for presuming death

The court must be satisfied that reasonable grounds exist for presuming death before exercising its *discretion* to grant the decree. Although *any* reasonable grounds may satisfy the court that the other spouse has died, e.g. an eye-witness account of the death, M.C.A. 1973, s. 19(3) expressly incorporates the presumption of death which arises from *seven years' continual absence*. It is insufficient merely to show that the other party has been continually absent for seven or more years; the petitioner must also show that he had no reason to believe that the other spouse was alive during that time.

An objective test is to be applied in determining whether there is no reason to believe the other spouse to be alive: *Thompson* v. *Thompson* (1956). This test will presumably be satisfied only if all reasonable enquiries have failed to reveal that the other spouse is alive.

NOTE: the statutory presumption of death differs from that at common law, as it is only in the former that the petitioner's belief is relevant.

3. Effect of a decree

A decree absolute irrevocably dissolves the marriage, even though the other spouse is subsequently found to be alive. The court does, however, have the power in such a case to make orders for financial provision: *Deacock* v. *Deacock* (1958) C.A.

If the other spouse is found to be alive between decree nisi and absolute, the decree nisi must be rescinded.

4. Relationship between s. 19 and s. 1(2)(e), M.C.A. 1973

As already noted the decree of presumption of death and dissolution of marriage originated when divorce based upon five years' living apart was unknown. In view of s. 1(2)(*e*) (*see* 4:**39** *et seq.*), where there has been an absence of at least five years a petitioner may rely on s. 1(2)(*e*) instead of s. 19. Should the period be less than five years, then the petitioner must rely on s. 19 if he wishes to avoid doubt being cast on the status of his remarriage.

5. Recognition of foreign decrees

If the foreign decree can be regarded as a divorce decree, recognition will be afforded in accordance with the rules laid down in the Family Law Act 1986 (*see* 4:**48**). If it cannot be so regarded, it may be recognised if granted either in circumstances which would have conferred jurisdiction on an English court (*see* 1:**16** *et seq.*) or in a country with which the petitioner had a real and substantial connection.

Judicial separation

6. Introduction

The decree of judicial separation originated in the M.C.A. 1857 and replaced the ecclesiastical decree of divorce *a mensa et thoro*.

The decree, which does not dissolve a marriage, is being increasingly sought and it provides a remedy for a spouse who has religious or conscientious objections to divorce. Furthermore, and unlike a divorce, it may be obtained within the first year of marriage.

The Law Commission (Law Com. No. 192, 1990) recommended that the ground for judicial separation should be proved in the same way as the ground for divorce. The one-year period may begin within the first year of the marriage but the separation would be granted only on the expiry of such period. The procedures for divorce and judicial separation should be integrated into a single system with the choice of remedy to be made at the end of the one-year period.

7. Grounds for a decree

The ground for obtaining a decree is proof of any such fact as is mentioned in s. 1(2) of the M.C.A. 1973: s. 17, M.C.A. 1973. Thus a petitioner must prove any of the five facts which raise a presumption of irretrievable breakdown of marriage (*see* 4:**3**), but the court is not concerned with whether the marriage has irretrievably broken down and this need not be alleged: s. 17(2). Once one of these facts is proved the court must grant a decree subject only to the limitation contained in s. 41 of the 1973 Act (*see* below).

Some of the provisions of the 1973 Act which relate to divorce are also relevant to judicial separation. Thus the following also apply for the purposes of judicial separation:

(a) Section 2 — (bars to reliance on s. 1(2)(*a*), meaning of 'living apart' etc.) (*see* Chapter 4).
(b) Section 6 — (reconciliation provisions) (*see* Chapter 4).
(c) Section 7 — (consideration by the court of certain agreements or arrangements) (*see* Chapter 4).

(d) Section 41 — (restriction on grant of a decree where children are affected) (*see* Chapter 9).

8.   Bars to a decree

Section 2 of the M.C.A. 1973 applies to a petition for judicial separation in the same way as it applies to a divorce petition: s. 17(1). Section 2, which has already been considered in relation to divorce, will, for example, prevent a successful petition for judicial separation if the petitioner relies on adultery and intolerability but the parties have lived together, after the discovery by the petitioner of the adultery relied upon, for more than six months.

9.   Effects of a decree

A decree of judicial separation, unlike decrees of nullity and divorce which affect marital status, takes effect immediately it is granted and has the following effects:

(a) The petitioner is no longer under a duty to cohabit with the other spouse: M.C.A. 1973, s. 18(1). This means that non-cohabitation following the granting of a decree cannot amount to desertion.
(b) If a party dies intestate while a decree is in force and the separation continues, that party's property in respect of which he or she died intestate will devolve as if the other spouse were dead: s. 18(2);

> NOTE: this provision implies that a decree will be discharged if separation ceases (*see* **10** below).

(c) Either spouse may subsequently petition for divorce on the same or similar facts upon which the decree of judicial separation or order under the Domestic Proceedings and Magistrates' Courts Act 1978 was granted: s. 4(1), M.C.A. 1973.
(d) If a divorce petition is subsequently presented, the court *may* treat the decree or order as sufficient proof of the ground upon which it was obtained. In such a case the court must hear evidence from the petitioner: s. 4(2).
(e) If a divorce petition is subsequently presented, a period of two

or more years' desertion immediately preceding the decree will be regarded as being desertion immediately preceding the presentation of the divorce petition, provided the decree of judicial separation has been continuously in force and cohabitation has not been resumed: s. 4(3).

(f) As in divorce and nullity proceedings, ancillary relief is available where a decree of judicial separation has been granted.

10. Discharge of a decree

There are *dicta* to the effect that a decree is *automatically* discharged on the resumption of cohabitation: *Haddon* v. *Haddon* (1887); *Matthews* v. *Matthews* (1912). This also appears to be the implication behind M.C.A. 1973, ss. 18(2) and 4(3). The court does have power, on application by a party, to discharge a decree on this ground: *Oram* v. *Oram* (1923).

> NOTE: the power, formerly contained in the M.C.A. 1965, to apply to the court for the rescission of a decree has been abolished by the M.C.A. 1973, Schedule 3.

11. Recognition of foreign decrees

The Family Law Act 1986 governs the recognition of overseas decrees of judicial separation and the grounds for recognition are substantially the same as for nullity and divorce decrees.

12. Effect of recognition

The 1986 Act does not concern itself with the effect in England of a foreign judicial separation which has been afforded recognition by the Act. In *Tursi* v. *Tursi* (1957) it was decided that, at common law, an Italian decree of judicial separation had the same effect on subsequent divorce proceedings here based on desertion as an English decree. Thus the wife could treat a period of desertion occurring before the foreign decree as immediately preceding the presentation of her divorce petition in England. The same approach may be adopted under the M.C.A. 1973. In *Sabbagh* v. *Sabbagh* (1984) a Brazilian judicial separation was held not to prevent the English courts from dealing with financial provision on the grant of an English divorce.

Declaratory judgments

13. Declarations as to marital status
Section 45 of the M.C.A. 1973 is repealed and replaced by the Family Law Act 1986, Part III. A party to a marriage may, under s. 55(1) of the 1986 Act, apply to a county court or the High Court for one or more of the following declarations.

(a) The marriage was valid at its inception.
(b) The marriage subsisted on a date specified in the application.
(c) The marriage did not subsist on a date so specified.
(d) The validity of a divorce, annulment or legal separation obtained outside England and Wales is entitled to recognition in England and Wales.
(e) The validity of a divorce, annulment or legal separation so obtained is not entitled to recognition in England and Wales.

The court has jurisdiction under s. 55(1) only if one party to the marriage is either:

(a) domiciled in England and Wales on the date of the application; or
(b) has been habitually resident there throughout the period of one year ending with that date; or
(c) died before that date and was either domiciled there at the date of death or had been habitually resident there throughout the period of one year ending with the date of death: s. 55(2).

NOTE: (1) There is no power to declare that a marriage was void at its inception (s. 58(5)).

(2) An applicant who is not a party to the marriage must have a sufficient interest in the determination of the application (s. 55(3)).

14. Declarations as to legitimacy or legitimation
Under s. 56(1) any person may apply to the county court or High Court for a declaration that he is the legitimate child of his parents. Under s. 56(2) any person may apply for one of the following declarations:

(a) That he has become a legitimated person.
(b) That he has not become a legitimated person.

'Legitimated person' includes a legitimation effected under the law of a foreign country and recognised by the law of England and Wales.

An applicant under s. 56 must either be domiciled in England and Wales on the date of the application or have been habitually resident there throughout the period of one year ending with that date.

There is no power to declare that a person is or was illegitimate: s. 58(5).

15. Declaration as to overseas adoptions

Under s. 57(1) a person whose status as an adopted child of any person depends upon an overseas adoption by that person may apply for a declaration that he

(a) is the adopted child of that person; or
(b) is not the adopted child of that person.

The applicant must either be domiciled in England and Wales on the date of the application or have been habitually resident there throughout the period of one year ending with that date.

16. General provisions relating to declarations

The following provisions apply to all the above declarations.

(a) A court shall make a declaration if the truth of the proposition to be declared is proved to its satisfaction unless it would manifestly be contrary to public policy (s. 58(1)).
(b) Any declaration is binding on all persons including the Sovereign (s. 58(2)).
(c) On dismissing an application for a declaration, the court has no power to make any other declaration (s. 58(3)).
(d) The papers in an application for a declaration may be sent either by the court of its own motion or on the application of any party to the proceedings, to the Attorney-General, who may intervene and argue any question which the court considers necessary to have fully argued. The Attorney-General may do this even if he was not sent the papers (s. 59).

Progress test 5

1.   What must a petitioner prove in order to obtain a decree of presumption of death and dissolution of marriage? Why should a petitioner want to obtain such a decree?   **(1–4)**

2.   In what way do the statutory and common law presumptions of death differ?   **(2)**

3.   When will an English court recognise a foreign decree of presumption of death and dissolution?   **(5)**

4.   When, and on what grounds, would a person seek a decree of judicial separation?   **(6–8)**

5.   What is the effect of a decree of judicial separation? When does such a decree cease to have effect?   **(9–10)**

6.   When will an English court recognise a foreign decree of judicial separation? What is the effect of such recognition? **(11–12)**

7.   What kind of declarations may a court be asked to make? **(13–16)**

8.   H and W were married a year ago. Subsequently H pretended to marry Miss X in order to have sexual intercourse with her. On learning of this W, who has religious objections to divorce, wishes to be released from her obligation to live with H. To H's annoyance Miss X continues to assert that she is married to him. Discuss.

9.   H married W abroad where he later obtained a nullity decree on the ground that the marriage was voidable. He came to England and met Miss Y whom he now wishes to marry. Discuss whether and how he may establish he is free to marry.

6
Domestic violence

Introduction

1. The remedies available

A party seeking protection from a violent spouse may seek an injunction, either as ancillary relief in other matrimonial proceedings or under the Domestic Violence and Matrimonial Proceedings Act 1976, or an order under the Matrimonial Homes Act 1983 or the Domestic Proceedings and Magistrates' Courts Act 1978. Under these Acts there need be no application for any other relief and, in the case of the 1976 Act, the applicant need not be a spouse. In addition, both the High Court and county court have a general power to grant injunctive relief.

The criminal law may appear to provide a remedy in the form of a prosecution for assault, particularly since s. 80 of the Police and Criminal Evidence Act 1984 makes a spouse both a competent and compellable witness against the other in proceedings involving an assault on the former. However, the traditional reluctance of the police to interfere in domestic disputes in the absence of serious injury and the punitive, as opposed to protective, functions of the criminal law in this context will rarely make the criminal law seem an apt solution for the typical case of the 'battered wife'. Nonetheless, a reassessment of the role of the police in cases of domestic violence has been undertaken both by the Home Office and individual police forces. In 1990 the Home Office published guidelines stressing the need to keep detailed records of incidents; the desirability of considering criminal charges rather than, as had been the general policy, trying to reconcile the parties; and the need to keep 'at risk' registers similar to those used in the protection of children.

Injunctions ancillary to other proceedings

2. Conditions which must be satisfied

Provided that a petition has been filed in proceedings for divorce, nullity or judicial separation, an application may be made to the court for an injunction ancillary to those proceedings. The injunction may enjoin one spouse not to molest the other or it may exclude one spouse from the matrimonial home. The court may also grant an injunction in these cases, notwithstanding that a petition has not been filed, provided the applicant gives an undertaking to file a petition within a given time.

Once the marriage has been ended by a divorce or nullity decree and the mutual rights and duties arising from the status of spouse have consequently ceased, the courts are reluctant to grant an injunction excluding a property-owning spouse, as against a non-owner, because an injunction exists to support or protect a legal right. However, an injunction will be granted in such circumstances, subject to the decision in *Richards* v. *Richards* (1983) H.L. that the children's interests are not paramount, if this is necessary to protect a child (*Phillips* v. *Phillips* (1973) C.A.) or if there are other proceedings pending between the parties. On the other hand the court will be less reluctant after decree absolute to grant an injunction enjoining a spouse not to molest the other. In view of the wide powers conferred on divorce courts by the M.C.A. 1973 to make orders affecting the matrimonial home (e.g. in *Allen* v. *Allen* (1974) C.A. it was held that the court had jurisdiction under s. 24 of the 1973 Act to order the husband to vacate the matrimonial home), applications for injunctions after decree absolute are likely to be uncommon.

Even though there are other proceedings in hand, an injunction will not be granted unless there is a 'sensible relationship' or 'sufficient connection' between the relief sought by way of injunction and that sought in those other proceedings: per Finer J in *McGibbon* v. *McGibbon* (1973). Thus, e.g., an injunction restraining the wife from preventing the husband entering the matrimonial home was refused the husband because it bore no reasonable relationship to the wife's application for maintenance on the basis of his wilful neglect to maintain; but an injunction restraining molestation (*McGibbon* v. *McGibbon*) did bear a reasonable relationship to an application for leave to petition for divorce within three years of marriage.

Injunctions may also be obtained as relief ancillary to proceedings under s. 17 of the Married Women's Property Act 1882 or in tort actions for assault or battery.

3.   The principles to be applied

The principles appear to be the same, where the application is by a spouse, whether the injunction is ancillary to other proceedings or is sought under the Domestic Violence and Matrimonial Proceedings Act 1976 (*Wiseman* v. *Simpson* (1988) C.A.) or the Matrimonial Homes Act 1983. In the case of the 1976 Act special principles, particularly in relation to the duration of the injunction, apply to applications by a cohabitee.

While it has been said that an injunction excluding one spouse from the matrimonial home (as opposed to one restraining molestation) is a 'drastic order' (*Hall* v. *Hall* (1971) C.A.), it is recognised that if it is 'fair, just and reasonable' that a spouse should be excluded, the court will so order (*Walker* v. *Walker* (1978) C.A.). In deciding whether to make such an order the court, according to *Richards* v. *Richards* (1983) H.L., must have regard to the matters contained in s. 1(3), Matrimonial Homes Act 1983 (*see* **7:17**). Thus, it must make such order as it thinks just and reasonable having regard to:

(a) the spouses' conduct in relation to each other and otherwise;

(b) the needs of the spouses and of any children (the fact that the ousted spouse will thereby be rendered homeless with no prospect of local authority housing does not of itself prevent ouster: *Thurley* v. *Smith* (1984) C.A.);

(c) the financial resources of the spouses; and

(d) all the other circumstances of the case (these include the reasonableness or otherwise of the other party's attitude: *Harris* v. *Harris* (1986)).

NOTE: no one particular matter is paramount.

4.   Ex parte applications

In cases of urgency an application for an injunction may be made *ex parte*, i.e. without the need for notice to the other party or that party's presence at the hearing. Such an application should not be made or granted unless there is a 'real immediate danger of serious injury or irreparable damage' (Practice Note, June 1978). Where there is no such danger application should be made on two clear days' notice to the other side as required by the Matrimonial Causes Rules. *Masich* v. *Masich* (1977) C.A. emphasised that only in exceptional cases should an *exclusion* order be made without this notice.

5. Duration and enforcement of injunctions

The court has a discretion as to the duration of any injunction it may grant. *Davis* v. *Johnson* (1978) H.L., which was concerned with a mistress's claim for an injunction under the 1976 Act to exclude her lover from their home (*see* **7** below), expressed the view that that Act did not change the substantive law as regards spouses and emphasised the temporary nature of an injunction excluding one party. In *Hopper* v. *Hopper* (1979) C.A. attention was drawn to the fact that, where matrimonial proceedings such as divorce or judicial separation were contemplated, the injunction may terminate on the court making a property adjustment order under the M.C.A. 1973. Where an injunction excluding a party has been obtained *ex parte*, it should be of very limited duration calculated in weeks rather than months: *Ansah* v. *Ansah* (1977) C.A.

As an injunction is a civil remedy enforceable by the civil authorities, the police have no power of arrest unless a breach of the peace is likely or has occurred, or a crime has been committed. Once there has been a breach of the terms of the injunction this is a contempt of court punishable by fine or imprisonment. Imprisonment, which in family matters has been said to be a remedy of 'very last resort' (*Ansah* v. *Ansah*), is possible only after a successful application for a warrant of committal. This is enforceable by the High Court tipstaff or county court bailiff, assisted by the police if necessary. As a county court is a 'superior court' within s. 14(1) of the Contempt of Court Act 1981 (County Courts (Penalties for Contempt) Act 1983, s. 1), its power to commit to prison for civil contempt is limited to a fixed term not exceeding two years.

Injunctions under the Domestic Violence and Matrimonial Proceedings Act 1976

6. The relief available

By s. 1(1), without prejudice to the jurisdiction of the High Court and whether or not other relief is sought in the proceedings, on application by a party to the marriage *any county court* has jurisdiction to grant an injunction containing one or more of the following:

(a) A provision restraining the other party from molesting the applicant. Molestation is not defined in the Act but it may occur without the threat or use of violence: *Davis* v. *Johnson* (1978) H.L. In *Vaughan* v. *Vaughan* (1973) C.A. 'molest' was said to be synonymous with 'pester', and it has been held to cover a wide range of annoying behaviour, e.g. a husband's offensive telephone and poster campaign aimed at the school where his wife taught (*Horner* v. *Horner* (1982)), and a husband's abusive letter to his wife, plus swearing at her when she collected the children from their access visit (*George* v. *George* (1986)).

Before an injunction containing this provision can be granted there must be some evidence of molestation: *Spindlow* v. *Spindlow* (1979) C.A.

(b) A provision restraining the other party from molesting a child living with the applicant. This provision covers any child living with the applicant, whether or not the applicant's child or a child of the family.

(c) A provision excluding the other party from the matrimonial home or a part of the matrimonial home or from a specified area in which the matrimonial home is included. It is not necessary for the excluded spouse to have been violent: *Spindlow* v. *Spindlow* (1979) C.A.

(d) A provision requiring the other party to permit the applicant to enter and remain in the matrimonial home or a part of the matrimonial home.

> NOTE: (1) The Act extends the previous law by providing a means whereby protection may be sought in the absence of proceedings for other relief.
>
> (2) 'Without prejudice to the jurisdiction of the High Court' implies that where an application is made to that court it must

be ancillary to other proceedings and this view is supported
by *Crutcher* v. *Crutcher* (1978). An argument against this view
is suggested by the provision in 1977 by rules of court of a
procedure, apparently not considered in *Crutcher*, whereby
proceedings *under the Act* may be brought in the High Court.

(3) Although the Act lays down no principles for the exercise
of the court's discretion, *Spindlow* v. *Spindlow* (1979) C.A.
asserted that the principles are the same as those which guide
the exercise of the High Court's discretion (*see* **3** above); this
applies even if the application is under s. 1(2), below: *Wiseman*
v. *Simpson* (1988) C.A..

7.   Who may apply?

Spouses may apply under s. 1(1), and this section applies to a
man and a woman who are living with each other in the same
household as husband and wife in the same way as it applies to the
parties to a marriage and any reference to the matrimonial home
shall be construed accordingly: s. 1(2).

Davis v. *Johnson* (1978) H.L.: Mr. D and Miss J had lived
together as husband and wife in a council flat of which they
were joint tenants. Owing to frequent beatings by D and
threats by him to kill her and throw her in the river and to
chop her up and put her remains in the deep-freeze Miss J
left, taking their baby daughter with her, and they went to
live in a refuge for battered women which was grossly
overcrowded and insanitary. She then successfully applied
to a county court judge for an injunction against
molestation by D and for his exclusion from the flat.
Following the decision of the Court of Appeal in *B* v. *B*
(1978) and *Cantliff* v. *Jenkins* (1978), that an unmarried
woman could not exclude the man with whom she was
living unless she could establish a right under the law of
property to exclusive possession, the injunction excluding D
was withdrawn. Miss J appealed and three members of a
five-member Court of Appeal, holding that the Court was
not bound by its two previous decisions, restored the
injunction ordering D's exclusion. D appealed on the basis,
inter alia, that s. 1 did not give a county court judge power
to exclude from premises a person who was a joint tenant of

those premises. HELD: s. 1 was concerned not with property rights but with protection from molestation and eviction. Therefore a county court did have jurisdiction to grant injunctive relief to an unmarried applicant so as to exclude a person from premises irrespective of that person's proprietary rights therein. Such exclusion would usually be for only a limited period. D's appeal was accordingly dismissed and *B* v. *B* and *Cantliff* v. *Jenkins* were overruled. The Court also reaffirmed the rule that, subject to established exceptions, the Court of Appeal is bound by its previous decisions.

NOTE: (1) Section 1(2) applies to unmarried persons who 'are living' with each other as husband and wife. In *Davis* v. *Johnson* the House of Lords did not take the point that when Miss J applied for the injunction the parties were no longer living with each other. To adopt a literal interpretation of the subsection would greatly restrict the protection afforded by it, and in *B* v. *B*, and *Davis* v. *Johnson* in the Court of Appeal it was suggested, but not decided, that the phrase could be interpreted to mean either 'are or have been living' with each other or 'were living together at the time of the incidents causing the separation'. Another view was that s. 1(2) was merely designed to give an unmarried person a *locus standi* to apply as if married. In *McLean* v. *Burke* (1980) it was held that s. 1(2) is satisfied if the parties were living together as husband and wife immediately before the event giving rise to the application.

(2) As in desertion (*see* 4:**19**) it is possible for parties to live in separate households under the same roof. However, in *Adeoso* v. *Adeoso* (1980) C.A. this was held not to be possible owing to the smallness of the accommodation. A man and his mistress lived in a council flat in separate rooms which they kept locked. The flat comprised one bedroom, a sitting-room, a kitchen and a bathroom and, though the parties communicated with each other by writing notes, they were held to be living with each other as if they were husband and wife.

(3) By analogy with the approach of the courts under the Supplementary Benefits legislation to the same phrase,

account may be taken of such matters as the stability of the relationship, financial support given by one to the other, the existence or otherwise of a heterosexual sexual relationship between them and whether the couple have held themselves out as married. None of these is conclusive one way or the other but a strong presumption in favour of parties living as husband and wife is raised if they are bringing up their children together.

8. Duration of injunctions

In *Davis* v. *Johnson* the judges emphasised the short-term nature of an injunction granted to an unmarried person to exclude a property owning party. This approach was extended to injunctions granted to a spouse by *Hopper* v. *Hopper* (1979) C.A. There it was held that exclusionary injunctions should be expressly limited in time, or it should be made clear that the injunction will be withdrawn after a reasonable time sufficient to enable either other accommodation to be arranged or, in the case of a spouse, the court to exercise its powers to make property adjustment orders.

In the case of injunctions ordering exclusion, an initial period of up to three months is likely to be sufficient: Practice Note (1978), though in *Fairweather* v. *Kolosine* (1982) C.A. exclusion until the youngest child reached 16 was ordered, i.e. for five years.

Orders may also be made 'until further order': *Spencer* v. *Camacho* (1983) C.A.

9. Power of arrest

If the judge is satisfied that the respondent has caused actual bodily harm to the applicant or child and he is likely to do so again, the judge may attach a power of arrest to *exclusionary* injunctions and injunctions against *violence* to a spouse or child: s. 2(1). 'Actual bodily harm' includes any hurt or injury calculated to interfere with health or comfort: *R* v. *Miller* (1954).

Section 2 applies to any case where a High Court or county court judge grants an injunction under s. 2(1), so that a power of arrest may be attached to an injunction granted in divorce proceedings: *Lewis* v. *Lewis* (1978) C.A. This case also emphasised that the attachment of a power of arrest is by no means to be regarded as a routine remedy for general, indiscriminate use: it is to be used only in exceptional cases.

Once a power of arrest has been attached, a constable may arrest, without warrant, any person he reasonably suspects to be in breach of the injunction: s. 2(3). The person arrested must be brought before a judge within 24 hours of his arrest and he cannot be released within that time unless the judge so directs. As a county court judge has similar powers under the County Court Rules (Ord. 46) to deal with breaches of injunctions under the 1976 Act to those of a High Court judge under the Rules of the Supreme Court (Ord. 90), he may commit for contempt a person brought before him by virtue of a power of arrest even though there has been no application for committal: *Boylan* v. *Boylan* (1980) C.A.

If, following his arrest, the respondent is committed to prison, the committal order must comply with the requirements laid down by the rules, e.g. it must not be left blank and it must state the duration of the committal, otherwise it will be invalid: *Wellington* v. *Wellington* (1978); *Cinderby* v. *Cinderby* (1978).

Orders under the Domestic Proceedings and Magistrates' Courts Act 1978

10. Introduction
Owing to the illusory protection afforded under earlier legislation by the magistrates' non-cohabitation order, which merely relieved one spouse from the obligation to cohabit with the other, the 1978 Act provides protection against a violent spouse in the form of personal protection orders and exclusion orders.

11. Personal protection orders under s. 16
Whether or not an application is being made for financial provision, either spouse may apply for an order under this section: s. 16(1). Subject to s. 16(8) (*see* **13**), orders may have conditions attached and last for such period as may be specified: s. 16(9).

Before the court (sitting as a family proceedings court) can make an order under s. 16(2) it must be satisfied that:

(a) the respondent *has used, or threatened to use, violence* against the person of the applicant or a child of the family, *and*
(b) it is *necessary for the protection* of the applicant or child of the family that an order should be made.

If the court is so satisfied, it may order that the respondent shall not use violence against the person of the applicant, or a child of the family, or both: s. 16(2) (the so-called 'personal protection' order). The respondent may also be ordered not to incite or assist another to use, or threaten to use, such violence: s. 16(10).

12. Exclusion orders under s. 16
Before the court can order exclusion it must be satisfied that:

(a) the applicant or a child of the family *is in danger of being physically injured* by the respondent (or would be if they were to enter the matrimonial home), *and*

(b) that the respondent has either

    (i) *used violence* against the person of the applicant or a child of the family, or

    (ii) *threatened to use violence* against the person of the applicant or a child of the family *and has used violence* against some other person, or

    (iii) *in contravention of a personal protection order, threatened to use violence* against the person of the applicant or a child of the family: s. 16(3).

If the court is so satisfied, it may order the respondent to leave the matrimonial home or prohibit him from entering it, or both: s. 16(3). The court does not have to be satisfied that the *danger* of a physical injury is immediate, as 'danger' is used in the section without any such qualification: *McCartney* v. *McCartney* (1980). Such an order does not affect any estate or interest in that home of the respondent or any other person: s. 17(4). The respondent may also be ordered to permit the applicant to enter and remain in the matrimonial home: s. 16(4).

NOTE: presumably the 'violence' under ss. 16(2) and (3) must be 'unlawful'.

13. Orders in cases of emergency
On an application for a personal protection or exclusion order, if the court thinks it *essential* that the application be heard without delay, it may be heard despite the fact that the court is not, in specified respects, a duly constituted family proceedings court, i.e. the court need not include both a man and a woman, the

members need not be members of the family court panel and the proceedings need not be separated from non-family proceedings: s. 16(5).

In the case of personal protection orders only, the court (which may consist of one magistrate) may make an 'expedited order' if satisfied that there is *imminent danger of physical injury* to the applicant or a child of the family, even though the summons has not been served on the respondent at all, or within a reasonable time before the hearing, or, if served, it requires him to appear at some other time or place: s. 16(6), (7).

An expedited order takes effect only from the date when notice of its making is served on the respondent or such later date as the court may specify. Such order ceases on whichever of the following dates occurs first:

(a) 28 days from the making of the order, or
(b) the commencement of the hearing of the application for an order under s. 16: s. 16(8).

Notwithstanding the limited duration of an expedited order, the court has power to make further such orders under s. 17(3) and has a general power to vary or revoke any order under s. 16: s. 17(1).

14. Power of arrest

If the court, under s. 16, has ordered the respondent not to use violence against the person of the applicant or a child of the family or not to enter the matrimonial home, it may attach a power of arrest to the order provided it is satisfied that the respondent has *physically injured* the applicant or a child of the family *and is likely to do so again*: s. 18(1).

Where this power of arrest is attached to an order, a constable may arrest the respondent without warrant in cases of suspected breach of such order: s. 18(2). The respondent so arrested must be brought before a magistrate within 24 hours of arrest, no account being taken of Christmas Day, Good Friday or any Sunday. The arrested person may be remanded: s. 18(3).

If a spouse considers that the other spouse has disobeyed a personal protection or exclusion order to which no power of arrest was attached, application may be made by the former spouse, on oath, to a magistrate for the commission area in which either spouse ordinarily resides, for a warrant for the latter's arrest. The warrant cannot be issued unless the magistrate has reasonable grounds for believing the other spouse has disobeyed the order: s. 18(4).

15. The 1976 and 1978 Acts compared
The following points of comparison should be noted:

(a) Only spouses may apply under the 1978 Act; unmarried persons may apply under the 1976 Act.
(b) The 1978 Act is concerned with children of the family; the 1976 Act applies to any child living with the applicant.
(c) Under the 1978 Act there must be physical violence, actual or threatened; mere molestation suffices for the 1976 Act.
(d) If there is an application for an order under ss. 2, 6 or 7 of the 1978 Act, the court has power to make orders relating to financial provision and children. Proceedings under the 1976 Act are 'family proceedings' within the C.A. 1989 and s. 8 orders in respect of children may be made (*see* 12:9).

> NOTE: it has been held that a husband may be guilty of rape if he has non-consensual sexual intercourse with his wife while a non-molestation order is in force or he has undertaken not to molest her (*R* v. *Steele* (1976) C.A.), though this is not so if the parties have resumed co-habitation (*R* v. *Reeves* (1984) C.A.). However, the landmark decision in *R* v. *R* (*Rape: Marital Exemption*) (1991) H.L. held that a husband's general immunity to a conviction for raping his wife should be abolished. In matrimonial proceedings the rape must be proved beyond reasonable doubt: *N* v. *N* (1991) C.A.

Orders under the Matrimonial Homes Act 1983

16. The protection afforded by the Act
The main object of the Act is to give a spouse, in or out of occupation, a right not to be evicted from the matrimonial home unless the court orders otherwise, and this right is registrable as a land charge, in which case it binds third parties (*see* 7:18). However, s. 1(2) of the Act provides that so long as one spouse has rights of

occupation, either spouse may apply to the court for an order declaring, enforcing, restricting or terminating those rights or prohibiting, suspending or restricting the exercise by either spouse of the right to occupy the dwelling house or requiring either spouse to permit the exercise by the other of that right. By s. 9(1) of the Act, where both spouses are entitled to occupy by virtue of a legal estate, either may apply under the Act to prohibit, suspend or restrict the exercise of the other's right to occupy, or to require the other to permit its exercise by the applicant. The court may make an order on those applications only after having had regard to the matters set out in s. 1(3) (*see* **3** above).

It is, therefore, possible for the 1983 Act to be used so as to provide the same kind of relief as already considered by, e.g. excluding one spouse from the matrimonial home or part of it. As the court's powers are limited, e.g. there is no power to grant a non-molestation order and it may not be possible to attach a power of arrest to an order, the 1983 Act is less likely to be resorted to for the purpose of seeking protection against a violent spouse than for protecting the right to occupy as against the other spouse and/or third parties.

It should be noted that one effect of *Richards* (*see* **3** above) was that if an ouster order were required in a divorce, separate proceedings under, e.g. the M.H.A. 1983 would be necessary. This was changed by the County Court (Amendment) Rules 1984 whereby under Ord. 47, r. 4 of the County Court Rules 1981 when matrimonial proceedings are pending application under M.H.A. 1983 may be made in these proceedings. However, an ouster order may be made only by a judge unless the respondent is not in possession of the dwelling house in question and his whereabouts cannot be ascertained after reasonable enquiries.

Orders under the courts' general power

17. The so-called 'inherent jurisdiction'

The High Court and county court may, under what is now respectively s. 31 of the Supreme Court Act 1981 and s. 38 of the County Courts Act 1984, grant injunctive relief 'in all cases where it appears to the court to be just and equitable to do so'. This is sometimes referred to as the courts' 'inherent jurisdiction' but this terminology was disapproved of by the House of Lords in *Richards* (above) because of the above statutory intervention.

Despite the apparent width of the courts' discretion *Richards* stressed that ouster orders cannot be made under it and in *Ainsbury* v. *Millington* (1987) H.L. the court held that its powers under the above sections were available only in support of a legal right. There the parties had been living together as husband and wife and their council house tenancy was in their joint names. When the respondent was sent to prison, the female applicant married. On the respondent's release from prison the applicant, her child and her husband moved out of the council house into unsatisfactory accommodation. The applicant then applied to the county court under the Guardianship of Minors Act 1971 and the Guardianship Act 1973 (since repealed by the C.A., 1989) claiming, *inter alia*, an interlocutory injunction to exclude the respondent from the council house. HELD: as neither the M.H.A. 1983 nor the D.V.M.P.A. 1976 were being relied upon (as required by *Richards*) it was necessary to rely on s. 38 of the County Courts Act 1984. An ouster injunction would not be granted since, as the applicant did not have the right to exclusive possession of the property, being one of two joint tenants, there was no legal right capable of being protected by the injunction requested.

There is judicial controversy over whether the courts' discretion may be exercised merely because the welfare of a child so dictates. Doubt as to whether such action is permissible was expressed in *Wilde* v. *Wilde* (1988) C.A. but there seems to be no reason why a legal right in relation to a child, e.g. the possession of 'parental responsibility' for the child (*see* Chapter 11), should not permit the exercise of the courts' general power to grant injunctive relief.

Progress test 6

1. In what kind of proceedings may a person obtain protection against domestic violence? **(1)**

2. What principles are applied by the court when an injunction is sought in divorce proceedings? **(2–5)**

3.   What provisions exist to afford protection against domestic violence in county court proceedings in the case of (*a*) a spouse, and (*b*) an unmarried person?   **(6–9)**

4.   What do you understand by (*a*) a personal protection order, and (*b*) an exclusion order in a magistrates' court?   **(10–12)**

5.   What provisions exist to enable a magistrates' court to grant an order in the nature of an injunction in an emergency?   **(13)**

6.   How may breaches of orders under the Domestic Proceedings and Magistrates' Courts Act 1978, s. 16 be dealt with?   **(14)**

7.   Compare the courts' powers under the Domestic Violence and Matrimonial Proceedings Act 1976 with those under the 1978 Act.   **(15)**

8.   How may the Matrimonial Homes Act 1983 be used to protect a spouse from domestic violence?   **(16)**

9.   What are the limits on the courts' general discretionary power to give injunctive relief?   **(17)**

10.   H and W were married three years ago and they have twin boys aged two. Six weeks ago H, who suspected W of having an affair, threw her and the children out of the matrimonial home, which belongs solely to him, saying that if they were to return he would 'give W the thrashing of her life'. W and the children are living with W's parents in very cramped accommodation. W consults you and seeks your advice as to:

(a) how she may prevent H from using violence against her or the children, and
(b) whether she can exclude H from the matrimonial home so that she and the children may return to live there.

Advise her. How, if at all, would your advice differ if H and W were not married to each other?

Part two

The economic aspects of marriage

7
Property disputes between spouses

Introduction

1. Property disputes
Spouses may disagree as to the ownership or possession of both real and personal property. However, the matrimonial home, in times of inflation not only a home but also an asset which maintains or increases its value, is most often the subject of dispute. The court's assistance in resolving these disputes may be sought before, on or after the termination of the marriage. The law provides various methods of enlisting the court's aid (*see* **2** below), the choice of method often being dictated by when the dispute arises.

The law relating to the ownership of the matrimonial home has increasingly been criticised for its complexity and artificiality and this has, in turn, led to proposals for reform (*see* **13** below).

2. Method of resolving property disputes
The following proceedings are available:

(a) Under s. 17 of the Married Women's Property Act 1882 (*see* **3–13** below). This is the most usual method, although it has declined in importance as a result of the wide discretionary powers conferred on the court by the M.C.A. 1973.
(b) Under s. 30 of the Law of Property Act 1925 (*see* **14** below).
(c) Under the Matrimonial Homes Act 1983 (*see* **15–20** below).
(d) Proceedings to restrain a breach of trust (*see* **21** below).
(e) By way of proprietary estoppel (*see* **22** below).

(f) By way of a licence (*see* **23** below).

In addition to the above one spouse may:

(a) Sue the other in tort, e.g. in trespass: Law Reform (Husband and Wife) Act 1962, s. 1. If the action is brought during the marriage, the court may stay the action if it considers that no substantial benefit would accrue to either party or it would be more conveniently disposed of under s. 17, M.W.P.A. 1882.
(b) Bring proceedings against the other for theft and similar offences: Theft Act 1968, s. 30. An order for restitution may be made upon conviction: s. 28.

> NOTE: proceedings for an injunction may be instituted and these have already been dealt with in Chapter 6. An ancillary application under s. 24, M.C.A. 1973 may be made in suits for divorce, nullity or judicial separation and the court may then alter title to property (*see* Chapter 9).

Section 17 of the Married Women's Property Act 1882

3. The s. 17 procedure
Section 17 provides a summary method of deciding 'any question between husband and wife as to the title to or possession of property'. Although the judge (i.e. of the High Court or county court) may make such order in respect of the property in dispute 'as he thinks fit', he may make only such order as will give effect to the parties' *existing* proprietary rights. There is no power to alter or vary those rights.

It may be thought that the much wider powers vested in the court by s. 24, M.C.A. 1973 have rendered s. 17 proceedings redundant. This is not so for the following reasons:

(a) Section 24 is available only on or after divorce, nullity or judicial separation, whereas s. 17 is available where there are no other matrimonial proceedings between the parties.
(b) As matrimonial misconduct is irrelevant in s. 17 proceedings (*Pettitt* v. *Pettitt* (1969) H.L.; *Gissing* v. *Gissing* (1970) H.L.), such proceedings may be preferred to those under the M.C.A. 1973 in cases where a spouse's misconduct may adversely affect a claim under s. 24. However, where there are proceedings for divorce,

nullity or judicial separation, s. 17 proceedings will seldom be appropriate: *Kowalczuk* v. *Kowalczuk* (1973) C.A.; *Suttill* v. *Graham* (1977) C.A.

(c) No application can be made under s. 24 by an applicant who has remarried: M.C.A. 1973, s. 28(3). Application under s. 17 may be made by an applicant who has remarried, provided it is made within *three years* after decree absolute of divorce or nullity: Matrimonial Proceedings and Property Act 1970, s. 39.

(d) There may be tax advantages in relying on s. 17 which declares a party's entitlement to property. Thus, such an order is not to be regarded as effecting the disposal of an asset and, therefore, does not attract capital gains tax.

(e) On a spouse's bankruptcy the other spouse may defeat the creditor's claim to property by establishing his or her title to that property.

4. The property

Section 17 applies to any property, whether it be real or personal, private, partnership or company. Disputes over money are specifically brought within the scope of the section by the Matrimonial Causes (Property and Maintenance) Act 1958, s. 7.

This Act also provides that the property in dispute need not still be in the possession or under the control of the other spouse.

5. What orders may be made?

As already stated, the court may make such an order as it thinks fit, provided that this gives effect to a party's existing proprietary rights. Thus, the court may order a sale, that there should be no sale until suitable accommodation has been found for the other spouse as in *Lee* v. *Lee* (1952) C.A., that a sum of money should be paid to the other spouse as in *Bothe* v. *Amos* (1975) C.A., or that an owner spouse should be prevented from entering the matrimonial home.

If a spouse has simply disposed of the property in question, or replaced it with other property, the court may order payment of an appropriate sum of money or make such order as it could have done in respect of the original property: Matrimonial Causes (Property and Maintenance) Act 1958, s. 7(3), (4).

6.   The principles applied by the courts

As English family law knows of no doctrine of community of property or of family assets, the mere fact that both spouses use property which belongs to one spouse only does not, of itself, give the non-owner any interest therein. In the absence of relevant statutory provisions, the rules applicable to the determination of a spouse's title to matrimonial property are the ordinary rules of property law as applied to disputes between strangers: *Pettitt* v. *Pettitt* (1969) H.L. This being so, many illustrative cases involve cohabitees rather than spouses.

As a legal estate must be created by deed (Law of Property Act 1925, s. 52), there will be no dispute as to who owns the legal estate in the absence of fraud or mistake. Disputes may, however, arise as to the entitlement to the equitable interest in the property. Section 53 of the 1925 Act provides that, except in the case of resulting, implied or constructive trusts, a declaration of trust must be evidenced in writing. Sometimes both the legal estate and the equitable interest will be set out in a conveyance of the property and, in the absence of fraud or mistake, the conveyance will be conclusive. Thus, in *Goodman* v. *Gallant* (1986) H and W bought a house, the conveyance being taken in H's name alone, and they agreed that W was entitled to a half share of the equity. H and W separated and W's boyfriend moved into the house. H, in return for payment, conveyed the house to W and her boyfriend as joint tenants. W later sought to sever this joint tenancy and she claimed three-quarters of the equity on the basis that H's conveyance had conveyed only half the equity (of which she was entitled to a quarter) as she already owned half by virtue of the earlier agreement. HELD: the conveyance to W and her boyfriend conclusively created a joint tenancy and there was no implied or resulting trust in her favour. She was, therefore, entitled to no more than half the equity.

In the absence of such written evidence, a spouse will be able to establish an equitable interest only by showing that property is held by the other spouse on a resulting, implied or constructive trust.

7.   Resulting and constructive trusts

An implied trust arises from the *presumed* intent of the parties. The resulting trust is a species of implied trust which occurs when property is bought in another's name. In such a case, unless there is evidence to the contrary, a trust may be presumed to have arisen (i.e. resulted) in favour of the person paying for the property. A constructive trust, on the other hand, does not depend upon the parties' presumed intentions but upon grounds of conscience.

Whether a resulting trust can be established depends upon the intention of the parties at the time the property was acquired. The court is required to draw the inferences a reasonable person would draw from the parties' conduct. Notwithstanding that it is not the courts' function to ascribe to the parties an intention they patently never had, the process is nevertheless artificial.

Evidence of this common intention may be provided by the following:

(a) An *actual agreement* between the parties. In *Pettitt* the opinion was expressed that *Balfour* v. *Balfour* (1919) C.A. (an agreement between spouses who are cohabiting is presumed *not* to intend to create legal relations) has little, if any, application to questions of title to spouses' property.

(b) Where one spouse has made a *substantial direct contribution* to the purchase of property in the legal ownership of the other spouse. This may take the form of, e.g. a contribution to the deposit and legal fees (*Muetzel* v. *Muetzel* (1970) C.A.) or regular, as opposed to occasional, contributions to the repayment of the mortgage (*Gissing* v. *Gissing* (1970) H.L.).

(c) Where one spouse has made a *substantial indirect financial contribution* to the purchase of property in the legal ownership of the other spouse: *Gissing* v. *Gissing*. This contribution, which must be in money or money's worth, may take the form of, e.g. a wife's working in her husband's business without wages (*Nixon* v. *Nixon* (1969) C.A.) or her guaranteeing the husband's mortgage and paying for extras for the house after it was built (*Falconer* v. *Falconer* (1970) C.A.).

There is disagreement between the House of Lords and the Court of Appeal, particularly Lord Denning MR, as to whether it is necessary for an *indirect* contribution to be specifically referable to the purchase of the property in question. In *Gissing* Lords Pearson and Diplock and Viscount Dilhorne thought it was necessary. In cases such as *Falconer* v. *Falconer* (1970), *Hargrave* v. *Newton* (1971) C.A. and *Hazell* v. *Hazell* (1972) C.A., Lord Denning

MR thought this was unnecessary. On this view expenditure by the non-owner on general expenses, thereby allowing the owner more resources with which to meet the cost of purchasing the property, suffices to give the non-owner an interest. This approach would have provided a different result in *Gissing*. There the matrimonial home had been purchased by the husband in his name alone. He paid the mortgage instalments, the outgoings on the house, for the holidays and gave his wife a housekeeping allowance. The wife provided some furniture and equipment for the house, bought her own and her son's clothes, paid for various extras for the family's benefit and for the lawn to be laid. The spouses had separate bank accounts. The husband appealed to the House of Lords from the decision of the Court of Appeal that the wife was entitled to a half share in the house. HELD: it was not possible to draw the inference from the facts that there was a common intention that the wife should have any beneficial interest in the matrimonial home.

> NOTE: this case emphasised that the equitable presumption of advancement is of less relevance today than formerly, because there will usually be evidence to rebut the presumption that the purchase of property by a husband in his wife's name is intended to be a *gift* by him to her.

In *Burns* v. *Burns* (1984) C.A. a Court of Appeal which did not contain Lord Denning MR said, in the context of a dispute between cohabitees, that substantial financial contributions had to be referable to the acquisition of the property in question. In *Lloyds Bank plc* v. *Rosset* (1990) H.L. the court held that a wife's indirect contribution by way of renovating the future matrimonial home was insufficient to give her a beneficial interest in it.

In addition to the parties' common intent, it must be shown that the person claiming the beneficial interest has acted to his or her detriment on the basis of such intent: *Grant* v. *Edwards* (1986) C.A. Such detrimental reliance should be more than 'trifling': *Lloyds Bank* v. *Rosset*.

(d) Where the legal owner has so conducted himself in relation to the other spouse that it would be *inequitable* to deny that other a beneficial interest. He will have so conducted himself if, by his words or conduct, he has induced that other to act to his own detriment in the reasonable belief that by so acting he was acquiring a beneficial interest (per Lord Diplock in *Gissing*). In such a case a constructive trust is imposed by law on grounds of conscience. Thus, in *Heseltine* v. *Heseltine* (1971) C.A. the wife had given her husband two sums of £20,000 and a further sum of £20,000. The first two were to enable her to escape estate duty should she predecease her husband; the third to enable him to become a Lloyd's underwriter. All these payments were made at her husband's request and without independent legal advice. The husband deserted the wife and she applied under s. 17 to determine, *inter alia*, title to the £60,000. HELD: it would be inequitable to hold otherwise than that the £40,000 was held by the husband on trust for the wife and the £20,000 was held by him on trust for the family until the breakdown of the marriage, when it was held on trust for the wife.

8. The Married Women's Property Act 1964

In addition to the above, this Act provides a method whereby a wife may acquire an interest in property derived from a housekeeping allowance. Section 1 provides that money derived from any *allowance* made by the husband *for the expenses of the matrimonial home or similar purposes,* or any property acquired out of such money, shall belong to the spouses in equal shares, unless there is an agreement to the contrary.

The following points should be noted:

(a) The Act applies only where it is the husband who makes the allowance.

(b) It is not clear whether the Act may be given retrospective effect. In *Tymoszcuk* v. *Tymoszcuk* (1964) it was held that it could, whereas this was doubted *obiter* in *Re John's Assignment Trusts* (1970) on the basis that the relevant time was when the allowance was made, not when the dispute arose, and retroactivity would disturb accrued titles.

(c) It is not clear whether mortgage instalments are 'expenses of the matrimonial home'. In *Re John's Assignment Trusts* it was said *obiter* that money given by a husband to his wife to pay mortgage instalments was within the Act, although the contrary view had earlier been taken in *Tymoszcuk* as the purchase of a house and the repayment of a loan were not to be regarded as 'expenses'.

(d) The Act creates a tenancy in common. Thus, on the death of one of the spouses the deceased's share will pass under his will or intestacy. Had a joint tenancy been created, the whole beneficial interest would have passed to the surviving spouse.

9.   The Matrimonial Proceedings and Property Act 1970

A further method whereby a spouse may acquire an interest in property is provided by s. 37 of this Act. This provides that where one spouse makes a substantial contribution in money or money's worth to the *improvement of real or personal property* in which, or in the proceeds of which, either or both has or have a beneficial interest, then, subject to any express or implied agreement to the contrary, that spouse shall be treated as having acquired by virtue of his or her contribution a share or an enlarged share, as the case may be, in that beneficial interest. The section goes on to say that the extent of that share shall be that agreed between the spouses or, in default of such agreement, that which seems to the court to be just in all the circumstances, whether the proceedings are between the spouses or not.

It is important to note the following points:

(a) The improvement must be 'substantial'. This preserves the pre-1970 law. Thus in *Pettitt* v. *Pettitt* (1969) H.L. it was said that the work should be of a capital or non-recurring nature (per Lord Reid). Thus 'do-it-yourself' jobs which a spouse would normally do, or work of an ephemeral nature, do not suffice. In *Pettitt* a husband's interior decorating, construction of a wardrobe, laying of a lawn and the construction of a well and a garden wall were held to be insufficient. A distinction should be drawn between improvement and mere maintenance.

In *Davis* v. *Vale* (1971) C.A. the payment of some £274 to connect a house bought for £1,300 to the electricity supply and to provide it with a water-heater, a sink-unit, three fireplaces, a wall and iron gates was 'substantial'.

It seems that the court will look at the situation in its totality and not look at each improvement in isolation: *Griffiths* v. *Griffiths* (1974); *In re Nicholson decd.* (1974).

(b) The improvement itself creates the share in the beneficial interest, notwithstanding the absence of any agreement that it should: *Davis* v. *Vale*.

(c) The section applies to improvements whenever effected: *Davis* v. *Vale*.

(d) Section 37 applies to any property, but only if there is no express or implied agreement precluding its application.

(e) As the contribution may be in money or money's worth, the section applies even if a spouse employs another person to do the work.

(f) In the absence of an agreement as to the extent of a spouse's share the court ascertains the value of the property before and after the date of the improvement(s) and enlarges the share of, or gives a share to, the improver by a proportionate amount corresponding to the increase in value: *In re Nicholson decd.* The court ignores the enjoyment value of the improvements: *Griffiths*.

(g) Section 37 applies to all types of proceedings and is not restricted to proceedings between the spouses.

(h) The section is of no help in ascertaining the ownership of property at the time of its acquisition, unless the improvements were done or agreed to be done at that time: *Davis* v. *Vale*, per Stamp L J.

10. Joint banking accounts

In order to determine the interests of spouses in bank accounts the courts have applied the following principles:

(a) If both spouses pool their resources, e.g. by paying their incomes into a joint bank account, the funds in this 'common purse' belong to them jointly: *Jones* v. *Maynard* (1951). If the marriage ends by judicial decree, the balance will be divided equally between the parties. If it ends by death, the surviving spouse will take the whole balance *jure accrescendi*.

Property purchased with funds from this type of account will *prima facie* belong to the purchaser alone: *Re Bishop* (1965). This presumption may be rebutted by evidence which discloses an intention to hold the property purchased on the same footing as the funds with which it was purchased, as in *Jones* v. *Maynard*.

(b) If the husband alone pays money into a joint account, the presumption of advancement (*see* **7** above) will apply. Though now weak, the presumption will apply in the absence of rebutting evidence, as in *Re Figgis* (1968) where both spouses were dead and there was no direct evidence of their intention.

The presumption is most commonly rebutted by evidence that the account was maintained solely for the wife's convenience to enable her to pay household expenses by cheque: *Hoddinott* v. *Hoddinott* (1949) C.A.

(c) If the wife alone pays money into a joint account, *prima facie* the money will be held on a resulting trust for her, as in *Heseltine* (*see* 7 above) where property bought from a joint account fed by the wife was held to belong to her.

11. Quantification of the beneficial interests

On the assumption that the court has established that a beneficial interest in property exists by virtue of the principles already discussed, the next task for the court is to quantify that interest. Again this is basically dependent upon discovering the intention of the parties at the time of the acquisition of the property as evidenced by their conduct. In *Gissing* (1970) it was stressed that too much use had been made of the equitable doctrine 'equality is equity' to divide property equally even though the contributions of the spouses had not been equal. Notwithstanding this view, the equitable approach will be adopted not only when this mirrors the parties' intention but also when the parties' contributions to the acquisition of the property cannot be accurately computed. This latter situation is likely to occur in the case of indirect contributions.

In the absence of a contrary intent, the parties' shares in the proceeds of sale will be computed as at the date of sale rather than at the date the relationship broke down or they separated: *Turton* v. *Turton* (1988) C.A.

12. Conveyancing problems arising on a sale of the property

Where the legal estate is vested in one spouse only but the other has obtained a beneficial interest because of, e.g. a substantial contribution to the purchase of the property, both spouses will have a beneficial interest in that property which takes effect behind a trust for sale. In such a case a second trustee should be appointed so as to convey the legal estate and overreach the equitable interest. If this is not done, and the purchaser takes the legal estate from the spouse in whom it is vested, he will nevertheless obtain a good title if he takes without actual or constructive notice of the equitable interest. In the case of *unregistered land,* the fact that a wife, who has a beneficial interest by virtue of her contributions to the purchase of the matrimonial home, is in occupation of that home does not amount to constructive notice: *Caunce* v. *Caunce* (1969). Though this decision has been criticised by the Court of Appeal in *Hodgson* v. *Marks* (1971) and *Williams & Glyn's Bank Ltd* v. *Boland and Another* (1979), it has not been overruled.

In *Kingsnorth Trust Ltd* v. *Tizard* (1986) the matrimonial home was unregistered land in H's name. After the marriage broke down W slept in the spare bedroom when H was away and at her sister's (and later at a boyfriend's) when he was at home. When he slept away W returned to care for the children. H sought a mortgage from the plaintiffs using the house as security and stated in his application that he was single. H arranged for a surveyor to visit the house when W was absent. H told the surveyor that he was married but separated and the surveyor found no evidence of occupation by an adult female. The mortgage was granted and the mortgagee later tried to enforce its charge on the house. The question arose whether this charge was subject to W's equitable interest, which she had by virtue of her contributions to the acquisition of the house. HELD: (1) W was in actual occupation of the house despite her regular and repeated absences;

(2) Under s. 199(1)(ii)(a) of the L.P.A. 1925 a purchaser or mortgagee is not fixed with notice of a claimant's rights unless he knows of them or would have known of them if such inspections as ought reasonably to have been made by him were carried out and the claimant is not found to be in occupation and there is no evidence reasonably sufficient to give notice of occupation. On the facts (*a*) the surveyor's discovery that H was married imposed a duty on him to look for signs of occupation by someone other than H and the children and to communicate the information to the mortgagee. In any event, the surveyor's report referred to H's 'son and daughter' and this should have put the mortgagee on further enquiry which would have led to the discovery of W's equitable interest in the house. The mortgagee was not entitled to rely on H's attempt to conceal W's occupation so as to relieve it of the duty to enquire further. Consequently, the mortgagee had notice of W's equitable interest; and (*b*) the mortgagee's pre-arranged inspection via the surveyor did not fall within 'such inspection as ought reasonably to have been made' because his inspection would

not necessarily reveal who was in occupation. Thus the mortgagee could not rely on this provision in s. 199(1)(ii)(a); and

(3) In view of the above the mortgagee's charge was subject to W's equitable interest.

This case adopted the criticisms of *Caunce* voiced in *Hodgson* v. *Marks* and *Boland*.

In *William's & Glyn's Bank Ltd* v. *Boland and Another* (1980) the House of Lords held, dismissing the Bank's appeal from the decision of the Court of Appeal, that, where title to land is *registered*, the equitable interest of a spouse in occupation is an overriding interest which binds a purchaser, regardless of notice, actual or constructive. In this case two husbands who were registered in the Land Registry as sole proprietors of their matrimonial homes, to the purchase of which their wives had contributed, had mortgaged the homes to a bank. This had been done without the wives' knowledge and in the absence of inquiry of them by the bank. The husbands defaulted in their mortgage payments and the bank sought possession orders. HELD: the wives' equitable interests were, by virtue of their actual occupation of the matrimonial home, overriding interests within s. 70(1)(g) of the Land Registration Act 1925 and therefore binding on the bank.

This decision contains *dicta* to the effect that the same principle applies where persons are living together without being married.

'Actual occupation' for the purpose of s. 70 (1)(g) has been held to be a question of fact and degree: *Abbey National Building Society* v. *Cann* (1990).

NOTE: as from December 1990 the system of compulsory registration of land was extended to the whole country. Despite this, land which is unregistered remains so until sold. Consequently, cases on unregistered land are still relevant.

13. Proposals for reform

As a result of *Williams & Glyn's Bank Ltd* v. *Boland and Another* the Law Commission (Law Com. No. 115 (1982)) has proposed that:

(a) The interests of co-owners, purchasers and lenders should be protected by registration. An equitable co-ownership interest and rights flowing therefrom would be enforceable against a purchaser or lender only if registered in the appropriate manner.

(b) There should be no effective sale or other disposition by the co-owner of the matrimonial home unless the other co-owner consents or the court orders the sale etc.

(c) A scheme of equal co-ownership of the matrimonial home should be introduced.

(d) These recommendations should be implemented by legislation incorporating the Matrimonial Homes (Co-ownership) Bill as appropriately amended. This bill, which originated in Law Com. No. 86 and failed to be enacted after a Second Reading in the House of Lords in 1980, provided for statutory co-ownership of the matrimonial home subject to contracting-out provisions.

Section 30 of the Law of Property Act 1925

14. Enforcement of the trust for sale

If spouses are joint tenants or tenants in common in equity of property, that property will be held on statutory trust for sale. This imposes an obligation to sell and unless the trustees agree to postpone sale, application for a sale may be made under s. 30. On such application the court may make such order as it thinks fit. An application under s. 17, M.W.P.A. 1882 would be inappropriate as there would be no dispute as to title to or possession of property.

The court will not order a sale under s. 30 if this would defeat one of the purposes for which the property was acquired. Thus in *Jones* v. *Challenger* (1960) C.A. a house bought as a matrimonial home was ordered to be sold because the parties had divorced and the house was no longer needed for its original purpose. If there are children the primary object is to provide a home for the children and the spouse who is to look after them: *Williams* v. *Williams* (1977) C.A.

In *Re Bailey (a Bankrupt)* (1977) a wife's claim to remain in the former matrimonial home until her son has completed his 'A' level studies did not prevent her former husband's trustee in bankruptcy from obtaining an order for sale. The claims of creditors were entitled to protection and the evidence of interference with the son's education was slight. Under the Insolvency Act 1986 the trustee in bankruptcy will be able to obtain an order for sale only if the court thinks it just and reasonable: s. 336. In deciding this the court must have regard to the creditors' interests, the spouse's (or former spouse's) conduct contributing to the bankruptcy, the needs and financial resources of the spouse or former spouse, the children's needs and all the circumstances of the case except the bankrupt's needs: s. 336(4). Where the trustee in bankruptcy applies for sale *more than a year after the bankruptcy*, 'the court shall assume, unless the circumstances of the case are exceptional, that the interests of the bankrupt's creditors outweigh all other considerations': s. 336(5).

Section 30 is also applicable to property bought by unmarried couples, the first of such cases being *Re Evers' Trust* (1980) C.A. In *Bernard* v. *Josephs* (1982) C.A. the following points regarding the application of s. 30 to unmarried couples were made:

(a) such applications should be brought in the Family Division of the High Court rather than the Chancery Division;
(b) if property is bought in both names, any express declaration of trust is decisive and it is good practice to make such declarations at the time of purchase. Otherwise shares are to be ascertained by reference to the parties' contributions to the purchase;
(c) the parties' shares are normally to be ascertained at the date of separation, though they may be valued at a later date as in *Gordon* v. *Douce* (1983) C.A. and *Walker* v. *Hall* (1983) C.A.;
(d) the court has power to postpone a sale, e.g. so as give time to allow other arrangements for accommodation to be made;
(e) seemingly the threat of refusing to make an order for sale, or postponing a sale indefinitely, cannot be used against the non-occupant.

The payment of an occupation rent by an owner in occupation to an owner out of occupation may be ordered under s. 30 if an order for sale is actually made and the order for payment is ancillary thereto. Payment may be enforced indirectly by the court indicating that unless an undertaking to pay an occupation rent is forthcoming an order for sale will be made: *Dennis* v. *Macdonald* (1981).

The Matrimonial Homes Act 1983

15. The right to occupy the matrimonial home
This Act consolidates, among other Acts, the Matrimonial

Homes Act 1967 which was originally intended to give a spouse who had no proprietary interest in the matrimonial home a right to occupy that home enforceable not only against the other spouse who had the legal estate but also against third parties. The scope of the 1967 Act was considerably widened by later enactments.

Section 1(1) provides that where one spouse is entitled to occupy a dwelling house by virtue of a beneficial estate or interest or contract or by virtue of any enactment giving him or her the right to remain in occupation, and the other spouse is not so entitled, then the spouse not so entitled shall have certain 'rights of occupation'. These rights are:

(a) the right not to be evicted or excluded from the dwelling house or any part thereof without leave of the court given by an order under s. 1;
(b) if not in occupation, the right to enter and occupy the dwelling house with leave of the court.

Rights of occupation continue only so long as the marriage subsists (even if it is polygamous: s. 10(2)) and the other spouse is entitled as above to occupy the dwelling house, except where provision is made under s. 2 for such rights to be a charge on an estate or interest therein: s. 1(10).

The Act does not apply to a dwelling house which has never been the spouses' matrimonial home; s. 1(10).

By s. 1(11) a spouse who has only an equitable interest in the dwelling house will be treated for the purposes of the 1983 Act as being not entitled to occupy by virtue of that interest. Thus, a spouse who has only an equitable interest by virtue of, e.g. some contribution or improvement to the dwelling house, will be able to seek the protection afforded by s. 1.

In determining entitlement to occupy, a mortgagee's right to possession conferred by his mortgage must be disregarded, whether or not he is in possession: ss. 8(1) and 9(4).

16. Protection of rights of occupation
Rights of occupation may be protected by:

(a) application to the court for an order under s. 1;
(b) registration as a charge.

17. Application for an order under s.1

Provided that one spouse has rights of occupation, *either* spouse may apply to the court for an order declaring, enforcing, restricting or terminating those rights, or prohibiting, suspending or restricting the exercise by either spouse of the right to occupy the dwelling house, or requiring either spouse to permit the exercise by the other of that right: s. 1(2).

On such an application the court may make such an order as it thinks just and reasonable having regard to all the circumstances of the case and, in particular, to:

(a) the spouses' conduct in relation to each other and otherwise,
(b) the needs of the spouses and of any children, and
(c) the financial resources of the spouses: s. 1(3).

In *Kaur* v. *Gill* (1988) C.A. it was said that 'all the circumstances' is apt to cover the situation of a purchaser bound by a class F charge.

Without prejudice to its general powers under s. 1, the court may:

(a) Except part of the dwelling house from a spouse's rights of occupation, particularly where the part in question was used for trade, business or professional purposes, e.g. a shop or surgery.
(b) Order a spouse occupying the house or part thereof under this section to make periodical payments to the other spouse for the occupation, i.e. order the payment of rent.
(c) Impose on either spouse obligations to repair and maintain the dwelling house or to discharge any liabilities in respect of it, e.g. order the repayment of the mortgage instalments; s. 1(3).

Where the legal estate in the dwelling house is jointly owned by the spouses, or they are joint tenants under a contractual or statutory tenancy, each may apply for an order prohibiting, suspending or restricting the exercise by the other of the right to occupy, or requiring the other to permit its exercise: s. 9(1) and (3).

In *Kalsi* v. *Kalsi* (1991) C.A. it was held that it was not possible to join third parties who were unaffected by the provisions of the Act in proceedings brought under the Act or to grant relief against such persons when they were not parties to the proceedings.

18. Registration of rights of occupation

In order to provide a spouse with protection against eviction by third parties, rights of occupation are a *charge* on the property: s. 2(1). The charge exists irrespective of whether an order has been made under s. 1 and it takes priority as if it were an equitable interest created on whatever is the latest of the following dates:

(a) the date the other spouse acquired the estate or interest entitling him to occupy the dwelling house;
(b) the date of the marriage; and
(c) the commencement of the 1967 Act, i.e. January 1st, 1968.

If a spouse's rights of occupation are a charge on the other spouse's interest under a trust, and no person other than the spouse is, or could be, a beneficiary under the trust, those rights are also a charge on the estate or interest of the trustees for the other spouse: s. 2(2). Such charge has the same priority as if it were an equitable interest created under powers overriding the trusts on the date it arose: ibid.

The charge *terminates* on the death of the other spouse, or on decree absolute of divorce or nullity unless, during the subsistence of the marriage, the court orders otherwise under s. 1: s. 2(4).

The charge is registrable as a Class F land charge or, in the case of registered land, by a notice. A spouse out of occupation may register a charge even though she has not been given leave by the court to enter and occupy the house: *Watts* v. *Waller* (1972) C.A.

Though the M.H.A. is limited to rights of occupation, a pending land action may be registered. In *Perez-Adamson* v. *Perez-Rivas* (1987) C.A. a wife's application for a property adjustment order was so registered. It was held binding on the mortgagee who had failed to search the Land Charges Register when the husband mortgaged the house.

19. The effect of registration

If properly *registered*, the charge binds everyone acquiring the property, even where the purchaser has obtained the other spouse's estate by surrender: s. 2(6). The binding effect of registration applies even to the other spouse's trustee in bankruptcy for a year following the bankruptcy: s. 336(2), Insolvency Act 1986. Thereafter, it is presumed, in the absence of exceptional circumstances, that the creditors' interests outweigh those of the bankrupt in which case the trustee may successfully apply under s. 1 of the M.H.A. 1983 for an order terminating the other spouse's rights of occupation: s. 336(5).

If the charge is *not registered*, it is void as against a *bona fide* purchaser for value, even if he knew of the spouse's rights of occupation: *Miles* v. *Bull* (*No. 2*) (1969). However, a 'sham' sale may be set aside: *Ferris* v. *Weaven* (1952), as will a sale if it falls within s. 37, M.C.A. 1973 (*see* 9:**16**).

20. Termination of registration
The registration of a Class F land charge will cease in the following circumstances;

(a) The Chief Land Registrar will cancel such registration if satisfied by evidence that the marriage has been terminated by death or court decree, or the rights of occupation have been terminated by court order: s. 5.
(b) A spouse entitled to rights of occupation may, in writing, release those rights or such of them as affect part of the dwelling house: s. 6. In *Wroth* v. *Tyler* (1974) a wife refused to release her rights and her husband, who had contracted to sell the matrimonial home in ignorance of registration of the charge, was liable in damages for breach of contract.
(c) As a charge may be registered in respect of only one dwelling house at any one time, the first charge against property will be cancelled on registration of a later charge: s. 3.

Proceedings to restrain a breach of trust

21. Proceedings by way of injunction
In *Waller v. Waller* (1967) both spouses had contributed to the purchase of the matrimonial home which had been conveyed to the husband alone. As a result of her contribution the wife acquired a beneficial interest in the property. The husband, without appointing the additional trustee as required by the Trustee Act 1925 and without obtaining his wife's consent, agreed to sell the house to a third party. The wife sought an interlocutory injunction to prevent him from disposing of the property without her consent. HELD: The wife was entitled to the injunction. If the husband had not been married to her, he would have been in

breach of s. 26(3) of the Law of Property Act 1925, which requires trustees to consult and give effect to the wishes of the beneficiaries of full age. The wife should not have her rights as a beneficiary prejudiced merely because she was has wife.

In such a case the intending purchaser would be unable to obtain specific performance against either one or both of the spouses. His remedy would be damages for misrepresentation under the Misrepresentation Act 1967, the measure of damages being the rise in value of the property between the date of the contract and that of completion: *Watts* v. *Spence* (1976).

Proprietary estoppel

22. Operation of the doctrine

It has sometimes been doubted whether this is a different category of estoppel from promissory estoppel, well-beloved of students of contract. What is certain is the fact that, unlike promissory estoppel, proprietary estoppel operates as a cause of action capable of creating new rights. Proprietary estoppel exists where:

(a) the plaintiff has acted to his detriment on the basis of a mistaken understanding of his own legal rights, and
(b) the defendant, the possessor of the legal rights, knowing what they are and that the plaintiff has made a mistake in relation to them, encourages the plaintiff to act to his detriment in respect of specific property. In such a case the defendant will be estopped (prevented) from exercising his legal right because it would be unjust and inequitable to allow the defendant to benefit from his conduct. It should, however, be noted that Lord Denning M.R. in *Greasley* v. *Cooke* (1980) C.A. thought, *obiter*, that detriment was unnecessary: he thought the plaintiff merely has to act on the basis of a mistake induced by the other.

This equitable principle is obviously apt to provide assistance to both spouses and cohabitees who may have been knowingly encouraged to, e.g. spend money on property, in the mistaken belief that they will thereby be given a beneficial interest in the property. An extreme example of the operation of proprietary estoppel is provided by *Pascoe* v. *Turner* (1979) C.A. where the defendant lived in the plaintiff's house as his wife. This relationship broke down and the plaintiff moved out telling the defendant that the house and everything in it was hers. On the basis of this, and to the defendant's knowledge, she spent money on renovation and refurnishing. The plaintiff gave the defendant two months' notice and, when she refused to move, instituted a claim for possession. HELD: he was estopped from denying her right to occupy the house as a licensee and the court thought that her equitable right to remain in the house could only be satisfied by a conveyance of the legal estate to her.

Licences

23. Types of licences

A right to occupation, or some other larger proprietary right as in *Pascoe* v. *Turner*, above, may be obtained by way of a licence. A licence may be either contractual or bare or have been obtained by estoppel.

(a) *Contractual licences.* There must be a valid contract and the court may experience difficulty in finding the necessary intent to create legal relations or valid consideration. In *Tanner* v. *Tanner* (1975) C.A. a generous court containing Lord Denning M.R. held that the defendant, who had given up a rent-controlled flat to move into the plaintiff's house with their two children, had a right to remain there until the children left school. Unfortunately the county court had already made an order for possession and the defendant had been rehoused by the local authority. The C.A. awarded the defendant £2000 compensation. In *Horrocks* v. *Forray* (1976) C.A., in somewhat similar circumstances, the court found that the deceased's conduct was more in the nature of a gift than a contractual undertaking, and in *Layton* v. *Martin* (1986) the court was unable to find that the deceased had intended legal relations when he promised his mistress financial security if she would live with him.

(b) *Bare licences.* A bare licence exists where one party has merely given another permission to enter premises. In such cases that permission may be withdrawn at any time. It will be trespass to remain on the premises after permission has been withdrawn, though reasonable time will be allowed to enable other accommodation to be found.

(c) *Licences by estoppel.* A licence may be created as a result of a person acting to his detriment on the basis of another's representation as to an existing fact or as to his intent (known as 'promissory estoppel'). As we have already seen a licence may arise as a result of proprietary estoppel. Generally speaking, proprietary estoppel is the only type of estoppel to act as a sword rather than a shield.

Progress test 7

1. What methods exist for the resolution of property disputes between spouses? **(2)**

2. What is the purpose of s. 17 of the Married Women's Property Act 1882 and to what extent does it still fulfil this purpose? **(3)**

3. What powers has the court in M.W.P.A. 1882, s. 17 proceedings? **(4–5)**

4. What principles are applied by the courts in determining the proprietary interests of the spouses in proceedings under M.W.P.A. 1882, s. 17? **(6–7)**

5. What is the effect on spouses' proprietary interests of purchasing property or making savings from a housekeeping allowance? **(8)**

6. What is the significance in matrimonial property law of improvements to property? **(9)**

7. To what extent is the fact that spouses have a joint bank account important as regards their proprietary interests in (*a*) the funds therein, and (*b*) property purchased therefrom? **(10)**

8. What relevance has the equitable maxim 'Equality is equity' in the quantification of a spouse's beneficial interest in M.W.P.A. 1882, s. 17 proceedings? **(11)**

9. To what extent is an intending purchaser of the matrimonial home affected by a wife's beneficial interest therein?   **(12)**

10. Explain the operation of s. 30 of the Law of Property Act 1925.   **(14)**

11. What is meant by 'rights of occupation' in the Matrimonial Homes Act 1983?   **(15)**

12. How are rights of occupation under the Act of 1983 protected?   **(16–18)**

13. What is the effect of registering a Class F land charge and when does such registration cease?   **(19–20)**

14. What do you understand by proceedings to restrain a breach of trust?   **(21)**

15. How does proprietary estoppel operate to provide a person with an interest in property?   **(22)**

16. What do you understand by a contractual licence?   **(23)**

17. H and W were married two years ago and they set up home in a house bought by H some years before his marriage. The spouses opened a joint bank account into which they both paid their earnings. A year later W ceased working as an interior designer and it was agreed that she should withdraw a monthly sum from the account for the housekeeping and the payment of the mortgage instalments. W bought a record player and various items of furniture from money she saved from the housekeeping. During the last six months she completely redecorated the interior of the matrimonial home and re-tiled the bathroom and kitchen. She now wishes to know if she has any proprietary interest in the matrimonial home and, if so, its extent and how she may enforce it. Advise her.

18. The conveyance of the matrimonial home was taken in the joint names of H and W. H, who is a dentist, uses the ground floor for his dental practice. H bought a holiday cottage in

Wales in respect of which W paid all the legal fees. H has
recently formed an adulterous relationship with his receptionist.
He wants to evict W and the children of the marriage and to
bring the receptionist to live in the matrimonial home. He also
wants to sell the cottage. W wishes to remain in the matrimonial
home, together with the children, and she wishes to prevent the
sale of the cottage. Advise her.

8

Financial provision during marriage

Methods of obtaining financial provision

1. The range of available methods

While a marriage subsists there are several ways in which one spouse may obtain financial provision from the other:

(a) At common law a husband has a duty to maintain his wife (*see* **2** below).

(b) Under the Social Security Act 1986 each spouse has a duty to maintain the other (*see* **3** below).

(c) Either spouse may obtain an order for financial provision from a magistrates' court under the Domestic Proceedings and Magistrates' Courts Act 1978 (*see* **4–19**).

(d) A spouse, usually the wife, may enforce the contractual right to maintenance under a separation or maintenance agreement (*see* **20–27** below).

(e) Either spouse may obtain an order for financial provision on the ground that the other spouse has failed to provide reasonable maintenance. Application may be made either in the High Court or any divorce county court under the M.C.A. 1973, or in a magistrates' court under the D.P.M.C.A. 1978 (*see* **28–34** below.)

(f) Either spouse may obtain an order for maintenance pending suit under s. 22 of the M.C.A. 1973 (*see* **35** below).

(g) Either spouse may obtain an order for financial provision following the granting of a decree of judicial separation (*see* Chapter 5).

The husband's common law duty to maintain

2. The scope of the husband's duty

At common law the husband was obliged to provide his wife with the necessities of life because she did not have the capacity to hold property or to contract to buy them. This obligation lasted only so long as she was entitled to be maintained by her husband. This entitlement ceased if she committed adultery which the husband had not connived at or condoned, and was suspended during her desertion. These rules were still relevant when a wife brought proceedings based upon wilful neglect to maintain, since these proceedings were merely the statutory means whereby the common law obligation could be enforced: *Gray* v. *Gray* (1976). However, the D.P.M.C.A. 1978 has replaced wilful neglect to maintain with proceedings which allege a failure to provide reasonable maintenance and, as this is not based on the common law, it would seem that the common law rules have little relevance. Thus conduct which would have disentitled a wife at common law is now merely a factor to be taken into account.

While a wife's property and contractual disabilities existed, her most important method of enforcing her husband's obligation to maintain her was the power given to her by the common law to pledge his credit for the purchase of necessaries. As these disabilities were gradually removed and the courts were given power to order a husband to pay his wife maintenance, the ability to pledge the husband's credit for necessaries (the agency of necessity) became unnecessary and was abolished by s. 41 of the Matrimonial Proceedings and Property Act 1970. It should, however, be noted that a wife may still act as her husband's agent either by virtue of express appointment, estoppel or the presumption which arises from the fact of cohabitation, but this is of no great practical importance.

The obligation imposed by the Social Security Act 1986

3. The mutual duty to maintain

Section 26(3) of the Act imposes a duty on each spouse to maintain the other and their children. If a spouse persistently refuses or neglects such maintenance and income support is consequently paid to the other spouse or their children, he will be guilty of an offence: s.26(1). Where income support is claimed by or paid to a person whom another person is liable to maintain, the Secretary of State may make a complaint to a magistrates' court to recover the amount from the 'liable person': s. 24(1). On hearing a complaint under s. 24(1) the court must have regard to all the circumstances, particularly the liable person's income, and it may order him to pay such sum, weekly or otherwise, as it considers appropriate: s. 24(4).

> NOTE: under the Child Support Act 1991, scheduled to be operative as from April 1993, unmarried mothers in receipt of social security benefits face fines of over £400 if they refuse to name the father of their child(ren).This Act places a duty to maintain on each parent of a child, one or both of whose parents is or are absent. Orders for maintenance in such cases may be made by a child support officer, thereby taking the matter away from the courts.

Financial provision in magistrates' courts

4.   The Domestic Proceedings and Magistrates' Courts Act 1978

Owing to the anomalies and inconsistencies caused by the divergent development of the matrimonial jurisdiction of the magistrates and the divorce court, the 1978 Act replaced the Matrimonial Proceedings (Magistrates' Courts) Act 1960 and brought the two jurisdictions more into line with each other, insofar as this is possible bearing in mind the different functions they are called upon to perform. Thus it was no longer necessary to prove a matrimonial offence before obtaining a magistrates' order, an order which can never affect the parties' marital status, whereas for some considerable time such offence had not needed to be proved in order to destroy the parties' marital status by divorce.

5.   Family proceedings courts

A magistrates' court sitting for the purpose of hearing family proceedings is known as a 'family proceedings court': s. 92(1)(a), C.A. 1989. A family proceedings court (as defined in s. 65(1), Mag. C.A. 1980) must consist of not more than three justices (magistrates), including, so far as is practicable, both a man and a woman: s. 66(1), Mag. C.A. 1980. A justice is not qualified to sit as a member of a family proceedings court unless he is a member of a family panel specially appointed to deal with family proceedings: s. 67(2), Mag. C.A. 1980. A stipendiary magistrate may sit alone: s. 66(2), Mag. C.A. 1980.

In order to ensure some degree of privacy for the hearing of family proceedings, only the following are allowed to be in court:

(a) officers of the court;
(b) parties to the case before the court;
(c) the parties' solicitors, counsel, witnesses and others directly concerned in the case;
(d) the press, who have restricted powers of reporting; and
(e) any other person who appears to the court to have adequate grounds for attendance: s. 69(2), Mag. C.A. 1980.

NOTE: special rules apply to the hearing of adoption cases.

In order to try to dissociate family proceedings from the criminal proceedings which form the largest part of a magistrates' court's work, s. 69(l) of the Mag. C.A. 1980 provides that the business of the magistrates' courts should, as far as is consistent with the due dispatch of business, be arranged so as to separate the hearing and determination of family proceedings from other business.

6. Jurisdiction

Unlike other matrimonial jurisdiction, the jurisdiction of magistrates' courts is not based on the applicant's domicile. Indeed it is specifically declared that jurisdiction is exercisable notwithstanding that any party to the proceedings is not domiciled in England: D.P.M.C.A. 1978, s. 30(5).

Section 30(1) of the D.P.M.C.A. 1978 confers jurisdiction on a magistrates' court if either the applicant or the respondent ordinarily resides within the commission area for which the court is appointed.

This jurisdiction is exercisable:

(a) where the respondent resides in Scotland or Northern Ireland, if the applicant resides in England and Wales where the parties last ordinarily resided together as man and wife, and

(b) where the applicant resides in Scotland or Northern Ireland, if the respondent resides in England and Wales: s. 30(3).

7.   Limitation period

Section 127(1) of the Mag. C.A. 1980 provides that a complaint must be made within *six months* of the act complained of.

If the matter complained of is a continuing matter, e.g. desertion or failure to provide reasonable maintenance, the six months' limit does not apply. Furthermore, by analogy with the former law relating to persistent cruelty, which has been replaced by 'unreasonable behaviour' (*see* **9** below), it may be that proof of conduct within the six months' period may render evidence of earlier conduct admissible. It should, however, be borne in mind that this approach was adopted to enable the persistence of the cruelty to be proved.

8.   Cases more suitable for the High Court

Section 27 of the 1978 Act provides that the magistrates must refuse to make an order on an application under s. 2 of the Act (*see* **10** below) if of the opinion that any of the matters in question between the parties would be more conveniently dealt with by the High Court. There is no appeal from such refusal.

9.   Financial orders under ss. 2, 6 and 7

The court has power to make orders for financial provision under ss. 2, 6 and 7 of the Act. In the case of the orders under s. 2, an order may be made only if the applicant establishes at least one of the grounds contained in s. 1 of the Act.

The four grounds provided by s. 1 are:

(a) the respondent's failure to provide reasonable maintenance for the applicant; or
(b) the respondent's failure to provide, or to make proper contribution towards, reasonable maintenance for any child of the family;
(c) that the respondent has behaved in such a way that the applicant cannot reasonably be expected to live with the respondent; and
(d) the respondent has deserted the applicant.

NOTE: (1) As regards **(a)** and **(b)** *see* **28–34** below.

(2) In applying **(c)** the magistrates' courts will be guided by decisions of the divorce courts on the same ground: *Bergin* v. *Bergin* (1983). As the 1978 Act does not contain a ground expressly based on adultery, as does the divorce legislation, it will be for the magistrates' courts to determine at what point adultery amounts to behaviour within paragraph **(c)**.

(3) Desertion is given the same meaning as in divorce. There is, however, no minimum period of desertion under the 1978 Act, unlike divorce.

(4) Consequent upon its proposals for divorce the Law Commission (No. 192, 1990) has proposed that the only ground of application under s. 1 should be failure to maintain.

10. Financial provision under s. 2

If an applicant for an order under D.P.M.C.A. 1978, s. 2 satisfies the court of any ground in s. 1, the court may make any one or more of the following orders under s. 2(1):

(a) an order that the respondent shall make to the applicant such periodical payments, and for such term, as may be specified.

(b) an order that the respondent shall pay to the applicant such lump sum as may be specified.

(c) an order that the respondent shall make to the applicant for the benefit of a child of the family to whom the application relates, or to such a child, such periodical payments, and for such term, as may be specified.

(d) an order that the respondent shall pay to the applicant for the benefit of a child of the family to whom the application relates, or to such a child, such lump sum as may be specified.

NOTE: (1) As regards lump sum payments: (a) there is a limit of £1,000 per payee, which limit may be increased from time to time by the Secretary of State. (b) they may be paid by instalments: s. 75, Mag. C.A. 1980. (c) it is specifically provided by D.P.M.C.A. 1978, s. 2(2) that they may be made to enable any liability or expenses reasonably incurred in maintaining the applicant, or any child of the family to whom the application relates, before the making of the order to be met.

(2) 'Child of the family' means the same as under the divorce legislation: s. 88(1), D.P.M.C.A. 1978. A 'child of the family' is defined by s. 52, M.C.A. 1973 (as amended by the C.A. 1989)

as a child of both parties to the marriage, and any other child *treated* by them as a child of the family, other than a child who has been placed with them as fosterparents by a local authority or voluntary organisation.

A child may still be capable of being treated as a child of the family notwithstanding a mistake by the husband as to the child's paternity: *W(RJ)* v. *W(SJ)* (1971). An as yet unborn child cannot be so treated, since 'treatment' involves behaviour towards the child and to hold otherwise would be to place an unfair burden on the husband who would then be liable for the child's maintenance: *A* v. *A* (1974). The court in *A* v. *A* was clearly influenced by the fact that, until the child's birth, the husband mistakenly believed he was the father and, in view of *W(RJ)* v. *W(SJ)*, he would otherwise have been responsible for the maintenance of another man's child for some years to come.

In order for a child to be treated as part of the family there must be a family of which he can be treated as a part. In *Re M (a minor)* (1980) C.A. the wife gave birth to an illegitimate child at a time when the spouses were separated and the wife was living with her parents. For the sake of their parents, who were Roman Catholics, the spouses pretended that the child was the husband's. The husband sent the child birthday and Christmas cards signed 'Dad' and occasionally bought clothes for him. On the husband's petition for divorce the county court judge granted a declaration that the child was a child of the family of the husband and wife. The husband appealed. HELD: as the spouses had been living apart when the child was born and there was nothing in their relationship which bore any relation to that of the husband and wife, the family had ceased to exist as a social unit. Therefore the child was not a child of the family.

11. Consent orders under s. 6

The court may order the respondent to make the financial provision specified by the applicant in his or her application if satisfied that the applicant or the respondent has agreed to make that provision and there is no reason to think that it would be contrary to the interests of justice to make the order.

'Financial provision' means the provision in paragraphs (*a*) to (*d*) of D.P.M.C.A. 1978, s. 2(1)(*see* **10** above), but the amount of any lump sum payment is limited by the terms of the agreement, not the £1,000 limit, and the length of time for which periodical payments are to be made is that specified in the agreement: s. 6(2). If the application relates to financial provision in respect of a child of the family, the court cannot make an order unless it considers that the agreed provision provides for, or makes a proper contribution towards, the child's financial needs: s. 6(3).

The court will be *prevented* from making the order requested if:

(a) not satisfied that financial provision has been agreed, or
(b) it would be contrary to the interests of justice to order the financial provision specified in the application, or
(c) the financial provision agreed in respect of a child of the family does not provide for, or make a proper contribution towards, the child's financial needs, or
(d) the respondent is neither present nor legally represented at the hearing: s. 6(9). This bar may be overcome if the court has such evidence of the respondent's consent to the making of the order, his financial resources and, in the case of financial provision to be made by the applicant in respect of a child of the family, the financial resources of such child, as may be prescribed by rules of court: ibid.

In the case of paragraphs **(b)** and **(c)** the court may order some *other* financial provision provided both parties agree: s. 6(5).

NOTE: where there is an application for an order under both ss. 2 and 6, the application under s. 2 must be treated as withdrawn if an order is made under s. 6: s. 6(4).

12. Orders under s. 7 in cases of voluntary separation
Where the spouses have been continuously living apart for more than three months, neither spouse being in desertion, and one spouse has been making periodical payments for the benefit of the other or of a child of the family, the other spouse may apply for an order under s. 7 and must specify the total amount of such payments made during the three months immediately preceding the making of the application: s. 7(1).

If satisfied that the respondent has made the payments

specified in the application, the court may order that the respondent:

(a) shall make to the applicant such periodical payments, and for such term, as ordered, and/or
(b) shall make to the applicant for the benefit of a child of the family to whom the application relates, or to such a child, such periodical payments, and for such a term, as may be so ordered: s. 7(2).

By virtue of s. 7(3) an order *cannot be made* requiring:

(a) more to be paid in total in any later three month period than was paid during the three months immediately preceding the application;
(b) more to be paid for the benefit of any person than the court would have ordered on an application under s. 2 of the Act;
(c) payment to be made to or for the benefit of a child of the family who is not the respondent's child, unless the court would have made such an order on an application under s. 2.

If the court considers that its powers under s. 7 would not provide reasonable maintenance for the applicant or a child of the family, it may treat the application under s. 7 as if it were an application under s.2, in which case it does not need the agreement of the parties to the order the court wishes to make, unlike s. 6 (*see* s. 6(5), **11** above).

NOTE: as regards payments within the three months preceding the application:

(a) provided that a payment to a third party, e.g. in respect of rent, rates, telephone or fuel charges, is for the benefit of the other spouse or a child of the family, such payment would seem to be within the section.
(b) seemingly any payment made for the benefit of the other spouse or a child of the family is within the section, even if made on a short-term basis to meet a temporary financial emergency.

13. The statutory guidelines for determining applications under ss. 2 and 7

These are contained in s. 3 of the 1978 Act, as substituted by s. 9, M.F.P.A. 1984, and are substantially the same as the criteria applicable under the M.C.A. 1973 (*see* 9:**14**). In the case of an order under s. 2(1) (a) or (b) or an order under s. 7 in favour of the other spouse, the court must give first consideration to the welfare of any minor child of the family: s. 3(1). In addition to all the circumstances of the case, the court must pay particular regard to:

(a) The income, earning capacity, property and other financial resources which each of the parties to the marriage has or is likely to have in the foreseeable future, including any increase in earning capacity which it would in the court's opinion be reasonable to expect a party to the marriage to take steps to acquire. The income of a husband's mistress (or second wife) is not one of his 'resources' (*Brown* v. *Brown* (1981)), though it may be relevant because, e.g. the benefit he derives therefrom may mean that a greater part of his income is available to maintain his wife (or first wife): *Macey* v. *Macey* (1981).

(b) The financial needs, obligations and responsibilities which each of the parties to the marriage has or is likely to have in the foreseeable future. 'Responsibilities' are not limited to those which are legally enforceable. In *Blower* v. *Blower* (1986) a spouse's responsibility towards his cohabitee and their child was a relevant consideration.

(c) The standard of living enjoyed by the parties to the marriage before the occurrence of the conduct which is alleged as the ground of the application.

(d) The age of each party to the marriage and the duration of the marriage. There is no rule which says that no order should be made in the case of a short, childless marriage: *Day* v. *Day* (1987).

(e) Any physical or mental disability of either of the parties to the marriage.

(f) The contributions made or likely to be made in the foreseeable future by each of the parties to the welfare of the family, including any contribution made by looking after the home or caring for the family.

(g) The conduct of each of the parties, if that conduct is such that it would in the opinion of the court be inequitable to disregard it: s. 3(2). In *Robinson* v. *Robinson* (1982) C.A., a case under the original s. 3, magistrates were held to be entitled to take account of a wife's desertion and to reduce the maintenance they would otherwise have awarded her.

In the case of an order under s. 2(1)(c) or (d) or an order under s. 7 to, or for the benefit of, a child of the family, the court must have regard to:

(a) the financial needs of the child;
(b) the income, earning capacity (if any), property and other financial resources of the child;
(c) any physical or mental disability of the child;
(d) the standard of living enjoyed by the family before the living apart of the parties to the marriage;
(e) the manner in which the child was being and in which the parties to the marriage expected him to be educated or trained;
(f) the matters mentioned in relation to the parties to the marriage in paragraphs (a) and (b) of s. 3(2): s. 3(3).

In addition to these matters the court must have regard to the same matters as under the M.C.A. 1973 where the child of the family is not the respondent's child, i.e.:

(a) whether the respondent had assumed any responsibility for the child's maintenance and, if he did, the extent to which, and the basis on which, he assumed that responsibility and the length of time during which he discharged that responsibility;
(b) whether in assuming and discharging that responsibility the respondent did so knowing that the child was not his own child;
(c) the liability of any other person to maintain the child: s. 3(4).

14. The quantum of financial provision

Apart from the limit on lump sum payments, the Act gives no guidance on the quantum of financial provision. Thus, as under the M.C.A. 1973, the amount of periodical payments which may be ordered is a matter for the courts' discretion and the principles to be applied will generally be those which have emanated from divorce cases (*see* 9:**15**). In practice the greatest restriction will be the level of income of the payer.

In magistrates' courts, as in the divorce court, the starting-point may still be one-third (*Gengler* v. *Gengler* (1976)) of the spouses' gross income: *Rodewald* v. *Rodewald* (1977) C.A., though the court will be greatly influenced by the net effect of the proposed order (*see* 9:**15**).

Income support may be taken into account only in the case of the low-income family, when the one-third rule will be inappropriate. Thus in *Shallow* v. *Shallow* (1978) C.A. it was held that a husband could be reduced to (what was then) the supplementary benefit level and the rest of his income, if any, would go to his wife and children. If she was still below supplementary benefit level, she would have to rely on that benefit to bring her up to that level.

15. Interim orders

On an application for an order under ss. 2, 6 or 7 a magistrates' court may make an interim maintenance order either before, or on dismissing, the application, or on a refusal under s. 27 (*see* **8** above) to make an order: s. 19(1)(a). The High Court may make such an order on directing the application to be reheard by a magistrates' court: s. 19(1)(b).

An interim maintenance order requires the respondent to make such periodical payments as the court thinks reasonable to the applicant or a child of the family under 18, or to the applicant for the benefit of such a child: s. 19(1)(i). If the parent with whom the child has his home is not a party to the marriage, the court may order the respondent to make periodical payments to that parent for the child's benefit: s. 19(2).

16. Maximum duration of orders

Periodical payments *for the benefit of a party to the marriage* under ss. 2, 6 and 7 cannot begin earlier than the date of the application for the order and cannot extend beyond the death of either such party or the payee's remarriage: s. 4. Any arrears due at the date of the payee's remarriage are recoverable. It should be noted that 'remarriage' includes a marriage which is void or voidable: s. 88(3).

It follows from the reference to remarriage in s. 4 that an order continues notwithstanding the parties' subsequent divorce. However, the High Court or county court, in later matrimonial proceedings between the parties, may direct that the magistrates' order, other than for a lump sum payment, should cease on a specified date: s. 28(1).

As the periods specified in s. 4 are the maximum periods, the court may decide on a shorter period and this power is unfettered. Thus it would seem possible to order payments of a variable nature in relation to successive periods of time, by analogy with the magistrates' power under the superseded Matrimonial Proceedings (Magistrates' Courts) Act 1960: *Khan* v. *Khan* (1980).

The duration of orders in respect of *children of the family* is governed by s. 5, D.P.M.C.A. 1978:

(a) Periodical payments under ss. 2, 6 and 7 may begin with the date of the application for the order or any later date and cannot extend beyond the death of the payer.

(b) Unless the court considers that in the circumstances of the case the welfare of the child requires that it should extend to a later date, periodical payments shall not in the first instance extend beyond the date of the child's birthday next following his attaining the upper limit of the compulsory school age: s. 5(2), as substituted by the M.F.P.A. 1984. Thus, while the limit remains at 16, orders will normally cease on the child's seventeenth birthday.

(c) Periodical payments should not, in any event, extend beyond the child's eighteenth birthday unless either:

  (*i*) the child is, or will be, or if an extension were granted would be, receiving instruction at an educational establishment or undergoing training for a trade, profession or vocation, whether or not he is also, or will also be, in gainful employment; or

  (*ii*) there are special circumstances which justify the making of an extended order: s. 5(3).

(d) Lump sum orders may be made in favour of a child who has attained the age of 18: s. 5(3)(a).

NOTE: provisions (b) and (c) are the same as those under the M.C.A. 1973 (*see* 9:**19**).

The normal maximum period for an *interim maintenance order* is three months from the making of the order: s. 19(5)(b). This may be extended for a further period or periods not exceeding three months: s. 19(6)(b).

17. The effect of the parties' cohabitation on certain orders

Section 25 concerns the effect on certain orders of the parties to the marriage living with each other either at the date of the making of the order or subsequently. 'Living with each other' has the same meaning as in divorce, i.e. living with each other in the same household: s. 88(2).

The effect of s. 25 is as follows:

(a) *Orders which involve a party to the marriage,* i.e. periodical payments to a party under ss. 2, 6 or an interim maintenance order, remain enforceable notwithstanding the parties' living together *unless* they live together for a continuous period exceeding six months, in which case the order ceases: s. 25(1).

(b) *Orders which do not involve a party to the marriage,* i.e. periodical payments to a child of the family under ss. 2, 6 or an interim maintenance order requiring payments to such a child, are unaffected by the parties' living together 'unless the court otherwise directs': s. 25(2).

(c) *An order under s. 7* is based on the voluntary separation of the parties to the marriage. It therefore follows that if the parties resume living with each other after a s. 7 order that order ceases immediately: s. 25(3). This also applies to any interim maintenance order made on an application for an order under s. 7.

(d) Section 25 is silent as to the effect of the parties' living together on *orders other than those already mentioned.* Therefore orders for lump sums and personal protection and exclusion orders will be unaffected by the parties' living together.

18. Variation and revocation of orders

Under s. 20 the court has wide powers to vary or revoke orders for periodical payments and, in certain circumstances, the variation of such orders may take the form of an order for a lump sum.

On the application of either party to the marriage, orders for periodical payments under ss. 2, 6 and 7 and interim maintenance orders may be varied or revoked. This power to vary includes a power to suspend and then revive a suspended provision: s. 20(6). A variation may be backdated to the date of the application for variation: s. 20(9).

In the case of an order for periodical payments to or in respect of a child of the family, the child himself may apply for variation if he has reached the age of 16: s. 20(12). The same rule applies to orders based on a failure to provide reasonable maintenance made by the High Court or a divorce county court: s. 27(6A), M.C.A. 1973, as inserted by s. 63(4), D.P.M.C.A. 1978 (*see* **28** below).

On an application to vary or revoke a periodical payments order under s. 2(l) (a) or (c) the court may order a lump sum under s. 2(1)(b) or (d): s. 20(l). In these applications it is not necessary for the original order to contain a lump sum. Furthermore, an order under s. 6 need not have contained a lump sum provision to enable the court to order a lump sum on an application to vary or revoke the periodical payments under s. 6: s. 20(2), as substituted by the M.F.P.A. 1984.

Any lump sum, ordered under ss. 20(1) and (2) may be additional to an existing lump sum order and will be subject to the statutory maximum amount per payee: s. 20(7). This statutory limit may be exceeded in the case of a variation of a s. 6 order provided the respondent or applicant agrees: s. 20(8). The court has a general power to vary the instalments where a lump sum has been ordered to be paid by instalments: s. 22.

In exercising its powers under s. 20 the court is directed to give effect, so far as it appears just to do so, to any agreement reached between the parties in relation to the application. Subject to this, the court must have regard 'to all the circumstances of the case . . . [including] any change in any of the matters to which the court was required to have regard when making the order': s. 20(11). First consideration must be given to the welfare of any minor child of the family: ibid.

19. Enforcement of orders for financial provision

Such orders may be enforced as a magistrates' court maintenance order: s. 32(l). Therefore the following methods of enforcement are available:

(a) warrant of distress, which is seldom used;
(b) attachment of earnings;
(c) imprisonment.

Orders may be registered in the High Court in which case they are enforceable as if made by the High Court. Arrears due under a magistrates' order cannot be enforced through the High Court or any county court without the leave of that court if arrears became due more than twelve months before enforcement proceedings were begun: s. 32(4). On hearing the application for such leave the court may refuse leave, grant it subject to such conditions as it thinks proper, or remit all or part of the arrears: s. 32(5).

Maintenance and separation agreements

20. Maintenance and separation agreements compared

The essence of a separation agreement is an agreement between the parties to live apart and this may contain provisions for maintenance. A maintenance agreement merely defines the extent and duration of a spouse's financial liability towards the other and/or the children with no binding agreement to live apart. It is only the former which precludes desertion (*see* 4:**22**).

As these agreements are in general governed by the ordinary law of contract they may be oral, written or under seal. However, for an agreement to be a maintenance agreement for the purposes of the M.C.A. 1973 it must be in writing (*see* **21** below). Consideration is essential unless the agreement is made under seal. Intention to create legal relations will usually exist because the parties will usually either have already separated or be at arm's length and about to separate.

A separation agreement is not void as against public policy provided the parties have already separated or are about to separate: *Wilson* v. *Wilson* (1848) H.L. An agreement which provides for future separation, and thereby tends to hinder reconciliation, is void unless contained in a reconciliation agreement, which obviously promotes reconciliation: *Re Meyrick's Settlement* (1921).

A separation agreement constitutes 'conduct' within s. 25, M.C.A. 1973 (*see* 9:**15**) and account must therefore be taken of it by the court when deciding whether, and if so what, financial provision should be awarded on divorce, nullity or judicial separation: *Brockwell* v. *Brockwell* (1980) C.A. In *Edgar* v. *Edgar* (1980) C.A. a wife had entered into a separation deed with her husband, who was a multi-millionaire, whereby she covenanted not to claim a lump sum in return for his promise to make certain periodical payments. The wife later resiled from this agreement and claimed a substantial lump sum. The trial judge assessed this at £670,000 and the husband appealed. HELD: although the wife was not precluded by her agreement from invoking the court's jurisdiction (*see Hyman v. Hyman* (1929) H.L. at **21** below), that agreement was binding on her. She had been unable to show that the disparity of bargaining power between herself and her husband had been exploited by him to her disadvantage. She had ignored the advice of her legal advisers and there was no evidence of any misconduct by the husband during the course of the negotiations leading to the agreement. There was no evidence that justice required the court to relieve the wife from the consequences of her agreement.

21. Common clauses in agreements
    The most common clauses found in agreements are as follows:

(a) The agreement to live apart, which releases each spouse from the duty to cohabit with the other. It is this clause which distinguishes a separation agreement from a mere maintenance agreement.

(b) An agreement not to take proceedings for *past* matrimonial misconduct — the so-called '*Rose v. Rose* clause' (after *Rose v. Rose* (1883)). This clause, which must be expressly written into the agreement, renders evidence of such misconduct inadmissible. An agreement not to petition for *future* misconduct renders the whole agreement illegal and void.

(c) A non-molestation clause. This is broken if some act is done by the spouse or on his authority which annoys the other spouse or would annoy a reasonable spouse. In *Fearon v. Alylesford* (1884) C.A. a wife's adultery and the subsequent birth of an illegitimate child were held not to be a breach, but there would have been a breach had there been evidence that she had held the child out as her husband's.

(d) A *dum casta* clause. In the absence of a clause to the contrary a wife may enforce her husband's promise to maintain her, even after she has committed adultery. It is, therefore, advisable for a husband to limit his obligation to maintain his wife and he may do this by way of a *dum casta* clause, the effect of which is to entitle the wife to maintenance only as long as she leads 'a chaste life'.

(e) Maintenance for the spouse and/or children. Duration is a question of construction. A husband's covenant to pay maintenance 'for his wife's life' is enforceable notwithstanding her adultery, the termination of the marriage, or the husband's death:

Kirk v. Eustace (1937) H.L. A method of restricting the husband's obligation would be to covenant to pay maintenance 'during the continuance of the marriage and so long as the spouses shall live separate and apart and the wife lead a chaste life'.

(f) A covenant by the wife not to sue for maintenance. At common law such a covenant is void on the ground of public policy as it purports to oust the jurisdiction of the courts: *Hyman* v. *Hyman* (1929) H.L. If such a covenant were the sole or main consideration for the husband's promise to maintain, the whole agreement would be unenforceable because there would be no consideration for the husband's promise. This would be so even if the agreement were under seal: *Bennett v. Bennett* (1952) C.A.

Such a covenant may occur in a maintenance agreement which is covered by s. 34, M.C.A. 1973. If so, it is void, but any other 'financial arrangements' in the agreement 'shall not thereby be rendered void or unenforceable' and are binding unless void or unenforceable for some other reason: s. 34(1). It is not clear whether 'other reason' includes a lack of consideration. The fact that a wife's promise not to seek maintenance is void is probably the reason for the decline in popularity of maintenance agreements.

Section 34(2) defines 'maintenance agreement' as any *written* agreement *between the parties to a marriage* containing financial arrangements, whether made during or after the marriage, or a separation agreement containing no financial arrangements where there is no other written agreement between the parties containing such arrangements.

'Financial arrangements' means provisions governing the rights and liabilities towards each other *when living separately* of the parties to a marriage (including a dissolved or annulled marriage) as regards the making or securing of payments or the disposition or use of any property, including such rights and liabilities as regards the maintenance or education of any child, whether or not a child of the family: ibid.

(g) An agreement delegating the exercise of parental responsibility. An agreement *surrendering* or *transfer*ring such responsibility is unenforceable: s. 2(9), C.A. 1989.

22. Variation of maintenance agreements

Section 35, M.C.A. 1973 provides that a maintenance

agreement as defined in s. 34 may be varied by the court on application by either party to the agreement.

Both parties must be domiciled or resident in England in order to give a divorce county court jurisdiction. A magistrates' court has jurisdiction if both parties are resident in England and Wales and at least one is resident in the commission area for which the court is appointed.

There can be no variation unless the court is satisfied that one of the following conditions is fulfilled:

(a) there has been a change in the circumstances, including a change foreseen by the parties when making the agreement, in the light of which the particular financial arrangements were made or financial arrangements were omitted, or
(b) the agreement does not contain proper financial arrangements with respect to any child of the family: s. 35(2).

> NOTE: Financial arrangements contained in a maintenance agreement made between the married or unmarried parents of a child in respect of that child may be varied or revoked on the basis of the above conditions: Sched. 1, para. 10, C.A. 1989. Alteration may take the form of either inserting a provision for secured or unsecured periodical payments, or increasing, reducing or terminating existing periodical payments.

23. Orders which can be made by the court

The orders which can be made may be retrospective (*Warden v. Warden* (1981) C.A.) and differ according to whether the variation is by a High Court or divorce county court or by a magistrates' court:

(a) *Variation by the High Court or divorce county court.* The court may make the following alterations:
>   (*i*) it may vary or revoke any financial arrangement in the agreement; or
>   (*ii*) it may insert financial arrangements for the benefit of a party or a child of the family.

(b) *Variation by a magistrates' court.* The court has power only in relation to periodical payments. Thus it may make the following alterations.
>   (*i*) where the agreement makes no provision for periodical

payments by either party, it may insert a provision for the making by one of the parties of periodical payments for the maintenance of the other or of any child of the family;

(*ii*) where the agreement does provide for periodical payments, it may increase, reduce or terminate those payments.

If the court alters an agreement by inserting or increasing a provision for periodical payments, these payments must terminate in accordance with the rules laid down in s. 28(1), M.C.A. 1973 as regards a spouse, and s. 29(2) and (3) as regards a child (*see* 9:**5, 19**).

Although the High Court and divorce county court may have power to vary an existing agreement by inserting a provision for a lump sum payment, such power does not exist in favour of a wife after her remarriage: *Pace (formerly Doe) v. Doe* (1977).

24. Variation of an agreement after one party's death

If a maintenance agreement within the meaning of M.C.A. 1973, s. 34 provides for the continuation of payments after the death of either party and that party died domiciled in England and Wales, the surviving party or the deceased's personal representatives may apply to the High Court or to *any* county court for a variation under s. 35: s. 36. A magistrates' court has no similar power.

An application cannot be made, except with the permission of the High Court or county court, after the end of the six months from when representation to the deceased's estate was first taken out: s. 36(2).

A county court has no jurisdiction under s. 36 unless it would have jurisdiction by virtue of s. 22, Inheritance (Provision for Family and Dependants) Act 1975.

Any alteration made in pursuance of this section creates the same consequences as if the alteration had taken place by agreement between the parties, for valuable consideration and immediately before the deceased's death: s. 36(4).

NOTE: Similar powers exist in relation to a maintenance agreement which provides for payments for the maintenance of a child after the death of a party to the agreement: Sched. 1, para. 11, C.A. 1989.

25. Matters to which the court must have regard in deciding whether to order a variation

If the court is satisfied as to the existence of one of the conditions set out in **22** above, it may make such alterations to the agreement 'as may appear to that court to be just having regard to all the circumstances': M.C.A. 1973, s. 35(2). In *Gorman* v. *Gorman* (1964) C.A. the spouses agreed to separate on the basis that the husband would not pay his wife maintenance but would provide free accommodation for her and the children and would maintain the younger children. The husband's earnings quadrupled and the wife's ill-health prevented her from earning. The husband voluntarily paid her £6 per week and she was in receipt of national insurance benefit. The wife applied to vary the agreement under s. 1(3) of the Maintenance Agreements Act 1957, the similarly-worded predecessor to s. 35, M.C.A. 1973. At first instance her application was refused and she then appealed to the Court of Appeal. HELD: as the circumstances in the light of which the financial arrangements were made were primarily to be judged objectively, the parties as reasonable people must have had in mind that the husband's earnings would increase. The change in circumstances had not rendered the agreement unjust because the wife was not destitute and the agreement was based on the express understanding that there was to be no maintenance for the wife. The Court applied *Ratcliffe* v. *Ratcliffe* (1962) C.A. which had held that a husband's voluntary reduction of his earnings by leaving his job to train for teaching did not justify an alteration in his favour of a maintenance agreement.

26. Discharge of agreements

This is in general governed by the ordinary law of contract. Thus an agreement may be terminated in the following ways:

(a) By agreement.
(b) A resumption of cohabitation discharges a separation agreement, but whether maintenance and property provisions are discharged is a question of construction.
(c) By breach. Only a *substantial* breach entitles the other party to treat the agreement as discharged. Thus a mere failure to pay maintenance is not a sufficient breach: *Clark* v. *Clark* (1939) (*see* **4:24**).

(d) A subsequent decree which terminates the duty to cohabit discharges a separation agreement, but whether maintenance provisions are discharged is a question of construction.
(e) The husband's bankruptcy discharges his obligation to pay maintenance under the agreement as arrears and future payments are provable in his bankruptcy.

27. Remedies for breach

These are the normal remedies available for breach of contract. These are equally available if an agreement has been varied by the court under M.C.A. 1973, ss. 35 or 36 since such variation is declared as having the same consequences as if made by agreement between the parties for valuable consideration.

The remedies are:

(a) damages.
(b) specific performance. There must be consideration even if the agreement is under seal.
(c) injunction.

Failure to provide reasonable maintenance

28. The grounds for an application

Either spouse may apply to the High Court or county court for an order under s. 27, M.C.A. 1973 if the respondent:

(a) has failed to provide reasonable maintenance for the applicant, or
(b) has failed to provide, or to make a proper contribution towards, reasonable maintenance for any child of the family: s. 27(1), as substituted by s. 63(1), D.P.M.C.A. 1978.

These grounds are the same as those contained in s. 1, D.P.M.C.A. 1978 (*see* **9** above). It is, therefore, possible to apply both in the High Court and divorce county court and in a magistrates' court for an order on the basis of a failure to provide reasonable maintenance.

The 1978 Act has brought the law in relation to failure to maintain applied in these courts broadly into line, although there are marked differences between the jurisdiction and powers of the courts (*see* **30–34**).

29. Nature of the proceedings
These proceedings are independent of, and not ancillary to, other proceedings. Thus the parties do not have to be in the process of seeking other matrimonial relief or be living apart.

30. Jurisdiction
The High Court or a county court has jurisdiction only if:

(a) the applicant or the respondent is domiciled in England or Wales on the date of the application; or
(b) the applicant has been habitually resident there throughout the period of one year ending with that date; or
(c) the respondent is resident there on that date: s. 27(2), as substituted by s. 6, Domicile and Matrimonial Proceedings Act 1973.

For the jurisdiction of magistrates' courts *see* **6** above.

31. Matters to which the court must have regard
In deciding:

(a) whether the respondent has failed to provide reasonable maintenance for the applicant, and
(b) what order, if any, to make under this section in favour of the applicant,

the High Court or divorce county court must have regard to all the circumstances of the case including the matters mentioned in s. 25(2) of the 1973 Act (*see* 9:**14**): s. 27(3), as substituted by the M.F.P.A. 1984.

This approach is similar to that applicable to applications for ancillary relief.

As the parties' conduct will probably be dealt with in much the same way as in applications for ancillary relief, the applicant's adultery will no longer be an automatic bar to an order.

In addition to the matters specifically mentioned the court is under a duty to consider 'all the circumstances of the case'. These will include the fact that the applicant may be in receipt of maintenance payments under an agreement. If so, by analogy with the law which applied in relation to wilful neglect to maintain, the court may still find that there has been a failure to provide reasonable maintenance on the basis of *Tulip v. Tulip* (1951) C.A. This view may be supported by the fact that it is the level of maintenance which must be unreasonable and not the failure to maintain. Today, the more likely remedy in such a case would be an application to vary the agreement.

In the case of orders in respect of children of the family, the court must have regard to the matters set out in s. 25(3)(a) to (e). Where the child is not the respondent's child the court must have regard to the matters set out in s. 25(4) (*see* 9:**21**). In addition to these matters, where an application relates to a minor child of the family first consideration must be given to the welfare of that child: s. 27(3) as substituted by the M.F.P.A. 1984.

For the similar approach in magistrates' courts *see* **13** above.

32. Orders under s. 27

It is only the respondent who can be ordered to make one or more of the following under M.C.A. 1973, s. 27(6):

(a) Periodical payments, secured or unsecured, to the applicant, to the child to whom the application relates, or for the benefit of that child.
(b) A lump sum. This may be paid by instalments which may be secured. Such sum may be paid to enable the applicant to meet liabilities or expenses reasonably incurred in maintaining the applicant or any child of the family to whom the application relates before the making of the application: s. 27(7).

The court also has power to make an interim order for periodical payments where the applicant or any child of the family to whom the application relates is in immediate need of financial assistance, but it is not yet possible to determine what order, if any, should be made: s. 27(5).

A periodical payments order in favour of a child which ceases to have effect when the child reaches 16 or at any time thereafter but before he attains 18 may be revived: s. 27(6B).

For the much more limited powers of magistrates' courts *see* **10** above.

33. Variation of orders

The High Court or a divorce county court has power under s. 31, M.C.A. 1973 (*see* 9:**29**) to vary orders under s. 27 for periodical payments, both secured and unsecured, and lump sums payable by instalments.

Where a spouse applies to vary any periodical payments order made in his or her favour, the court cannot order a lump sum or property adjustment: s. 31(5).

Where any periodical payments order has been made in favour of a child of the family, that child may apply for a variation provided he has reached the age of sixteen: s. 27(6A), inserted by the M.F.P.A. 1984.

34. Maximum duration of orders

Payments to a party to the marriage ordered by the High Court or a divorce county court are governed by s. 28, M.C.A. 1973 and those in respect of a child of the family by s. 29 (*see* 9:**5, 19**).

For the duration of orders made by magistrates' courts *see* **16** above, but note that the parties' resumed or continued cohabitation has no effect on orders made in the High Court or a divorce county court (*see* **17** above).

35. High Court and magistrates' court compared

The following points should be noted:

(a) In both instances a failure to provide reasonable maintenance must be proved and the matters to be considered by the court are broadly similar.

(b) The jurisdictional requirements are different.

(c) It will usually be cheaper and quicker to apply to the magistrates' court and this probably explains why little use is made of the High Court.

(d) In view of the more limited orders available in a magistrates' court, applications to the High Court will usually be reserved for where the respondent is a person of some means.

(e) Where the parties are living together application may only be made to the High Court or a divorce county court.

Maintenance pending suit

36. Orders under s. 22, M.C.A. 1973

On a petition for divorce, nullity or judicial separation, the High Court or a divorce county court may order *either* party to the marriage to make to the other such periodical payments for his or her maintenance and for such term as the court thinks reasonable.

This order is known as an order for maintenance pending suit. In deciding whether to make an order the court is *not* required to consider the matters set out in s. 25 (*see* **9:14**).

Section 22 specifies that the order cannot begin earlier than the presentation of the petition and ends on the determination of the suit. The court may continue the order if there is an appeal from the court's decision: *Schlesinger* v. *Schlesinger* (1958).

The only order that can be made is in relation to periodical payments and these cannot be secured. Any deficiencies in the amount of maintenance pending suit may be remedied by the back-dating of financial provision on the granting of a decree of divorce, nullity or judicial separation.

Progress test 8

1. How may a spouse obtain maintenance from the other during the subsistence of the marriage? **(1)**

2. To what extent is the husband's common law duty to maintain his wife relevant today? **(2)**

3. How does the Social Security Act 1986 affect the duty of one spouse to maintain the other? **(3)**

4. What special rules apply to 'family proceedings courts'? **(5)**

5. When does a magistrates' court have jurisdiction to hear family proceedings? What limits are there to the court's ability to make an order in such proceedings? **(6–8)**

6. What power has a magistrates' court to make orders for financial provision? **(9–12)**

7. What matters must the court consider when deciding applications under ss. 2 or 7 of the D.P.M.C.A. 1978? **(13)**

8. How does a magistrates' court determine the amount of financial provision to be paid by the respondent? **(14)**

9.   When an interim order be made by magistrates?   **(15)**

10. What are the rules governing the maximum duration of magistrates' orders (a) for the benefit of a party to the marriage, and (b) in respect of children of the family?   **(16)**

11. In what circumstances will a magistrates' order be terminated, varied or revoked?   **(17–18)**

12. How may a magistrates' order for financial provision be enforced?   **(19)**

13. What is the difference between a separation agreement and a maintenance agreement?   **(20)**

14. Discuss the most usual clauses to be found in separation or maintenance agreements.   **(21)**

15. What powers exist to vary a maintenance agreement? **(22–24)**

16. What matters must the court consider in deciding whether to vary a maintenance agreement?   **(25)**

17. In what ways may an agreement be terminated and what are the remedies for breach of an agreement?   **(26–27)**

18. In what circumstances may a spouse be ordered to maintain the other spouse and/or children of the marriage when no other matrimonial proceedings are pending?   **(28–29)**

19. What matters must a court take into account in deciding whether to make an order and, if so, the amount of the order under s. 27, M.C.A. 1973?   **(31)**

20. Briefly compare the High Court and magistrates' court in the context of a claim that one spouse has failed to maintain the other.   **(30, 32–34)**

21. What powers exist to vary orders under s. 27, M.C.A. 1973? **(33)**

22. What is maintenance pending suit and when may it be awarded? **(36)**

23. Four years ago H and W were reconciled after they had resolved their marital difficulties. They entered into an agreement in which H agreed, *inter alia*, to pay W £25 per week should they separate in return for her promise not to sue for maintenance. Six months ago H went to live with Miss X. Thereafter H has paid in accordance with the agreement but W finds this insufficient as she is unable to obtain employment. Recently H gave W £150 in order to cover the cost of repairs to the former matrimonial home. Advise W, who does not want a divorce, how she might obtain more maintenance from H. What difference, if any, would it make to your advice if W has committed adultery?

9

Financial provision after the termination of marriage

Introduction

1. Equality of spouses' duty to maintain

The husband's common law duty to maintain his wife ceases on the dissolution of the marriage. However, on dissolution the High Court or divorce county court has wide powers to order *either* spouse to make ancillary financial provision and/or property adjustment for the other spouse. In practice this will usually mean that the husband is ordered to maintain his ex-wife.

2. The statutory guidelines

The Matrimonial and Family Proceedings Act 1984 repealed the former requirement whereby the court had, as far as was practicable, to place the parties in their pre-breakdown financial position. This direction has been replaced be various guidelines to the effect that the courts' wide-ranging powers to order financial provision are to be exercised:

(a) with regard to all the circumstances of the case, first consideration being given to the welfare while a minor of any child of the family under the age of eighteen: s. 25(1);

(b) with regard *in particular* to the matters specified in s. 25(2), (3) and (4) (*see* **14, 20, 21** below).

(c) with regard, in certain circumstances, to the ability of the payee to become self-sufficient: s. 25A (*see* **5** below). This is the so-called 'clean break' principle.

NOTE: as the child's welfare in (a) is not the 'paramount consideration' as it is under the Children Act 1989, it is likely that such welfare, though it may be given greater weight than other matters, will not necessarily prevail over other considerations (*see* 13:6).

3.   The orders which may be made
The court may make orders under ss. 23 and 24 of the 1973 Act which are in the nature of cash payments and capital. As regards cash, under s. 23 the court may order:

(a) unsecured periodical payments;
(b) secured periodical payments;
(c) lump sum or sums.

All these orders are referred to in the Act as 'financial provision' orders (*see* **4–8**).
As regards capital, under s. 24 the court may order:

(a) transfer of property;
(b) settlement of property;
(c) variation of ante- or post-nuptial settlements;
(d) reduction or extinction of an interest in a nuptial settlement.

All these orders are referred to in the Act as 'property adjustment' orders (*see* **9–12**).
The court may also order a sale of property (*see* **13**).

NOTE: applications for ancillary relief may be made by a party who is not to benefit thereby. In *Simister* v. *Simister* (1986) it was held that the court had jurisdiction to hear an application by a husband for a periodical payments order to be made against him so that he could be relieved of a maintenance agreement.

Financial provision for a party to the marriage

4.   When may the court make an order?
All the above orders may be made on the granting of a decree nisi of divorce or nullity (or on the granting of a decree of judicial separation) or at any time thereafter. This is so even if the order is made by consent and it states that it is not to take effect until

after decree nisi: *Board* v. *Checkland* (1987) C.A. However, although proceedings may be taken at any time after the presentation of the petition (M.C.A. 1973, s. 26), neither the orders nor any settlement made in pursuance thereof take effect until decree absolute of divorce or nullity (ss. 23(5), 24(3)).

5. Duration of an order for financial provision

Though the court will specify the period for which the order is to run, the term cannot exceed the maximum laid down by M.C.A. 1973, s. 28, i.e. in the case of *unsecured* periodical payments, the joint lives of the parties or until the payee's remarriage; in the case of *secured* periodical payments, the payee's life or remarriage.

NOTE: (1) 'Remarriage' includes a marriage which is void or voidable: s. 52.

(2) There can be no application for financial provision or property adjustment against the former spouse by a spouse who has remarried.

In pursuance of the policy of the legislation to encourage self-sufficiency, the court, on or after the grant of a divorce or nullity decree, must consider whether it would be appropriate to exercise its powers to order periodical payments, lump sums, or a sale of property in favour of a party to the marriage, in such a way that the financial obligations of each party towards the other will be terminated as soon after decree as it considers just and reasonable: s. 25A(1). It has been emphasised that the court is required only to consider the appropriateness of a clean break; it should not strive to achieve a clean break regardless of all other considerations: *Clutton* v. *Clutton* (1991) C.A. The court may order periodical payments for such term as would in its opinion be sufficient to enable the payee to adjust without undue hardship to the termination of his or her financial dependence on the payer: s. 25A(2). In *Waterman* v. *Waterman* (1989) C.A. the trial judge imposed a five-year limit on the wife's receipt of periodical payments. The court also has power to direct that a party shall not be entitled to apply under s. 31 of the 1973 Act (*see* **25** below) for an extension of the term specified in an order for periodical payments in favour of a party to a marriage made on or after a decree of divorce or nullity: s. 28(1A).

6. Periodical payments

These provide a spouse with a steady income and, in a proper case, they may be awarded in addition to a lump sum.

7. Secured periodical payments

Here the court directs that the payer should pay an annual sum to the payee and that such sum should be secured on a capital fund provided by the payer, e.g. stocks and shares, and vested in trustees. In the case of default in making the payments ordered, resort may be had to the fund but, in the absence of such default, the capital ultimately reverts to the payer or his estate. The advantages of secured over unsecured provision are:

(a) it lasts for the payee's life;
(b) enforcement is more likely to be successful;
(c) unlike unsecured provision it may be assigned to another.

8. Lump sum payments

Although M.C.A. 1973, s. 23 gives the court power to make an order for 'lump sum or sums', it is not possible for more than one lump sum order to be made but such an order may be payable in instalments: *Coleman* v. *Coleman* (1973). Such instalments may be secured: s. 23(3)(c).

Section 23(3) allows the court, without prejudice to its general power to award a lump sum, to order the payment of such sum to enable the applicant to meet liabilities reasonably incurred in maintaining himself or herself or a child of the family before the application for an order was made.

In assessing the amount of a lump sum the court should take no account of the Law Society's statutory charge (*see* **10** below) so as to increase the amount of the order and thereby increase the amount that might be recovered by way of that charge: *Collins* v. *Collins* (1987) C.A. The 'one-third rule' is applicable when assessing the amount of a lump sum payment: *Bullock* v. *Bullock* (1986) C.A.

At one time the courts were prepared to make a lump sum award only where the payer had substantial available capital as in, e.g. *Davis* v. *Davis* (1967) C.A.: the husband's capital amounted to some £400,000 and the wife was awarded the lump sum of £25,000, in addition to periodical payments, in order to enable her to establish a home. However, the Law Commission recommended that greater use should be made of lump sum awards and it is possible to summarise the principles applicable to such awards as follows:

(a) the payer should have sufficient available capital assets without crippling his earning power;

(b) the payee need have no specific purpose for the lump sum in mind;

(c) such payments should be made outright and not subject to conditions except that where there are children the award may be made subject to a settlement;

(d) they may reduce or obviate periodical payments and this may be a crucial consideration where it appears that the making of such payments may be attended by bitterness.

Section 23(6), inserted by s. 16 of the Administration of Justice Act 1982, allows a court to order that a lump sum to be paid at a later date or by instalments shall carry interest at a rate specified by the court.

> NOTE: an application for an immediate lump sum may be adjourned if there is a real possibility in the foreseeable future of capital being available: *Davies* v. *Davies* (1985) C.A.

Property adjustment orders

9.   A transfer of property order
Under M.C.A. 1973, s. 24(1) (a) the court may transfer the property of one spouse to one of the following:

(a) the other party;
(b) any child of the family;
(c) any person for the benefit of any child of the family.

This power covers not only property in the possession of a spouse but also property to which that spouse is entitled in reversion. It may be used in relation to investments, or, as is usually the case, the matrimonial home, either in place of, or in addition to, a lump sum order.

> *Allen* v. *Allen* (1974) C.A.: the matrimonial home, which was in the husband's name alone, was ordered to be transferred by him to himself and his wife in equal shares.

Hector v. *Hector* (1973) C.A.: the matrimonial home, which was jointly owned by the spouses, was ordered to be transferred to the wife, subject to a charge of £1,000 to be paid to the husband on his wife's death, the sale of the house or the youngest child reaching 16.

NOTE: this form of order was criticised in *Alonso* v. *Alonso* (1974) C.A. and *McDonnell* v. *McDonnell* (1977) C.A. because in times of rapid inflation it was thought preferable to give a spouse a proportion of the value of the matrimonial home rather than a charge for a fixed amount.

Brisdion v. *Brisdion* (1974) C.A.: the spouses had bought their council house and it had been conveyed into their joint names. The husband had paid a £5 deposit and the mortgage repayments for some 15 months. As his contribution towards the acquisition of the property, and therefore his interest in it, was so small, the house should be transferred wholly to the wife.

NOTE: a similar order was made in *President* v. *President* (1977) C.A. where the husband's eventual share in the matrimonial home would be small because of the Law Society's charge for legal aid costs.

10. A settlement of property order

Under M.C.A. 1973, s. 24(1) (b) the court may order such property as is mentioned in **9** above to be settled for the benefit of the other party and/or children of the family.

This power may be used in relation to , e.g. shares, but it is most commonly used in connection with the matrimonial home as a means of providing a home for the wife and child(ren) but at the same time preserving what will usually be the spouses' main capital investment.

Mesher v. Mesher (1973) C.A.: the matrimonial home stood in the spouses' joint names. The husband went to live with his mistress and his wife remained behind with the eight year old daughter of the marriage. By the time the case reached court both spouses had remarried. HELD: it was preferable that the wife and daughter should have a roof over their heads rather than that the wife should be given capital. Therefore the house should be held by the parties in equal shares on trust for sale and should not be sold until the daughter reached 17 or leave of the court was obtained.

NOTE: (1)   In *Martin* v. *Martin* (1978) C.A. it was stressed that the prime consideration is to give both parties a roof over their head, whether or not there are children involved. If a sale of the matrimonial home will provide a home for both parties, it should be sold and they should be given their shares absolutely.

The importance of the need to provide the parties with a home, even when there are no children, is illustrated by *Dallimer* v. *Dallimer* (1978) C.A. where the court accepted that it would be wrong to make a 75-year-old husband leave the matrimonial home. His wife, to whom the co-respondent had transferred his home in which they were both living, was given a one-third interest in the former matrimonial home.

(2)   It is not every case which will lend itself to a *Mesher* type of order. In *Hanlon* v. *Hanlon* (1978) C.A. such an order was thought inappropriate because the parties had not remarried and, if the original order (house to be held by the parties on trust for sale for themselves in equal shares or until the youngest child reached 17) were adhered to, the effect of the Law Society's charge for legal aid costs would be that neither party would receive more than £2,500, and the wife and daughter would have to leave the house and be housed by the local authority, whereas the husband was living in police accommodation. The court ordered the house to be transferred to the wife absolutely with the husband being compensated by a reduction in the amount of periodical payments he had to make.

The Court of Appeal also criticised the *Mesher* order in *Carson* v. *Carson* (1981) C.A. and *Mortimer* v. *Mortimer-Griffin* (1986) C.A. However, in *Clutton* v. *Clutton* (1991) C.A. it was said that a *Mesher* order might still provide the best solution, e.g. where the money realised by the sale of the matrimonial home was sufficient to provide both parties with a roof over their heads but the interests of the children required them to remain in the matrimonial home.

NOTE: if a house is transferred by the court, that is 'property

. . . recovered or preserved' within s. 16(6) of the Legal Aid Act 1988, and the Law Society is then entitled to recover costs from a legally aided party by way of a first charge on the property in question. Where the property is the matrimonial home, the Law Society has a discretion to postpone the enforcement of the charge and to transfer a postponed charge to another house, e.g. the next house bought by the ex-spouse. A similar discretion exists where the property in question is cash, e.g. moneys received in respect of a spouse's interest in the matrimonial home to be used for the purchase of a home. If enforcement is postponed, interest is charged at a rate of 12% per annum simple interest.

In *Hanlon* v. *The Law Society* (1981) H.L. and *Simmons* v. *Simmons* (1983) C.A. the hope was expressed that the hardship caused by the charge for the cost of legal aid would be obviated by legislation.

It should be noted that the statutory charge does not apply:

(a) if costs are recovered from the other side;
(b) to the first £2,500 of money or property recovered or preserved;
(c) to periodical payments.

> NOTE: a party may make a 'Calderbank offer' (named after *Calderbank* v. *Calderbank* (1976) C.A.). Here a party makes a 'without prejudice' offer of financial provision. If rejected, the court first learns of it only after it has made an order. If the order is no more advantageous to the offeree than the offer, the offeror may escape having to pay all or some of his costs.

11. An order for the variation of a marriage settlement

The court, for the benefit of the parties to the marriage and/or children of the family, may vary an existing ante-nuptial or post-nuptial settlement made on the parties to the marriage. For this power under M.C.A. 1973, s. 24(1) (c) to be exercisable there must be:

(a) *A settlement*
    (*i*) This has been widely defined and, as well as marriage settlements in the strict sense, it has been held to cover

such matters as a house bought by both spouses but conveyed to the husband alone, a house in the spouses' joint names and an insurance policy effected by a husband for his wife's benefit.

(*ii*) An outright transfer or gift of property is *not* a settlement: *Prescott* v. *Fellowes* (1958) C.A.

(*iii*) Section 24(1) (c) expressly provides that the term includes a settlement made by will or codicil. There can, however, be no variation of a settlement so made during the testator's lifetime.

(*iv*) The settlement must be in existence at the date of the final decree.

(b) *The settlement must have a nuptial element.*

(*i*) The settlement 'must provide for the financial benefit of one or other or both of the spouses as spouses and with reference to their married state' per Hill J in *Prinsep* v. *Prinsep* (1929).

(*ii*) The settlement must have been made with reference to the particular marriage before the court.

(*iii*) An agreement to provide maintenance in the event of the marriage *not* continuing does not possess the required nuptial element.

(*iv*) The settlement may be made either by the parties themselves or a third party.

NOTE: the court may achieve the same result, in an appropriate case, by using its power to order a transfer under s. 24(1)(b) rather than by ordering a variation.

12. An order extinguishing or reducing an interest under a marriage settlement

This power, under M.C.A. 1973, s. 24(1)(d), allows the court to extinguish or reduce the interest of either party under a marriage settlement notwithstanding the fact that there is no resulting benefit either to the other party or a child of the family.

13. An order for the sale of property

As a result of Law Com. No. 99, *Orders for Sale of Property under the Matrimonial Causes Act 1973* (1980), the Matrimonial Homes and Property Act 1981 inserted a new s. 24A into the M.C.A. 1973.

This section provides that on the making of any order for financial provision (other than for unsecured periodical payments), or at any time thereafter, the court may order the sale of any property specified in the order, provided that at least one spouse has a beneficial interest in it or the proceeds of sale: s. 24A(1). Though the section applies to any property, the matrimonial home will usually be the subject of an order for sale.

The court may impose conditions on the order, e.g. that the property be offered for sale to a specified person or class of persons (s. 24A(2)), or that it is not to take effect until the occurrence of a specified event or after the expiration of a specified time (s. 24A(3)).

14. The statutory guidelines for determining applications under ss. 23, 24 and 24A

Section 25 of the M.C.A. 1973 (substituted by M.F.P.A. 1984, s. 3), in addition to enjoining the court to consider all the circumstances of the case and to give first consideration to the welfare of any minor child of the family, sets out specific criteria to be applied in considering *whether* and, if so, *how* to exercise its powers under ss. 23, 24 and 24A. Under s. 25(1) the court must give 'first consideration to the welfare while a minor of any child of the family who has not attained the age of eighteen.' This does not mean that such welfare is a paramount or overriding consideration: it is an important consideration to be kept in mind when having regard to all the circumstances of the case: *Suter* v. *Suter* (1987) C.A. The reference to children of the family may mean that their welfare will take precedence over that of any children of a subsequent relationship, whether marital or non-marital.

Apart from the pre-eminence given to the welfare of a minor child of the family, the section gives no indication as to the priority between the criteria or the weight to be attached to them. This flexibility results in the court having such a wide discretion that the outcome of a case is unpredictable and the value of decisions as precedents is greatly reduced. In *Sharpe* v. *Sharpe* (1981) C.A. it was emphasised that courts should look to s. 25, not reported cases, to see what order should be made. The specific criteria contained in s. 25(2) are:

(a) The income, earning capacity, property and other financial resources which each of the parties to the marriage has or is likely to have in the foreseeable future, including in the case of earning capacity any increase in that capacity which it would in the opinion of the court be reasonable to expect a party to the marriage to take steps to acquire. As the tax system allows the payer of periodical payments to deduct them from his taxable income, the courts concern themselves with the parties' *gross* income: *Rodewald* v. *Rodewald* (1977) C.A.

A husband's *potential* earning capacity will be taken into account, provided that there is evidence of the availability of work. In *Williams* v. *Williams* (1974) an unemployed husband had been ordered to pay his wife £4 per week on the basis that he should have been able to find a job. On appeal the court attached great weight to the fact that the Supplementary Benefits Commission had concluded that he was not voluntarily unemployed. This fact was to be borne in mind when the case was reheard and the order was subsequently reduced to 1p per week. In the case of a non-working wife her potential earning capacity will seemingly be considered if it is reasonable to expect her to work. Whether it is reasonable depends upon such matters as her age, the need to stay at home to look after children, whether she is the wife of a wealthy man and her ability to re-train.

'Financial resources' includes welfare benefits (*Walker* v. *Walker* (1983) C.A.) and also damages, whether they represent loss of earnings or compensation for personal injures: *Daubney* v. *Daubney* (1976) C.A. Prospective financial resources are also to be taken into account: *Calder* v. *Calder* (1976) C.A.: the husband's future entitlement under a family settlement of Canadian properties should have been taken into account by the trial judge when considering the size of the lump sum payment the husband should make. The fact that the assets in question are outside the jurisdiction is irrelevant: *Browne* v. *Browne* (1989) C.A. (here the payee had interests in a Jersey trust fund and in a Swiss trust held in Liechtenstein). 'Resources' may be acquired after the spouses have separated. Such 'after-acquired' assets may properly be taken into account and treated in the same way as those acquired before the separation: *Schuller* v. *Schuller* (1990) C.A.

(b) The financial needs, obligations and responsibilities which each of the parties to the marriage has or is likely to have in the foreseeable future. This covers such matters as additional expenses arising from the further education or training of a spouse, those incidental to earning a living or providing accommodation. 'Needs' means 'reasonable requirements': *Preston* v. *Preston* (1981) C.A. and these may be determined by reference to a party's previous standard of living: *Gojkovic* v. *Gojkovic* (1990) C.A. 'Obligations and responsibilities' covers those owed to a new wife and the children of present and former unions. It will also cover those owed to a mistress, though the weight to be attached to such an obligation may well be less than in the case of a wife. In *Delaney* v. *Delaney* (1990) C.A. it was said that a former husband was entitled to balance his future aspirations for a new life against his responsibilities towards his former family.

(c) The standard of living enjoyed by the family before the breakdown of the marriage. This seems to be a repetition of the old principle that the standard of living should not be allowed to drop more than is inherent in the circumstances: *Kershaw* v. *Kershaw* (1964). In the case of the rich there may be no significant reduction in living standards. Where the means are moderate the courts try to achieve the same standard of living for both parties. In the case of the poor the courts attempt to produce equality between the spouses at the income support level. This heading will be particularly important when the court has to decide the level of financial provision payable during the subsistence of a deferred clean break order as in *Attar* v. *Attar* (1985).

(d) The age of each party to the marriage and the duration of the marriage. The significance of the parties' ages *per se* is not clear. It may, however, allow the court to consider a wife's youth and the consequent possibility of remarriage as a factor in favour of making lump sum provision which, unlike periodical payments, is not adversely affected by the payee's remarriage.

As regards the duration of the marriage there is some doubt as to the meaning of 'marriage' in this context. The cases indicate that the cohabitation which will be considered under this heading need not be marital. In *Campbell* v. *Campbell* (1977), where the marriage had lasted two and a quarter years, the court refused to take account of three and a half years' pre-marital cohabitation because, in its view, the rights, duties and obligations of marriage begin on the celebration of the marriage. Conversely, in *Kokosinski* v. *Kokosinski* (1980), where marital cohabitation had lasted for four months, the court felt it could do justice only if it did have regard to the wife's conduct in helping her husband during their twenty-four years' pre-marital cohabitation. The court felt itself able to adopt a broad approach by virtue of its obligation to 'have regard to all the circumstances of the case'. In *Foley* v. *Foley* (1981) C.A. it was held that a judge is entitled to distinguish between pre-marital cohabitation and marriage, and the amount of weight to be given to each is a matter for the judge's discretion.

Although the marriage may in law have lasted for a considerable time, the court is seemingly concerned only with the time during which the parties cohabited with each other. In *Krystman* v. *Krystman* (1973) C.A. the court refused to make a financial provision order against the husband where the parties had cohabited for only two weeks out of a marriage which had lasted for some twenty-six years.

(e) Any physical or mental disability of either of the parties to the marriage. This seems to add little to the matters to be considered under paragraph **(b)** above. Section 40, M.C.A. 1973 makes special provision for the payment of money and transfer of property where the recipient is incapable of managing his affairs because of mental disorder.

(f) The contributions made, or likely in the foreseeable future to be made, by each of the parties to the welfare of the family, including any contribution made by looking after the home or caring for the family. This will be particularly relevant to a wife who has been unable to obtain an interest in matrimonial property by virtue of financial contributions to its acquisition because she has had to stay at home to care for the family. In the absence of a financial contribution, a failure to satisfy this paragraph may act to a spouse's detriment. In *Taylor* v. *Taylor* (1974) the spouses had cohabited for only twenty days and the wife had contributed nothing to the marriage. The court consequently extinguished her interest in the matrimonial home which was held in the spouses' joint names. Similarly, in *West* v. *West* (1977) C.A. the court felt justified in making only a small order in favour of the wife who, because she would not leave her parents' house and join her husband, had contributed nothing to looking after the home. On the other hand, in *Gojkovic* v. *Gojkovic* (1990) the wife's contribution to the success of an hotel business prompted the award of a £1.3m lump sum and she was not obliged to deal with it in any particular way. This case emphasised that no rigid mathematical formula should be used to calculate a party's needs or requirements (*see* **(b)** above).

(g) The conduct of each of the parties, if that conduct is such that it would in the opinion of the court be inequitable to disregard it. Clearly, in view of the abolition of divorce based patently, rather than covertly as now, on the 'matrimonial offence', the spouses' matrimonial misconduct should be less relevant than formerly. This approach was given effect by the judicial gloss placed upon the original s. 25 by *Wachtel* v. *Wachtel* (1973) C.A. There the court, in a judgment delivered by Lord Denning MR, held that conduct is *not* to be considered *unless* it is 'both obvious and gross' in the sense that 'to order one party to support another whose conduct falls into this category is repugnant to anyone's sense of justice'. Though doubted in *Rogers* v. *Rogers* (1974) C.A., this principle was affirmed in *Harnett* v. *Harnett* (1973) C.A., and subsequent cases. It was the intention of the 1984 Act to put into statutory form the previous practice of the courts in relation to conduct, though the view has been expressed that the statutory formulation may have produced a change of emphasis whereby conduct assumes a greater relevance than under *Wachtel*. However, in *K* v. *K* (*Financial Provision: Conduct*) (1988) C.A. the court was of the opinion that the amendment affected by the 1984 Act had merely given effect to the previous practice of the courts. It is, therefore, likely that causes under the original s. 25 will continue to provide relevant examples of the operation of this heading.

The obvious difficulty was to decide what, and when, conduct may properly be described as 'obvious and gross' (and therefore relevant because it would be inequitable to disregard it). In *Harnett* v. *Harnett* (1973) Bagnall J, in a judgment upheld by the Court of Appeal, said that '. . . conduct must be obvious and gross in the sense that the party concerned must be plainly seen to have wilfully persisted in conduct, or a course of conduct, calculated to destroy the marriage in circumstances in which the other party is substantially blameless. I think that there will be very few cases in which these conditions will be satisfied'.

According to the court in *Cuzner* v. *Underdown* (1974) C.A., these conditions were satisfied where the wife, shortly before her husband conveyed his house into their joint names, confessed she was committing adultery. Her interest in the house was ordered to be transferred to her husband because her conduct in taking a half share in it while committing adultery was 'obvious and gross'. This seems difficult to reconcile with *Harnett* v. *Harnett* (1973), *Backhouse* v. *Backhouse* (1978) and *Bateman* v. *Bateman* (1979), where the wife's misconduct did *not* disentitle her to financial provision, but there are significant differences between these cases and *Cuzner* v. *Underdown*. In *Harnett* the husband, who had discovered his wife in bed with the lodger, had been violent towards her and was not 'substantially blameless'. Similarly in *Bateman*, where the wife had twice knifed and wounded her husband, the husband was not free from shortcomings, whereas in *Cuzner* v. *Underdown* there were no allegations against the husband. In *Backhouse* the marriage had broken down because of the wife's adultery but, unlike the wife in *Cuzner* v. *Underdown*, she had contributed towards the purchase of the matrimonial home. In *K* v. *K (Financial Provision: Conduct)* (1988) C.A. the wife had connived at the suicide attempts by her husband, a manic depressive. The court found that she wanted him to commit suicide so that she could live with her lover. The wife's conduct was consequently taken into account in reducing her entitlement to financial provision. The court said that 'conduct' includes conduct *after* the breakdown of the marriage and that it need not have contributed to such breakdown.

Conduct is not limited to matrimonial misconduct or conduct during the subsistence of the marriage. In *Jones* v. *Jones* (1975) C.A. the court took account of the former husband's knife attack on his ex-wife after decree absolute. In *Evans* v. *Evans* (1989) C.A. the court took account of the former wife's conviction for inciting others to kill her ex-husband and discharged the financial provision which she had. In *J.(H.D.)* v. *J.(A.M.)* (1980) the husband, who had remarried, applied for a variation of a financial provision order in favour of his first wife. He contended that her conduct should be considered because, from the date of his remarriage, she had conducted a malicious campaign of persecution against him, been convicted of assaulting his wife and been in breach of injunctions against molestation. HELD: her conduct would be taken into account because it was part of 'all the circumstances of the case'.

The conduct which satisfies this section need not be morally blameworthy. In *West* v. *West* (1977) C.A. it was said that 'gross' as used in *Wachtel* v. *Wachtel* did not imply any moral judgment. Furthermore, the wife's conduct in *J.(H.D.)* v. *J.(A.M.)* was partly due to illness but the court took the view that, after making allowances for that illness, it would be repugnant to anyone's sense of justice not to take her conduct into account. A different view might have been taken had the conduct been entirely due to mental illness. Presumably it would not be 'inequitable' to disregard such conduct.

(h) In the case of proceedings for divorce or nullity of marriage, the value to either of the parties to the marriage of any benefit (for example, a pension) which, by reason of the dissolution or annulment of the marriage, that party will lose the chance of acquiring. The loss of a pension may persuade the court, e.g. not to order a clean break or to order a larger lump sum. In addition to the loss of a right to a pension, which includes both state and private schemes, there may be other benefits involved. Thus in *Trippas* v. *Trippas* (1973) C.A. the husband had promised his wife that, in the event of a sale of the family business, she would get a share. Shortly after the spouses separated the business was sold and the husband gave each of the sons £5,000. HELD: as it was a reasonable inference that the wife would have received some benefit from the sale had the parties not separated, she should be compensated for the loss of that benefit.

This case shows that the court, contrary to the express terms of the paragraph, was concerned with the loss of a benefit caused by the *breakdown* of the marriage, not its dissolution. The proceeds of sale could have been considered as part of the 'financial resources' within paragraph **(a)** above.

Section 24A(6), inserted by the M.F.P.A. 1984, provides that where a third party has a beneficial interest in property, as well as a spouse, that party must be given an opportunity to make representations before an order for sale is made. Such representations are among the circumstances to which the court is required to have regard under s. 25.

15. The quantum of the award

After having had regard to the above matters, the court is no longer required to place the parties 'so far as it is practicable' in the financial position they would have been in had the marriage not broken down (*see* **2**). As there will be two households on breakdown instead of one, it was rarely practicable to achieve this ideal. The courts did, therefore, the best they could. In doing this the courts adopted the so-called 'one-third rule' as an aid to the adjustment of the parties' financial position. However, the courts' approach to this 'rule' was difficult to predict. In both *Furniss* v. *Furniss* (1981) C.A. and *Stockford* v. *Stockford* (1981) C.A. it was criticised by Ormrod LJ, yet in *Slater* v. *Slater* (1982) C.A. it was said to be helpful in cases where the income was neither very large nor very small. This last case was distinguished in *Potter* v. *Potter* (1982) C.A. which held that the 'rule' was inappropriate for the redistribution of the capital where the payee's reasonable requirements should be balanced against the payer's ability to pay.

Although it is difficult to state with any certainty the extent to which the 'rule' will still apply, particularly in view of the fact that the first consideration is the welfare of any minor child of the family, not the financial shares of the spouses, and the fact that its scope has been restricted in recent cases, it may still be of some relevance.

It must be emphasised that the one-third approach, which originated in the ecclesiastical courts and was given a new lease of life by *Wachtel* v. *Wachtel*, is merely a flexible starting point. Consequently, the proportion of the parties' income and capital which may be awarded can be adjusted upwards or downwards depending on the circumstances.

The basic arithmetical approach is to take one-third of the total of the parties' gross income and capital. If the wife's assets are less than this third, her husband will be required to make available sufficient of his assets to bring her up to one-third. The circumstances which will justify a departure from the one-third 'rule' include, e.g. a short marriage, an existing proprietary interest in the matrimonial home, very low income and no capital. This is, however, subject to the approach, championed by Ormrod LJ in *Furniss* and *Stockford*, that the court should take into account such matters as the parties' tax liability and the cost of their housing in order to assess the net effect of the proposed order.

16. Avoidance of dispositions

Under s. 37, M.C.A. 1973 the court is given power to prevent attempts to defeat a claim for financial relief by the disposal of assets.

(a) 'Financial relief' means:
   (*i*) Maintenance pending suit under s. 22.

(*ii*) Financial provision under s. 23.

(*iii*) Property adjustment under s. 24.

(*iv*) Financial provision after a finding of failure to maintain under s. 27.

(*v*) Variation of orders during the life of both parties under s. 31, but not after the death of one party under s. 31(6).

(*vi*) Alteration of maintenance agreements during the life of both parties under s. 35, but not after the death of one party under s. 36.

(b) Section 37 does *not* apply to any disposition:

(*i*) made in a will or codicil, or

(*ii*) made before the 1st January, 1968, or

(*iii*) made to a bona fide purchaser for valuable consideration (other than marriage) without notice of the other party's intention to defeat the applicant's claim for financial relief. 'Notice' includes both actual and constructive notice. Constructive notice arises where the facts impose a duty to make sufficient enquiries and these would have given rise to actual notice: *Kemmis* v. *Kemmis* (1988) C.A. Whether enquiries are sufficient depends upon the whole of the circumstances relating to the disposition at the time it is made: *Sherry* v. *Sherry* (1991) C.A.

(c) On the application of a person against his or her spouse or former spouse, the court, if satisfied (i.e. on a balance of probabilities) that the other party has or had the intention to defeat the applicant's claim for financial relief, may either:

(*i*) restrain the other party from making any disposition or transferring any property out of the jurisdiction or otherwise dealing with any property, where that party is about to do so, or

(*ii*) set aside any disposition already made. If an applicant has not yet obtained an order for financial relief, he or she must show in proceedings for that relief that, if the disposition were set aside, he or she would get financial relief or different financial relief.

In *Kemmis* v. *Kemmis* (above) it was said that the intention to defeat a financial relief claim need not be the sole or dominant intent: it suffices if it played a substantial part in the disposor's intentions as a whole.

The section applies even though the property is situated

outside the jurisdiction but the court would generally refuse to exercise its powers under the section if the order would be ineffective: *Hamlin* v. *Hamlin* (1985) C.A.

(d) As it may be difficult to show the necessary intention to defeat the claim for financial relief, s. 37(5) provides that that intention shall be rebuttably presumed if:

> (i)   the disposition or proposed disposition has had or will have the effect of defeating the applicant's claim for financial relief, *and*
>
> (ii) the disposition took place less than three years before the application.

If the disposition was made three years or more before the application, the applicant will have to prove the necessary intention on the part of the other party.

(e) A disposition caught by the section is voidable, not void. *National Provincial Bank Ltd* v. *Hastings Car Mart Ltd* (1964) C.A.: the husband deserted his wife and conveyed the matrimonial home to the defendant company which he had formed. The company then mortgaged the house to the plaintiff bank. HELD: the conveyance to the company would be set aside as it had been made with intent to defeat the wife's claim to financial relief, but the mortgage to the bank, being bona fide, was valid.

Financial provision for children of the family

17. The orders which may be made

By s. 23, M.C.A. 1973 the court may make any of the following orders in respect of the children of the family:

(a)   Unsecured periodical payments.

(b)   Secured periodical payments (*see* 7 above).

(c)   Lump sum or sums (*see* 8 above and note that, unlike lump sum payments to spouses, the power to order lump sum or sums for a child of the family is exercisable 'from time to time').

Either party to the marriage may be ordered to make these payments.

By s. 24 the court is empowered to order:

(a)   Transfer of property (*see* 9).

(b)   Settlement of property (*see* 10).

(c) Variation of ante- or post-nuptial settlements (*see* **11**).

Either party to the marriage may be ordered to make these property adjustments.

NOTE: these powers in relation to children apply only to 'children of the family' as defined in s. 52(1), M.C.A. 1973 (*see* **8:10**).

Where the court has ordered secured periodical payments, a lump sum or a property adjustment in respect of a child of the family, it may also order a sale of property under s. 24A (*see* **13** above).

18. When may the court make an order?
The court may make the above orders:

(a) Before the granting of the decree of divorce or nullity (or judicial separation).
(b) At the time of granting such decrees.
(c) At any time after the granting of such decrees.
(d) If the proceedings for divorce, nullity (or judicial separation) are dismissed after the commencement of the trial, an order under s. 23 may be made either forthwith or within a reasonable time after the dismissal. Orders under s. 24 are available only on decree absolute of divorce or nullity.

19. Maximum duration of orders
The duration of orders in respect of children of the family is governed by s. 29, M.C.A. 1973.

(a) Unless the court considers that in the circumstances of the case the welfare of the child requires that it should specify a later date, periodical payments, secured or unsecured, shall not in the first instance extend beyond the date of the child's birthday next following his attaining the upper limit of compulsory school age. Thus, while this limit remains at 16, orders will normally cease on the child's seventeenth birthday: s. 29(2).
(b) Periodical orders should not, in any event, extend beyond the child's eighteenth birthday unless either:
    (*i*) the child is, or will be, or if an extension were granted would be, receiving instruction at an educational

establishment or undergoing training for a trade, profession or vocation, whether or not he is also, or will be, in gainful employment; or

(*ii*) there are special circumstances which justify the making of an extended order.

(c) There are no restrictions on the courts' powers to order a settlement of property or to vary nuptial settlements.

(d) Notwithstanding anything in the order, any unsecured periodic payments order in favour of a child will cease on the death of the payer. However, arrears due under the order at the date of death may be recovered.

20. The statutory guidelines for determining applications under ss. 23, 24 and 24A

Section 25(3) of the M.C.A. 1973 directs the court to have regard to 'all the circumstances of the case' and in particular:

(a) the financial needs of the child;

(b) the income, earning capacity (if any), property and other financial resources of the child;

(c) any physical or mental disability of the child;

(d) the manner in which he was being and in which the parties to the marriage expected him to be educated or trained;

(e) the considerations in s. 25(2) **(a)**, **(b)**, **(c)** and **(e)** (*see* **14** above).

NOTE: When determining a child's financial needs the courts may be assisted by information regarding the costs of raising a child provided by, e.g. the National Foster Care Association. In 1990 the National Children's Home estimated that the *minumum* weekly cost of bringing up a child aged 2 was £13.09, aged 5 £14.87, aged 8 £18.05 and aged 11 £19.11.

In the case of an order for sale, third-party representations must be considered: s. 24A(6) (*see* **13** above).

21. When the child is the child of one party only

When the court is asked to order financial provision for a child of the family against a party who is not the child's natural or adoptive parent, the court is specifically directed to consider some additional matters. This will enable the court to do justice in view of the fact that 'child of the family' is widely defined. Under M.C.A. 1973, s. 25(4) these additional matters are:

(a) whether that party had assumed any responsibility for the child's maintenance and, if so, the extent to which, and the basis upon which, that party assumed such responsibility and the length of time for which that party discharged such responsibility;
(b) whether in assuming and discharging such responsibility that party did so knowing that the child was not his or her own;
(c) the liability of any other person to maintain the child.

22. The interests of the child

By M.C.A. 1973, s. 41 the court may not make absolute a divorce or nullity decree, or grant a decree of judicial separation, if it appears necessary to exercise any of its powers under the C.A. 1989 regarding a child of the family, it is not yet in a position to exercise such power and there are exceptional circumstances making it desirable in the interests of the child that it should give a direction under this section.

The variation, discharge and enforcement of orders

23. The court's power to vary or discharge orders for financial relief

By s. 31, M.C.A. 1973 the court has power:

(a) to vary orders;
(b) to discharge orders;
(c) temporarily to suspend any provision in an order;
(d) to revive any suspended provision.

These powers, in divorce or nullity proceedings, relate to:

(a) maintenance pending suit and any interim order for maintenance;
(b) any periodical payments, secured or unsecured;
(c) any lump sum payments payable by instalments, whether secured or unsecured.

24. Orders which cannot be varied

Of the possible orders for financial provision or property adjustment which may be made the following cannot be varied:

(a) lump sum payments not payable by instalments;
(b) transfer of property orders;
(c) orders for the settlement of property, the variation of marriage settlements or the extinction of an interest under such settlements in suits for divorce or nullity. If these orders are made in suits for judicial separation, there is power to vary (see Chapter 5).

Parties may attempt to achieve finality by coming to an agreement purporting to settle any financial questions between them and having this agreement incorporated into the court's order. The court is under no obligation to go behind the information furnished with the application, unless it has reason to think that there are other circumstances into which it ought to inquire: s. 33A, as inserted by the M.F.P.A. 1984. If one of the parties later becomes dissatisfied with the order and wishes to re-open the issue, this raises the question of whether the court has power to vary in such circumstances. In *Minton* v. *Minton* (1979) H.L. the parties agreed, *inter alia*, that the husband should convey the matrimonial home to the wife but, until this was done, he should pay her periodical payment of 5 pence per year. This agreement was incorporated into a court order, the husband duly conveyed the house to the wife and the order for periodical payments ceased. The wife then applied for a variation of the periodical payments order. HELD: as the substance of the parties' agreement, approved by the court, was a final settlement, the court had no jurisdiction to vary the order. Section 23(l) of the 1973 Act, which allowed the court to achieve finality where appropriate, practical and just, enabled the court to apply the so-called principle of 'the clean break' so as to 'encourage the parties to put the past behind them and to begin a new life which is not overshadowed by the relationship which has broken down' per Lord Scarman.

Minton was distinguished in *Jessel* v. *Jessel* (1979) C.A., which held that an order for periodical payments payable 'until further order' was variable, on the ground that *Minton* was concerned with a nominal order which had come to an end.

It seems that the 'clean break' principle:

(a) Applies only where there is a genuine final order which contains no continuing provision for periodical payments, e.g. where the court has dismissed an application for periodical payments, or a nominal order for such payments has come to an end. An order for periodical payments 'until further order' is not a final order.

It should be noted that the court now has jurisdiction to dismiss an application for periodical payments without the consent of the applicant and with a direction that the applicant shall not be entitled to make any further application in relation to his or her marriage for periodical payments: s. 25A(3) (*see Seaton* v. *Seaton* (1986) C.A.).

(b) Cannot apply to orders in respect of children of the family because such orders may be made 'from time to time': M.C.A. 1973, s. 23(4). Moreover, the presence of young children will mean that the parties will still have to co-operate even after decree absolute: *Moore* v. *Moore* (1980) C.A. Even so, s. 25(A) provides for the possibility that the court may be able to indicate a date when there could be a clean break despite the fact that there are dependent children for whom the parties share a continuing obligation: *Suter* v. *Suter* (1987) C.A.

As regards consent orders it was held in *Thwaite* v. *Thwaite* (1981) C.A., applying *de Lasala* v. *de Lasala* (1979) P.C., that the legal effect of such orders is derived not from the agreement between the parties but from the order itself. This is a necessary consequence of *Minton.* If it were otherwise, a consent order would be a 'subsisting maintenance agreement' within s. 35, M.C.A. 1973 (*see* 8:**22**) and subject to variation under that section.

When a consent order is drafted its terms must come within the powers granted to the court by the M.C.A. 1973. If terms are to be incorporated which are not within those powers, they must be formulated as undertakings to the court, which are enforceable as effectively as direct orders: *Jenkins* v. *Livesey* (1984) H.L.

Consent (and other) orders may be challenged on the grounds of:

(a) mistake,
(b) fraud (but not undue influence: *Tommey* v. *Tommey* C.A. (1982), though doubt as to the correctness of this decision was expressed in *Jenkins* v. *Livesey*),
(c) fresh admissible evidence,
(d) material non-disclosure (*Robinson* v. *Robinson* (1982) C.A., and
(e) evidence of no intent to carry out the agreement on which the order was based (*Thwaite*).

It was stressed in *Jenkins* v. *Livesey*, above, that not every failure to make a full and frank disclosure would justify the setting aside of a consent order. This could be done only where the failure had led the court to make an order which was substantially different from the order it would have made had there been proper disclosure. Here the order was set aside because the wife had failed to disclose her engagement to marry.

A striking example of mistake is provided by *Barder* v. *Barder* (1987) H.L. There a clean break order by consent had been made in which H was ordered to transfer the former matrimonial home to W within 28 days of the order and W gave certain undertakings regarding the mortgage on it. H was given five days in which to appeal but he did not do so. More than a month later, when the order was still unexecuted, W killed the children and committed suicide. H was given leave to appeal against the order out of time and the trial judge held that the order had been vitiated by a fundamental common mistake, i.e. that W and the children would continue to benefit from the order for an appreciable time. The deceased's mother, who stood to inherit the property successfully appealed against this order. The former husband then appealed against her appeal and the original order was restored. As regards leave to appeal out of time, the court held that leave should be given only

   (*i*)   where the appeal was likely to succeed,
   (*ii*) the supervening event had happened shortly after the order (a delay of a year or more was likely to preclude leave),
   (*iii*) application for leave was made promptly and
   (*iv*) innocent third parties would not thereby by prejudiced.

25. Variations which are not allowed

By M.C.A. 1973, s. 31(5) the court is prohibited from making the following variations:

(a) An order for periodical payments, secured or unsecured, in favour of a spouse or a child of the family, cannot be varied by making a property adjustment order. However, in *S* v. *S* (1987) it was held that a broad approach to s. 31(5) allowed the court to *terminate* a former wife's periodical payments in return for an acceptable capital sum offered by her former husband. A broad

approach was to be preferred because this would assist in the application of the clean break principle and accorded with the primacy to be given to the welfare of any minor child of the family.
(b) An order for periodical payments, secured or unsecured, in favour of a spouse, cannot be varied by making an order for a lump sum. Such a variation is possible when the order is for a child of the family, as financial provision orders for such children may be made 'from time to time'.
(c) Any order for periodical payments in favour of a spouse on or after a decree of divorce or nullity, if the court has made a direction under s. 28(1A) (*see* **5** above).

26. The effect of death on secured provision

If the payer under a secured periodical payments order dies, an application for variation must be made by the payee or by the deceased's personal representatives within six months of representation to the deceased's estate first being taken out, unless the court grants an extension of time: M.C.A. 1973, s. 31(6).

27. Matters to be considered

Where there is an application for variation the court must have regard to all the circumstances of the case, first consideration being given to the welfare while a minor of any child of the family, and the circumstances include any change in any of the matters which it must have considered under M.C.A. 1973, s. 25 when making the order in question. In the case of periodical payments ordered on divorce or nullity, the court must consider whether, in the light of the circumstances and any change thereto, it is appropriate to vary the order only for such further period as will in the court's opinion suffice to enable the payee to adjust without undue hardship to the termination of those payments. Where the payer has died, the court must also have regard to the changed circumstances resulting from his death: s. 31(7), as substituted by the M.F.P.A. 1984, s. 6(3).

It is wrong to fix a termination date merely to bring an acrimonious dispute to an end. Such a date should be fixed only after considering whether the payee would be able to adjust to the termination of payments without undue hardship: *Morris* v. *Morris* (1985) C.A.

28. The enforcement of orders for financial provision

Arrears of payments of money due under a court order may be enforced in the High Court by the usual methods of execution, i.e.:

(a) a writ of *fieri facias*;
(b) a writ of sequestration;
(c) a garnishee order;
(d) a charging order;
(e) an order for the attachment of earnings;
(f) a judgment summons under the Debtors Act 1869;
(g) the appointment of a receiver by the way of equitable execution. This was used in *Levermore* v. *Levermore* (1980) to compel the sale, under s. 30 of the Law of Property Act 1925, of the matrimonial home held by the wife's husband and brother-in-law as tenants in common and thereby to procure out of the proceeds of the sale the payment to her of the lump sum the husband had been ordered to pay.

> NOTE: if an order is registered in a magistrates' court, it becomes enforceable in that court with the assistance of the clerk of the court.

Section 32 of the 1973 Act provides that a person shall not be entitled to enforce, through the High Court or *any* county court, arrears which accrued more than twelve months before the commencement of the proceedings to enforce them, without the leave of that court. Application for leave can be made only by the payee and the court may refuse leave, grant it subject to such conditions as it thinks proper or remit the arrears or any part thereof.

In the case of secured provision or a property adjustment order, the order may be enforced by the court deferring the grant of the degree of nullity, divorce or judicial separation until the payer has executed any instrument required to give effect to the order: s. 30.

29. Recovery of overpayments

The question of repayment of sums already paid may arise in two situations:

(a) Where the payments were excessive because of changed circumstances: M.C.A. 1973, s. 33. The court has a discretion to order repayment of such sum, not exceeding the excess, as the court thinks just.

This section applies to orders for maintenance pending suit (and any interim order for maintenance on failure to provide reasonable maintenance) and periodical payments, secured or unsecured.

(b) Where the original order for secured or unsecured periodical payments has ceased to have effect because of the payee's remarriage: s. 38.

Section 38(1) expressly deprives the party liable to make payments, or his personal representatives, of any right of action to recover payments made after the payee's remarriage in the mistaken belief that the order still subsisted. Instead, such a party must apply under s. 38 and the court may order repayment in full or, if it thinks this unjust, in part, or dismiss the application.

30. The *Anton Piller* order

This is an order made on an *ex parte* application to allow a party to enter premises to inspect and remove material evidence. Before such an order can be made the following conditions must be satisfied:

(a) the applicant must present a strong prima facie case;
(b) the potential or actual damage to the applicant must be serious; and
(c) there must be clear evidence that the defendant possesses vital material which he might destroy or dispose of so as to defeat the interests of justice before an *inter partes* application can be made.

Though this type of order originated in commercial cases, it has been used in matrimonial cases to allow documents relating to a husband's income and capital to be inspected and photographed where he had failed to comply with an order for financial provision (*Emanuel* v. *Emanuel* (1982)) and to allow for the valuation of a husband's stock-in-trade which had been omitted from his affidavit of means (*K* v. *K* (1982)).

Note also the use of the *Mareva* injunction (named after *Mareva Compania Naviera S.A.* v. *International Bulkcarriers S.A.*

204 The economic aspects of marriage

(1980)) to freeze a respondent's assets. This is additional to the statutory power contained in s. 37, M.C.A. 1973 (*see* **16** above).

Financial provision from the estate of a deceased spouse

31. Applications for financial provision

The Inheritance (Provision for Family and Dependants) Act 1975 gives the court wide powers to order financial provision out of a deceased's estate for his family and dependants. Section 1(1) provides that where a person dies domiciled in England and Wales and is survived by any of the persons enumerated in **32** that person may apply to the High Court, or to the county court if the value of the net estate gives it jurisdiction, for an order under s. 2 of the Act on the ground that the disposition of the deceased's estate effected by his will or the law relating to intestacy, or the combination of his will and that law, is not such as to make reasonable financial provision for the applicant.

An application under s. 2 cannot, except with leave of the court, be made more than six months from the date on which representation with respect to the deceased's estate was first taken out: s. 4.

32. The applicants for an order under s. 2

The Act caters for a wide range of applicants but for present purposes it is necessary only to consider applications by:

(a) *A surviving spouse:* s. 1(1)(a)

This includes a person who, in good faith, contracted a *void* marriage with the deceased unless either the marriage of the deceased and that person was dissolved or annulled during the deceased's lifetime, or that person contracted a later marriage during the deceased's lifetime: Act of 1975, s. 25(4). A polygamously married spouse may apply under s. 1(1)(a): *Re Sehota (decd)* (1978).

Where a decree of divorce, nullity or judicial separation has been made within twelve months of the death, and there has been no financial provision or property adjustment order under the M.C.A. 1973, the court may, if it thinks it just, treat the applicant as a surviving spouse. For this to apply to judicial separation, the decree must have been in force and the separation continuing at the date of death: s. 14.

(b) *A former spouse of the deceased whose marriage to the deceased was dissolved or annulled and who has not remarried:* ss. 1(1)(b), 25(1). 'Remarriage' includes a marriage which is void or voidable, and a party's marriage will be treated as a remarriage notwithstanding that the previous marriage of that party was void or voidable: s. 25(5).

A former spouse who was remarried may still be able to apply by virtue of s. 1(1)(e) which covers any dependant, other than those specified in s. 1(1), wholly or partly maintained by the deceased.

(c) A *child of the deceased:* s. 1(1)(c).

'Child' includes an illegitimate child and a child *en venture sa mère* at the deceased's death: s. 25(1), as well as an adopted child: *Williams* v. *Johns* (1988).

(d) *Any person (not being a child of the deceased) who, in the case of any marriage to which the deceased was at any time a party, was treated by the deceased as a child of the family in relation to that marriage*: s. 1(1)(d). In determining whether a child was treated as a child of the family the court will, presumably, apply the same approach as that under the M.C.A. 1973, though it should be noted that the definition under the 1975 Act does not require treatment by *both* parties to the marriage.

33. Reasonable financial provision
This means:

(a) If the applicant is a surviving spouse (except where the marriage with the deceased was the subject of a decree of judicial separation and at the date of death the decree was in force and the separation was continuing), such financial provision as it would be reasonable in all circumstances of the case for a husband or wife to receive, whether or not that provision is required for his or her maintenance: Inheritance (Provision for Family and Dependants) Act 1975, s. 1(2)(a). In deciding whether reasonable financial provision has been made, the test is an objective one. The court is not concerned with making a *fair* division of available assets: *Jessop* v. *Jessop* (1991) C.A.

Section 3(2) also provides that in deciding this matter the court must have regard to the provision the applicant might reasonably have expected to receive if the marriage had been ended by divorce, rather than death.

(b) In the case of any other applicant, such financial provision as it would be reasonable in all the circumstances of the case for the applicant to receive for his or her maintenance: s. 1(2) (b).

Re Christie (decd) (1979) held that the maintenance under s. 1(2)(b) referred to the applicant's way of life, health, financial security and allied matters such as the well-being, health and financial security of the applicant's immediate family. This was doubted in *Re Coventry (decd)* (1979) C.A. which held that a son seeking financial provision from his father's estate had to establish that the absence of provision for him was objectively unreasonable. The applicant had to show some moral claim to be maintained over and above the mere fact of the blood relationship and the fact that the son was in need did not entitle the court to interfere.

34. Types of order under the Act

The orders which may be made are set out in the Act of 1975, s. 2 and to a large extent they are similar to those available under ss. 23 and 24 of the M.C.A. 1973. The court may order:

(a) periodical payments;

(b) a lump sum, which may be ordered to be paid by instalments (s. 7);

(c) a transfer of property;

(d) a settlement of property for the applicant's benefit;

(e) the acquisition of property from the deceased's estate and its transfer to the applicant or settlement for his benefit;

(f) the variation of any nuptial settlement (including a settlement by will) for the benefit of the surviving spouse, child of the marriage or person treated by the deceased as a child of the family.

35. Orders for periodical payments

By s. 2(2) of the Act of 1975 an order under s. 2(1) (a) for periodical payments may provide for:

(a) payments of such amount as may be specified in the order;

(b) payments equal to the whole of the income of the net estate or of such portion thereof as may be specified;

(c) payments equal to the income of such part of the net estate as the court may direct to be set aside or appropriated for that purpose.

NOTE: (1) The court is also given an overriding discretion to determine the amount of the payment in any other way it thinks fit and it also has additional powers under s. 2(4) in order to give effect to the order or to secure fairness between beneficiaries.

(2) Where the order is for the payment of an amount specified in the order, the court may direct that a specified part of the net estate shall be set aside for making payments out of the income thereof; but the amount set aside shall not be more than is sufficient, at the date of the order, to produce the income required.

(3) A periodical payments order in favour of a widow or widower does not automatically terminate on remarriage except if judicially separated at the date of death: s. 19(2). Remarriage automatically terminates a periodical payments order in favour of a former spouse of the deceased: ibid.

36. Matters to be considered by the court

The matters to which the court must have regard, set out in s. 3 and resembling those contained in s. 25, M.C.A. 1973, are as follows:

(a) The financial resources and needs which the applicant, any other applicant for an order or any beneficiary of the deceased's estate, has or is likely to have in the foreseeable future. 'Financial resources' includes earning capacity and in considering a person's financial needs his financial obligations and responsibilities shall be taken into account: s. 3(6).

(b) Any obligations and responsibilities of the deceased towards any applicant for an order or towards any beneficiary.

(c) The size and nature of the deceased's net estate.

(d) Any physical or mental disability of any applicant for an order or any beneficiary.

(e) Any other matter, including the conduct of the applicant or any other person, which the court may consider relevant.

In addition to these matters the court, in the following circumstances, must take account of further facts:

(a) Where the applicant is the deceased's spouse or former spouse, the court must also have regard to the applicant's age, the duration of the marriage and the applicant's contribution to the welfare of the deceased's family (including any contribution made by looking after the home or caring for the family).
(b) Where the applicant is a child, the court must also have regard to the manner in which that child was being, or might be expected to be, educated or trained, and where the applicant is not the deceased's child but was treated as such by the deceased it must also have regard to the same matters as those contained in s. 25(4), M.C.A. 1973 (*see* **21**).

In considering all of the above matters the court must take account of the facts as known to it at the date of the hearing: s. 3(5).

> NOTE: any oral or written statement made by the deceased, e.g. that provision has not been made in the will for a spouse because he or she has adequate resources, is admissible as evidence of any fact stated therein: s. 21. Such a statement is not binding on the court and may be ignored if, e.g. the court thinks that provision would have been made had the marriage been ended by divorce rather than death: *see* **33** above and *Moody* v. *Stevenson* (1991) C.A.

37. Prohibitions on applications under the 1975 Act imposed in divorce proceedings

Under s. 15, as substituted by the M.F.P.A. 1984, on granting a decree of divorce, nullity or judicial separation or at any time thereafter, the court, on the application of either party to the marriage, may order that the other party shall not be entitled on the death of the applicant to apply for an order under s. 2 of the 1975 Act, provided the court thinks it just to do so.

Although s. 15 contemplates proceedings after divorce, such proceedings must be appropriate and should not be initiated unless there is a real chance of success. Instances where proceedings will be appropriate will be comparatively few, e.g. where the death causes periodical payments to cease or capital under an insurance policy to be unlocked: *Re Fullard* (1981) C.A.

38. The variation or discharge of secured periodical payments orders made under the M.C.A. 1973

Under s. 16, on an application for an order under s. 2 of the 1975 Act by a person entitled at the deceased's death to payments under a secured periodical payments order made under the M.C.A. 1973, the court has power, if application is made under s. 16 by that person or the deceased's personal representative, to vary or discharge that periodical payments order or to revive any provision thereof suspended under s. 31 of the 1973 Act (*see* **23**).

39. The variation or revocation of maintenance agreements

Under s. 17, on an application for an order under s. 2 of the 1975 Act by a person entitled at the deceased's death to payments under a maintenance agreement which provided for payments under the agreement to continue after the deceased's death, the court has power, if application is made under s. 17 by that person or the deceased's personal representative, to vary or revoke that agreement.

'Maintenance agreement' means any agreement, oral or written, whenever made by the deceased with any person whom he married, which contained provisions governing their rights and liabilities towards each other when living separately (whether the marriage be dissolved or annulled) in respect of the making or securing of payments or the disposition or use of any property, including such rights and liabilities with respect to any child's maintenance, whether or not the deceased's child or a person treated by the deceased as a child of the family in relation to the marriage: s. 17(4).

40. Avoidance of dispositions

Sections 10 to 13 contain powers which allow the court to require the donee of property, either actually disposed of or agreed to be left by will with the intention of defeating an application for financial provision, to provide such sum of money or other property as the court may specify, provided that full valuable consideration was not given or promised by the donee.

41. Applications following overseas divorces or annulments

The Matrimonial and Family Proceedings Act 1984 amended the 1975 Act so that application may be made by a former spouse whose marriage to the deceased was either dissolved or annulled under the law of any part of the British Isles, or any country or territory outside the British Isles provided the divorce or annulment is recognised as valid in England and Wales.

Progress test 9

1.   When, and with what objective, may the High Court order a spouse to maintain the other spouse? What orders may be made by the court?   **(1–3)**

2.   When do orders for a spouse's maintenance take effect and how long do they last?   **(4–5)**

3.   What are the advantages of secured provision over unsecured provision?   **(6–7)**

4.   What are the principles applicable to the award of a lump sum?   **(8)**

5.   Illustrate by reference to decided cases the powers that exist to enable the court to order the transfer of one spouse's property to the other spouse.   **(9)**

6.   What powers exist to order a settlement of a spouse's property?   **(10)**

7.   What do you understand by the term 'nuptial settlement'? What powers exist to vary such a settlement?   **(11–12)**

8.   To what extent does the court have a power to order a sale under the M.C.A. 1973?   **(13)**

9.   Illustrate by reference to decided cases the matters the court must take into account in deciding whether, and if so, how to exercise its powers to award financial provision for a spouse. **(14)**

10. To what extent is a spouse's conduct relevant to the award of financial provision?   **(14)**

11. How do the courts determine the quantum of an award of financial provision? **(15)**

12. What powers does the court possess to deal with attempts to defeat a claim for financial relief? **(16)**

13. What ancillary orders for the maintenance of children may be obtained in divorce proceedings? In respect of what kind of children may such orders be obtained? **(17)**

14. When may an order for the maintenance of a child be made and for how long does it continue? **(18–19)**

15. What matters does the court consider when determining applications in respect of a child's maintenance in divorce proceedings? Are there any special matters to be considered if the person from whom financial provision is sought is not the child's father? **(20–22)**

16. Explain the powers of the court to vary orders for financial provision and the impact thereon of the 'clean break' principle. **(23–27)**

17. How can an order for periodical payments be enforced? **(28)**

18. How and in what circumstances may a spouse who has paid too much maintenance recover the overpayments? **(29)**

19. What powers has the court to order financial provision from a deceased's estate for his family and dependants? **(31–35)**

20. In making an order for financial provision from a deceased's estate what matters must the court take into consideration? **(36)**

21. Is there any interrelationship between applications under the Inheritance (Provision for Family and Dependants) Act 1975 and (*a*) divorce proceedings , and (*b*) liability under a maintenance agreement? **(37–39)**

22. H and W, who were married five years ago, had cohabited for six years before their marriage. The matrimonial home was conveyed into H's name alone, although W's earnings have been used to make the mortgage interest repayments. W recently gave birth to an illegitimate child and H intends to divorce her. Advise W (*a*) whether H has grounds for a divorce; (*b*) what orders the court might make in favour of W and/or her child in the event of a divorce, and (*c*) the matters to which the court would have regard when exercising its powers to award financial provision.

23. To what extent has the courts' approach to conduct under s. 25 of the M.C.A. 1973 been consistent with the aim of the 1969 divorce law reform which, in part, was '. . . to enable the empty legal shell [of the marriage] to be destroyed with the maximum fairness, and the minimum bitterness, distress and humiliation'?

24. Advise H in the following unrelated circumstances:

(a) H and W were divorced two years ago and W obtained an order for a lump sum payable in three yearly instalments and for periodical payments. He has to date made all the payments due under these orders but has just learnt that over a year ago W remarried. He wishes to know what effect this remarriage has on his financial liability to W.

(b) H and W are about to be divorced and H wishes to know how he might take advantage of the 'clean break' principle to prevent W making further claims for financial provision after the divorce.

(c) H, who is ill and unemployed, is about to have his marriage to W, a wealthy woman of independent means, annulled. He has discovered that three years ago she transferred a large part of her shares to her sister for a sum just below the then market price. He wishes to know the effect of this transaction on his forthcoming application for financial provision. Would your advice differ if the transfer took place less than three years ago?

25. H and W were married fifteen years ago and some four years ago W began an adulterous relationship with X, by whom she had a child, Y. H, believing Y to be his child, set up a trust fund for Y. Two years ago H discovered that he was not Y's father and divorced W. W remarried but the marriage lasted only a few months owing to the death of her husband. As her husband had only modest means H helped to maintain her and Y. H recently died in Australia, where he usually spent the winter, and left the whole of his estate to charity. Advise W who wishes to obtain financial provision for herself and Y from H's estate.

Part three

Children

10
The child's legal status

1. Family Law Reform Act 1987

Over the years there has been a tendency for legislation to assimilate the legal position of the child born of unmarried parents to that of the child born of married parents. This tendency has culminated in the Family Law Reform Act 1987. Section 1(1) provides that, subject to any contrary intent, references made in enactments passed and instruments made after 4th April 1988 to 'any relationship between two persons shall . . . be construed without regard to whether or not the father or mother of either of them, or the father or mother of any person through whom the relationship is deduced, have or had been married to each other at any time.'

This rule of construction effectively means that the distinction between a legitimate and an illegitimate child disappears in all respects, in the absence of contrary intent, except that the father of an illegitimate child does not automatically have parental responsibility for that child (*see* 11:**4**) and an illegitimate child is not entitled as of right to British citizenship.

The 1987 Act abolishes affiliation proceedings (s. 17) whereby the mother of an illegitimate child could obtain financial provision for the child from its father. Such provision is now available for *all* children under s. 15(1) and Schedule 1 of the Children Act 1989 (*see* 14:**2**).

As regards a child born after 4th April 1988 to a wife as a result of artificial insemination by a donor (AID) other than the husband, it 'shall be treated in law as the child of the parties to that marriage' unless it is proved to the court's satisfaction that the husband did not consent to the AID: s. 27.

Section 1(3) states that references to a person whose father and mother were married to each other at the time of his birth include those treated as legitimate under s. 1 of the Legitimacy Act 1976, those legitimated under s. 2 of that Act and those adopted under the Adoption Act 1976.

> NOTE: declarations of parentage may be made under s. 56 of the Family Law Act 1986, as amended by the F.L.R.A. 1987 (*see* Chapter 5).

2. Legitimacy Act 1976

(a) The children of *void* marriages are treated as legitimate if:
  (i) the father was domiciled in England or Wales at the child's birth or, if he died before then, was so domiciled immediately before his death, *and*
  (ii) both or either of the parents, at the time of the insemination resulting in the birth or, if no such insemination, the child's conception (or date of the marriage if later) reasonably believed the marriage was valid: s. 1.

> NOTE: (1) A belief in the validity of the marriage may still be reasonable notwithstanding a mistake of law: s. 1(3).
>
> (2) As regards children born after 4th April 1988 there is a statutory presumption that, unless the contrary is shown, one of the parents did reasonably believe the marriage to be valid at the relevant time: s. 1(4).
>
> (3) The Act does not apply to children born *before* its parents' void marriage: *In re Spence dec'd* (1990).

(b) The children of *voidable* marriages are legitimate as a decree of nullity in such cases has no retrospective effect: M.C.A. 1973, s. 16.

3. Legitimacy Act 1976, s. 2

An illegitimate child is legitimated by his parents' subsequent marriage, provided the father is domiciled in England or Wales at the date of the marriage: s. 2. If, at that time, the father was domiciled abroad, it must be shown that the law of the father's domicile recognised the legitimation: s. 3.

An adopted child may be legitimated under ss. 2 or 3 if adopted by either parent as sole adoptive parent: s. 4.

Legitimation has the effect of placing the illegitimate child in much the same position as one born legitimate. He has the same rights and is under the same obligations in respect of the support of himself or any other person as if he had been born legitimate, and legislation relating to claims for damages, compensation, allowances, benefits and the like apply to him as though born legitimate: s. 8.

4. Adoption Act 1976

Section 39 states that an adopted child shall be treated in law as if he had been born as the child of a married couple or, in the case of a single adopter, born to that adopter in wedlock. Consequently adoption has the effect of legitimating an illegitimate child.

Progress test 10

1. To what extent is it correct to say that the Family Law Reform Act 1987 has abolished the legal stigma attached to illegitimacy? **(1)**

2. What is the legal status of a child born as a result of A.I.D.? **(1)**

3. What are the rules relating to the legal status of children in nullity suits? **(2)**

4. How may a child be legimated? **(3)**

5. What is the effect of adoption on an illegitimate child? **(4)**

6. In 1987 Wendy married Hugo in the knowledge that he was suffering from AIDS. They agreed that there would be no marital sexual intercourse. Wendy satisfied her desire for a child by becoming pregnant as a result of artificial insemination. The donor of the semen was Ian, Hugo's brother. Hugo was aware of the artificial insemination but did not indicate his approval. Shortly before the birth of the child Wendy and Hugo separated. Wendy wishes to know whether she may obtain financial provision for the child from Hugo or Ian. Advise her.

11
Parental responsibility for children

Introduction

1. The law's perspective

Until recent times the law has tended to look at the relationship between a child and its parents from the perspective of the parents rather than of the child. Thus it was common for courts to talk about a parent's rights in relation to, e.g. custody and access. As we have seen, custody, with its proprietorial overtones, has given way to decisions over where the child is to have its residence, and the parent's 'right' to access has given way to decisions over whether the child is entitled to contact with a named person or persons. This is rather more than a change of terminology. It signifies a change in philosophy from parental rights to children's rights, the recent beginnings of which are to be found in the House of Lords' decision in *Gillick* v. *West Norfolk & Wisbech Area Health Authority* (1985).

2. The decision in Gillick

Mrs Gillick, the mother of five girls under the age of 16, sought a declaration that guidance given by the then Department of Health and Social Security (DHSS) and acted upon by the Area Health Authority was unlawful. This guidance was to the effect that the decision to give contraceptive advice and treatment to girls under the age of 16 without parental involvement was a matter for the clinical judgment of the individual doctor. The House of Lords, by a 3:2 majority, held that the DHSS guideline was lawful and Mrs Gillick's application consequently failed.

Though the case was concerned with a narrow point, the judgments of the majority had a wider impact. The effect of the decision was that if a child had sufficient intelligence and understanding, any parental right in the matter under consideration yielded to the right of the child to make its own decisions. In this case, if an under-age girl with sufficient understanding consented to her doctor prescribing the contraceptive pill, the girl's parent could not overrule such consent. On the other hand, if a child with sufficient understanding refused treatment, it was still open to the child's parents to consent. In such a case treatment could be lawfully undertaken but parental consent in no way dictated that treatment should be given (*see In re R (a Minor) (Wardship: Medical Treatment)* (1991) C.A., below).

A child's right to act autonomously is not dependent upon the attainment of a particular age but upon the child's ability to understand. Furthermore, 'parental rights are derived from parental duty and exist only so long as they are needed for the protection of the person and property of the child' (per Lord Scarman).

This shift of emphasis from parental rights to parental responsibilities has been continued by the Children Act 1989 (operative from 14 October 1991). Section 3(1) introduces the new statutory concept of 'parental responsibility' and defines it as meaning 'all the rights, duties, powers, responsibilities and authority which by law a parent of a child has in relation to the child and his property.'

3. Parental rights, duties, powers, etc.

In the absence of a statutory checklist it is generally agreed that a parent has the right to:

(a) the possession of and contact with his child;
(b) control the child's education and religion;
(c) exercise reasonable discipline;
(d) consent to the child's marriage;
(e) consent to medical treatment;
(f) agree to the child's adoption;
(g) consent to change the child's surname;
(h) administer the child's property; and
(i) to appoint a guardian for his child.

Similarly, a parent has a duty to:

(a) ensure his child is being educated;
(b) maintain his child;
(c) protect the child; and
(d) to represent the child in legal proceedings.

4. Who has parental responsibility?

Section 2(1) of the C.A. 1989 provides that where a child's mother and father were married to each other at the time of the child's birth, they shall each have parental responsibility for the child. This applies to children born as a result of AID (*see* **5**).

Where the child's parents were not married to each other at the time of the child's birth, only the mother has parental responsibility (s. 2(2)) but the father may acquire it either by a court order or agreement with the mother under s. 4, or a residence order under s. 8: s. 12(1). If the father had already acquired a parental rights and duties order under s. 4(1), Family Law Reform Act 1987, this will automatically be deemed to be an order under s. 4 of C.A. 1989 (Sched. 14, para. 4).

Parental responsibility may also be acquired by a guardian, a person with a residence order (*see* 12:**12**), adopters (*see* 13:**12**) and local authorities where a care order or emergency protection order is in force (*see* 15:**7, 15**).

Section s. 5, C.A. 1989 provides that a court may appoint a guardian if the child has no parent with parental responsibility or a parent or guardian with a residence order has died during the subsistence of the order. A parent with parental responsibility or a guardian may appoint another (or others (s. 5(10))) to act as guardian in the event of their death. Such appointment must be in writing, dated and signed by the maker or, where not so signed, signed at his direction and duly witnessed: s. 5(5). The section goes on to provide for the circumstances in which the appointment of a guardian may be revoked or disclaimed.

NOTE: (1) More than one person may have parental responsibility for the same child at the same time: s. 12(5);

(2) Where more than one person has parental responsibility for a child, each person may act independently without the other(s) in discharging that liability. This power is

subject to any statute requiring the consent of more than one person in any matter affecting the child: s. 12(7);

(3) The fact that a person has parental responsibility for a child does not entitle him to act in a way incompatible with any order made in respect of the child under the 1989 Act: s. 12(8);

(4) Though a person who has parental responsibility may not surrender or transfer any part of it to another, he may arrange for some or all of it to be met by one or more persons acting on his behalf: s. 12(9). A person acting on his behalf may already have parental responsibility for the child: s. 12(10). An arrangement will not affect any liability the person making it may have as a result of failing to meet any of his parental responsibilities for the child concerned: s. 12(11).

5. Determination of parentage

As can be seen, it is important to determine a child's parentage. Modern advances in relation to, e.g. egg donation and implantation, i.e an embryo derived from a donor woman's egg and fertilised outside the bodies of the donor and donee by semen from the donee's husband is implanted in the donee's womb, make it important to determine who the mother is. The Human Fertilisation and Embryology Act 1990 provides that only the woman who has given birth is to be regarded as the child's mother: s. 27. Under s. 28 a husband whose wife has produced a child by artificial means will be regarded as the child's father even though the child is not his genetic child, provided he consented to his wife's treatment. If the man is not married, or he did not consent to his wife's treatment, he will still be regarded as the child's father provided that the man and woman were treated together and the man's sperm was not used. If the man's sperm *was* used, the common law presumption (*see* below) applies. In the case of a child born to a married couple as a result of AID, the child is rebuttably presumed to be the child of that couple: s. 27, Family Law Reform Act 1987. The presumption will be rebutted if the husband did not consent to his wife's artificial insemination (ibid).

As regards the identification of the father, at common law a child conceived or born to a married couple is rebuttably presumed to be the child of that couple. It follows from this that a child will be presumed to be the child of the husband if:

(a) born between decree nisi and decree absolute;

(b) conceived after a decree nisi and born after decree absolute;

(c) when a separation agreement or maintenance order is in force, or

(d) born after the husband's death provided the birth is within the normal period of human gestation.

The presumption does not apply, and the child will consequently be rebuttably presumed not to be the husband's child, where the child is conceived when the spouses were separated as a result of a decree of judicial separation. If a child is born some time after the husband has been continuously absent from his wife, there may come a time, which the House of Lords in *Preston-Jones* v. *Preston-Jones* (1951) (*see* 4:7) refused to identify, when it becomes impossible to raise the presumption that the husband is the father.

> NOTE: (1) The above presumptions may be rebutted by proof on a balance of probability: Family Law Reform Act 1969, s. 26. Blood tests and DNA fingerprinting play an important role in this connection (*see* 4:9).
>
> (2) The presumptions may be rebutted by the spouses' evidence as to whether they had marital sexual intercourse at the relevant time: s. 48 M.C.A. 1973, and spouses are compellable as regards giving evidence of access or non-access to each other: Civil Evidence Act 1968, s. 16(4).

Progress test 11

1. What is the significance of the decision of the House of Lords in *Gillick* from the point of view of a parent's right to control his child? **(1–2)**

2. What does 'parental responsibility' mean in the Children Act 1989? **(2)**

3. What rights and duties are parents said to have over their children? **(3)**

4. Who has or may acquire parental responsibility in respect of a child? **(4)**

5. Can the exercise of parental responsibility be delegated to another? **(4)**

6. What presumptions apply to determine who is the child's mother and father? **(5)**

7. How may these presumptions be rebutted? **(5)**

8. John and Jane, who are not married to each other, have three children, Keith, aged four, Linda, aged 15, and Mary, aged 17. Keith requires an operation, Linda has an appointment to see the family doctor in order to obtain a prescription for the contraceptive pill and Mary wants to marry her boyfriend. John, who does not wish to consent to any of these proposed courses of action, and Jane, who does, seek your advice as to their respective legal positions. Advise them.

12

Disputes over the care and upbringing of children

Introduction

1. Methods of determining disputes

The question of who is to have care of, or contact with, a child may be decided in 'family proceedings'. These are defined in s. 8(3) and (4) of the Children Act 1989 as any proceedings under:

(a) the inherent jurisdiction of the High Court (e.g. wardship proceedings);
(b) Parts I, II and IV of the 1989 Act;
(c) the D.V.M.P.A. 1976 (*see* 6:**6**);
(d) the Adoption Act 1976 (*see* Chapter 13);
(e) the D.P.M.C.A. 1978 (*see* 6:**10**);
(f) sections 1 and 9 of the M.H.A. 1983 (*see* 7:**15**); and
(g) Part III of the M.F.P.A. 1984 relating to financial provision following an overseas' divorce, nullity or legal separation (*see* 9:**41**).

2. The paramount consideration

'When a court determines any question with respect to:

(a) the upbringing of a child; or
(b) the administration of a child's property or the application of any income arising from it,

the child's welfare shall be the court's paramount consideration': s. 1(1), C.A. 1989.

Though this principle is of general application, it should be borne in mind that it is not applicable when leave to apply for a s. 8 order is sought (*see* 12:**14**), in adoption (*see* 13:**6**), to decisions concerning ouster orders (*see* 6:3), to decisions relating to blood or DNA tests to determine paternity (*see* 4:9) or to the imposition of restrictions on publication by the media of matters affecting a ward of court (*see* **5** below).

3. The application of the welfare principle

Unlike earlier legislative tests where the child's welfare was the 'first and paramount consideration', the test in s. 1 makes the child's welfare the overriding consideration. In deciding what course of action will most advance the child's welfare, the court will take into account the factors having a bearing on that welfare. In doing this the court is, for the first time, assisted by the general principle in s. 1(2) (i.e. that any delay is likely to prejudice the child's welfare) and by the statutory checklist contained in s. 1(3).

Section 1(3) contains nothing which judges will not already have considered when deciding on the disposition of a child subject to a custody dispute, in which case pre-Act decisions will still be valid authorities on the interpretation of the subsection. These decisions frequently illustrate the point that several matters, sometimes competing with each other, need to be taken into account but the underlying principle is always that the court must decide which course of judicial action is the least wrong to adopt in order to secure the child's welfare. It should be noted that the matters contained in s. 1(3) are not exhaustive and they are to be referred to *only* when the court is involved in a *contested* s. 8 order (*see* **9** below) or in a care or supervision order (*see* **15:5** *et seq.*): s. 1(4).

The matters set out in s. 1(3) are:

(a) *the ascertainable wishes and feelings of the child concerned (considered in the light of his age and understanding)*. The older the child the more likely it is that the child will have the maturity to make a convincing case for having a say in any decision affecting its future. Thus in *M.* v. *M.* (1987) C.A. the strongly expressed views of a 12-year-old girl that she wanted to live with her father was the basis for overturning a decision that she live with her mother. In *In re P (a Minor)* (1991) C.A. the court gave effect to the wish of a 'mature and sensible' 14-year-old boy to go to a local school rather than take up a place as a boarder at a major public school. Even so, the court will always be alert to the possibility that a child's expressed wishes may be the result of pressure or prejudicial influence by the parent with whom the child lives. Under this paragraph a child's wishes and feelings need not be ascertained by interviewing the child (usually in private) but may be garnered from evidence given by the guardian *ad litem* for the suit or a social worker.

(b) *his physical, emotional and educational needs.* 'Physical' needs will obviously include a child's need for a particular kind of medical treatment which, for example, may not be readily available in the area where one of the parents proposes to live. 'Emotional' needs is apt to cover the view, occasionally approved by judges, that young children, particularly girls, are better with their mother than their father. This has been said to be not a rule of law but a matter of 'common sense' and 'human experience': *Re M* (1967) C.A. Though this may be a natural state of affairs, it has recently been stressed that it should not be regarded as a presumption and it is readily displaced if the child's welfare so dictates: *In re H (a Minor)* (1990) C.A. There is no similar rule in relation to young boys being with their father. A child may also be emotionally attached to a brother or sister and this would be a relevant matter under this heading: *C. v. C.* (1988) C.A.

'Educational' needs is wide enough to cover both religious and secular education. Although the modern approach to religious upbringing is not to regard it with the obsessive importance which characterised Victorian decisions, this does not mean that religion is unimportant. In *Roughley* v. *Roughley* (1973) C.A. religious education was held to be a matter worthy of consideration but not as important as the child's happiness and stability. If adherence to the tenets of a particular religious sect adversely affects a child, this will be of particular relevance when deciding what is in the best interests of that child. Thus in *Re C* (1964) a parent's membership of a religious sect, which banned its members from social intercourse with non-members, was a decisive factor in favouring the other parent who had left the sect. A similar approach to membership of the Church of Scientology was adopted by the court in *Re B and G* (1985) C.A. In *In re H (a Minor)* (1980) the fact that a child would not be isolated from the rest of the community was a decisive factor in the court's decision to order that a five year old boy should live with his mother who was a practising Jehovah's Witness. The mother was moderate in her attitude to her religious beliefs and she had undertaken that her son would play a full part in all school activities and she would not take him with her when she went to make converts.

Secular education was an important element in the court's decision in *May* v. *May* (1986) C.A. to let children live with their father who placed greater store on educational achievement than the mother and her lover with whom the children were living. A parent's disruption of a child's educational progress at a crucial stage would be a relevant matter for the court's consideration.

(c) *the likely effect on him of any change in his circumstances.* The court is more likely to be concerned with the child's short-term interests rather than with what the situation is likely to be in a few years' time: *T.* v. *T.* (1987) C.A. The importance of preserving a satisfactory status quo was emphasised by the House of Lords in *J.* v. *C.* (1969) H.L. There the 10½-year-old son of Spanish parents living in Spain had, from the age of three, lived in England with English foster parents and their six children. In wardship proceedings it had been ordered that the boy should live with the foster parents and the boy's natural parents appealed to the House of Lords on the ground, *inter alia*, that his welfare was best served by him being with his parents. HELD: in general a child's welfare was best served by the child being with his parents. However, this rule did not apply here because, to all intents and purposes, the boy was an English boy and the evidence suggested that his successful adjustment to and integration in the Spanish way of life was unlikely and his removal from a settled and happy environment would damage his emotional stability and happiness. Consequently the parents' appeal was dismissed.

Medical and similar evidence will usually be available in order to assist the court when determining the likely effect on a child of a proposed change of environment. It is highly unlikely that much credence would now be given to the view of Eve J in *Re Thain* (1925) that in the case of a young child 'one knows from experience how mercifully transient are the effects of partings and other sorrows, and how soon the novelty of fresh surroundings and new associations effaces the recollection of former days and kind friends'.

(d) *his age, sex, background and any characteristics of his which the court considers relevant.* The relevance of a child's age and sex have already been considered. 'Background' is wide enough to encompass matters such as racial or cultural background. It is unlikely that 'characteristics' will be given the restricted meaning familiar to criminal lawyers in the context of provocation and duress. Rather it will be seen as covering whichever of the child's attributes or traits the court wishes to use as a justification for its decision.

(e) *any harm which he has suffered or is at risk of suffering.* Unlike decisions in relation to care orders the harm here need not be 'significant'. 'Harm' is wide enough to cover both physical and mental ill-treatment as well as sexual abuse.

(f) *how capable each of his parents, and any other person in relation to whom the court considers the question to be relevant, is of meeting his needs.* This may be thought to give an advantage to the mother who is generally regarded as better equipped at looking after children, particularly young children (*see* **(b)** above) but this, like all the criteria under s. 1(3), is subject to the child's best interests. The reference to 'any other person' covers such persons as a step-parent, cohabitee, grandparent or child-carer. It is important to remember that while a parent may have been a bad spouse he or she may still be a good parent.

(g) *the range of powers available to the court under the 1989 Act in the proceedings in question.* There is a wide range of orders available to the court (*see* **9** *et seq.*) but there is a presumption against the court making an order 'unless it considers that doing so would be better for the child than making no order at all.': s. 1(5).

Wardship proceedings

4. Procedure

Section 41 of the Supreme Court Act 1981 provides that:

'(1)   Subject to the provisions of this section, no minor shall be made a ward of court except by virtue of an order to that effect made by the High Court.

(2)   Where an application is made for such an order in respect of a minor, the minor shall become a ward of court on the making of the application, but shall cease to be a ward of court at the end of such period as may be prescribed unless within that period an order has been made in accordance with the application.

(2A)   Subsection 2 does not apply with respect to a child who is the subject of a care order ....

(3)   The High Court may, either upon an application in that behalf or without such an application, order that any minor who is for the time being a ward of court shall cease to be a ward of court.'

Note that wardship proceedings, other than those relating to the creation and termination of wardship, may be transferred to a county court under s. 38(2), M.F.P.A. 1984.

There is judicial disagreement over whether the court (i.e. the Family Division of the High Court) may exercise the inherent jurisdiction of its ancestor, the Court of Chancery acting as *parens patriae* (father of the nation), without the minor first being made a ward under what is now s. 41. In *Re E* (1955) Roxburgh J concluded that this was not possible but the opposite view was taken by Stamp J in *Re N (No.2)* (1967), and Sir Jocelyn Simon P in *L* v. *L* (1969)).

Any person (other than a local authority without leave: s. 100, C.A. 1989) may initiate wardship proceedings provided he has a legitimate reason for so doing. The applicant must state his relationship to the ward and the application may be dismissed if it is considered to be an abuse of the process of the court: Practice Direction (1967), e.g. if the application was in the nature of a publicity stunt: *Re Dunhill* (1967).

NOTE: in view of the wide powers available to courts under the Children Act 1989 (*see* 9 *et seq.* below) the need for wardship proceedings is likely to be greatly reduced.

5.   The welfare principle

Though s. 1(1) of the C.A. 1989 applies to wardship cases, it does not apply if the child's upbringing is not the real issue. Thus in *Re X (a Minor) (Wardship: Jurisdiction)* (1975) C.A. the defendants proposed to publish a book about the deceased father of the female ward. The book contained passages showing the deceased to have been a man who was 'utterly depraved in his sexual activities, who indulged in sordid and degrading conduct, and who was obscene and drank to excess'. As there would be very grave psychological injury to the girl if she were to learn of the book's references to her father, her stepfather made her a ward of court and sought an injunction to prevent publication. At first instance this was granted because of the need to protect the girl. On appeal this decision was reversed since neither the girl's care nor upbringing were in issue. On the other hand, publication by the media of the names of the natural father and his wife was prohibited by Latey J in the case where a child, born to a surrogate mother who had been artificially inseminated with the natural father's sperm, had been made a ward: *In re a Baby* (1985). In *In re W (a Minor)* (1991) C.A. the court stressed that the protection of the ward from harm had to be weighed against the right of the press or others to publish or to comment and it took account of article 10 of the European Convention on Human Rights which safeguards the freedom to hold opinions and to receive and impart information and ideas without interference by public authority. Except in the most exceptional cases, the ward could not be protected from any distress caused by reading about himself.

If the court feels that the ward should be separately represented, the Official Solicitor will be appointed as the ward's guardian *ad litem*. His duty is to safeguard the ward's interests, to investigate all the relevant circumstances and to report thereon to the court.

6. Scope of the jurisdiction

The wardship jurisdiction is exercisable:

(a) notwithstanding that there are no other proceedings in existence, i.e. it is not ancillary to other matters;

(b) in respect of any unmarried minor, i.e. he need not be a child of the family, as under the M.C.A. 1973 or the D.P.M.C.A. 1978. It should be noted that an unborn child cannot be made a ward of court: *Re F (in utero)* (1988) C.A.;

(c) by persons who have no *locus standi* under other legislation;

(d) in emergencies. The speed and convenience with which the wardship jurisdiction may be invoked (it is exercisable at weekends and when the courts are on vacation) is particularly helpful in cases where a child is likely to be 'kidnapped' and taken out of the jurisdiction. Such conduct may also be deterred by criminal sanctions under the common law offence of kidnapping and under the Child Abduction Act 1984.

7. The effect of wardship

Wardship effectively vests parental rights and responsibilities in relation to the ward in the court which usually delegates the day-to-day care of the child to an individual. Consequently, major decisions affecting the child must be taken by the court. Such decisions include giving consent in relation to a wide range of matters. These include marriage, the initiation of adoption proceedings (*see In re F (a Minor)* (1983) C.A.), major surgery, medical action which does not prolong the ward's life (in *In re J (a Minor) (Wardship: Medical Treatment)* (1990) C.A. the court, in the best interests of a brain-damaged baby, authorised doctors to withhold placing the child on a ventilator if the doctors thought this appropriate on the basis of their clinical judgment), the ward's removal from the jurisdiction and consent to the ward being interviewed in connection with criminal proceedings (the court's leave is not required before a ward may be called to give evidence in a criminal trial: *In re R (a Minor) (Wardship: Witness in criminal proceedings)* (1991) C.A.). Interference with and disobedience to the court's order is a contempt of court.

One of the difficulties with the wardship jurisdiction is the extent to which the court's powers are co-extensive with those of a parent. If they are co-extensive, on the basis of *Gillick* (*see* 11:**2**) the powers of the court will yield to the child's autonomy where the child is sufficiently mature to make decisions for itself. However, in *In re R (a Minor) (Wardship: Medical Treatment)* (1991) C.A. it was held that the wardship jurisdiction was wider than that of parents because it was derived not from parental rights and responsibilities but from the delegated performance of the Crown's duty to protect its subjects (i.e the *parens patriae* jurisdiction). In this most difficult case, the court ordered that the ward, a 15 year old mentally ill girl, must undergo psychiatric treatment despite the fact that during lucid intervals she had refused to consent to such treatment.

The court may order either parent to pay such weekly or periodical sums to the other parent or to any other person having care of the ward as the court thinks reasonable towards the maintenance and education of the ward or to the ward: Family Law Reform Act 1969, s. 6(2). The payment may continue until the ward attains 21, and a former ward who is 18 or over but not 21 may obtain an order for maintenance.

The court may no longer commit a ward to the care or supervision of a local authority under s. 7(2) of the Family Reform Act 1969: s. 100, C.A. 1989. Where a ward is in care under s. 7(2) the order is deemed to be a care order and the High Court ceases to have jurisdiction over such ward: *In re C (a Minor)* (1991).

Wardship automatically terminates when the minor achieves his majority, i.e. 18: s. 1 of the 1969 Act, and on the making of a care order: s. 91(4) of the 1989 Act.

8. Local authorities and wardship

Prior to the Children Act 1989 local authorities frequently resorted to the wardship jurisdiction in cases of difficulty concerning the welfare of children in their care. Section 100(3) provides that a local authority wishing to use the court's wardship jurisdiction in respect of a child in care must first seek the court's permission. Permission will be granted only if the court is satisfied that the result sought to be achieved by the authority could not be achieved by some other order *and* there is reasonable cause to believe that the child is likely to suffer significant harm if the wardship jurisdiction is not exercised (s. 100(4)). If permission is granted, the child does not become a ward of court: s. 100(2)(c).

An alternative to an application under s. 100(3) is to apply for a 'specific issue order' under s. 8 (*see* **13**).

Orders relating to children in family proceedings

9. 'Section 8 orders'

Section 8 of the C.A. 1989 allows a court in 'family proceedings' (*see* **1** above) to make, vary or discharge a range of orders. These are:

(a) the 'contact order',
(b) the 'prohibited steps order',
(c) the 'residence order', and
(d) the 'specific issue order'.

These orders may contain directions as to their implementation, impose conditions either on the person in whose favour they are made, the child's parent or person with parental responsibility, or person with whom the child is living, be made to apply for a specified time, or make such other provision as the court thinks fair (s. 11(7)).

Consistent with the general principle regarding the prejudicial effect of delay, the court has a duty in s. 8 proceedings to draw up a timetable and to give directions so as to ensure adherence to it so far as is reasonably practicable (s. 11(1)).

Section 8 orders, which may be made at any time during the course of proceedings even though the court cannot dispose of the matter (s. 11(3)), automatically end when the child reaches 16 unless the court is satisfied that the circumstances are exceptional: s. 9(6). Section 8 orders also end automatically on the making of a care order (*see* 15:5) (s. 91(2)) or an adoption order (*see* 13:2 below): s. 12(3)(aa), Adoption Act 1976.

10. The contact order

This replaces the access order and is an order 'requiring the person with whom a child lives, or is to live, to allow the child to visit or stay with the person named in the order, or for that person and the child otherwise to have contact with each other'. It differs from the access order in that it is framed in terms of the child's right to visit his parent rather than vice versa.

A contact order which requires the parent with whom the child lives to allow the child contact with the other parent automatically ends if the parents live together for a continuous period exceeding six months: s. 11(6).

A local authority can neither obtain a contact order nor apply for one: s. 9(2).

11. The prohibited steps order

This is modelled on the wardship jurisdiction and is an order that 'no step which could be taken by a parent in meeting his parental responsibility for a child, and which is of a kind specified in the order, shall be taken by any person without the consent of the court'.

The court cannot make a prohibited steps order so as to achieve a result which could be achieved by way of a residence or contact order or use it to circumvent the restrictions placed by s. 100(2) upon the exercise by the High Court of its wardship jurisdiction in cases involving a local authority (*see* 8 above): s. 9(5).

12. The residence order

This replaces custody and custodianship orders and is an order 'settling the arrangements to be made as to the person with whom a child is to live'. Joint residence orders may be made where parents are separated. In such cases the order may specify the periods during which the child is to live in the different households (s. 11(4)) and both parents continue to have parental responsibility for the child. If the parents live together for a continuous period exceeding six months, the residence order automatically ends: s. 11(5).

During the subsistence of a residence order no-one may change the child's surname or remove him from the U.K. for a month or more without either the written consent of everyone with parental responsibility or leave of the court: s. 13(1).

If the court makes a residence order in favour of a father who does not already have parental responsibility because, e.g. he was not married to the child's mother at the date of birth, the court must also make an order under s. 4 giving him such responsibility: s. 12(1). A s. 4 order lasts for as long as the residence order continues and may be terminated only by court order: s. 12(4).

The court may also make a residence order in favour of persons other than the child's parent or guardian: s. 12(2). Though such persons have parental responsibility, they may not consent to an order freeing the child for adoption, agree to the child's adoption or appoint a guardian for the child: s. 12(3).

The only s. 8 order which a court may make in respect of a child in local authority care is a residence order (s. 9(1)) but application cannot be made by an authority: s. 9(2).

A residence order may be enforced in a magistrates' court by way of a fine or imprisonment: s. 14.

13. The specific issue order

This is an order 'giving directions for the purpose of determining a specific question which has arisen, or which may arise, in connection with any aspect of parental responsibility for a child.' These are apt to cover matters such as consent to medical treatment or the withholding of such treatment which have traditionally been the province of wardship proceedings (*see* 7 above).

As in the case of a prohibited steps order, the court cannot make a specific issue order so as to achieve a result which could be achieved by way of a residence or contact order (s. 9(5)) or use it to circumvent the restrictions placed by s. 100(2) upon the exercise by the High Court of its wardship jurisdiction in cases involving a local authority: s. 9(5).

> NOTE the power of the court to make a 'family assistance order' under s. 16 in any proceedings where the court may make a s. 8 order. Family assistance orders replace supervision orders under the M.C.A. 1973 and the D.P.M.C.A. 1978. The order requires a probation officer or local authority officer (e.g. social worker or welfare rights officer) to advise, assist and (where appropriate) befriend any person named in the order. The court must be satisfied that the circumstances are exceptional and must have obtained the consent of every person to be named in the order: s. 16(3). Where a local authority officer is to be appointed, the authority must agree to the appointment or the child must or will live in its area. Where a s. 8 order is also in force the supervisor may refer to the court the question of whether that order should be varied or discharged. Family assistance orders may last for no more than six months from the date the order is made: s. 16(5).

14. Who may apply for a s. 8 order?

Any of the orders may be made on the application, *without leave*, of:

(a) any parent (including the child's unmarried father) or guardian of the child: s. 10(4);
(b) any person with a residence order in his favour in respect of the child: s. 10(5); and
(c) any person with an existing care and control order: sched. 14, para. 8.

Additionally, *leave is not required* by the following who are permitted to apply *only for a residence or contact order*:

(a) any party to a marriage (whether or not subsisting) in relation to whom the child is a child of the family (*see* 8:**10**);
(b) any person with whom the child has lived for a period of at least three years (this period need not be continuous but it must

have *begun* more than five years before, or *ended* more than three months before, the making of the application);

(c) any person who has the consent of the person(s) in whose favour a residence order or existing care and control order exists;

(d) any person who has the consent of the local authority where the child is in its care; and

(e) any person who, in any other case, has the consent of anyone with parental responsibility for the child: s. 10(5) and sched. 14, para. 8.

Anyone falling outside the above provisions, persons who are, or within the last six months were, local authority foster parents or the child himself may apply for a s. 8 order but only *after the court has granted leave*. Where the child applies for leave the court may grant it only if satisfied that he has sufficient understanding to make a s. 8 application: s. 10(8). In all other cases the court's decision on whether to grant leave must have been based on:

(a) the nature of the proposed application for the s. 8 order;

(b) the applicant's connection with the child;

(c) any risk of the proposed application disrupting the child's life to such an extent that he would be harmed by it; and

(d) if the child is being looked after by a local authority, the authority's plans for the child's future and the wishes and feelings of the child's parents: s. 10(9).

15. Section 8 orders under the Matrimonial Causes Act 1973

The court (i.e the Family Division of the High Court or the county court) may make, vary or discharge any s. 8 order (*see* **9** above). Where a court has power to make a s. 8 order a family assistance order may be made whether or not a s. 8 order is made (*see* **13** above).

In support of the general welfare principle in s. 1 of the C.A. 1989 (*see* **2** above), the 1973 Act provides a mechanism whereby the court must give specific consideration to the exercise of its powers under the 1989 Act before a final decree is granted. Thus s. 41 (as amended by the 1989 Act) provides as follows:

'(1) In any proceedings for a decree of divorce or nullity of marriage, or a decree of judicial separation, the court shall consider:

(a) whether there are any children of the family to whom this section applies; and
(b) where there are any such children, whether (in the light of the arrangements which have been, or are proposed to be, made for their upbringing and welfare) it should exercise any of its powers under the Children Act 1989 with respect to any of them.'

Where it appears to the court that the circumstances require, or are likely to require, the exercise of any of its powers under the 1989 Act but (*a*) it is not in a position to exercise them without further consideration, and (*b*) there are exceptional circumstances making it desirable in the child's interests that the court should make a declaration under s. 41, the court *may* direct that the decree of divorce or nullity is not to be made absolute, or the decree of judicial separation is not to be granted, until the court orders otherwise: s. 41(2).

NOTE: (1) The section *must* be applied to children of the family under the age of 16 at the time of the hearing and *may* be applied to such children aged 16 and over if the court so directs: s. 41(3).
  (2) For the meaning of 'child of the family', *see* 8:**10**.

16. Section 8 orders under the Domestic Proceedings and Magistrates' Courts Act 1978

A magistrates' court (sitting as a 'family proceedings' court), on an application by either party to the marriage for a financial provision order under ss. 2, 6 or 7 of the Act (*see* 8:**9** *et seq.*), may make, vary or discharge any s. 8 order and also has the power to make a family assistance order (*see* above).

If there is a child of the family under the age of 18, the court must not dismiss or make a final order until it has decided whether to exercise any of its powers under the Children Act 1989 with respect to the child: s. 8, D.P.M.C.A. 1978, as amended by the 1989 Act.

NOTE: 'child of the family' has the same meaning as under the M.C.A. 1973 (*see* 8:**10**).

Progress test 12

1. What machinery does the law provide for the resolution of disputes concerning the welfare and upbringing of a child? **(1)**

2. How is the welfare of a child protected in 'family proceedings'? **(2)**

3. Explain and illustrate the application of s. 1(1) of the Children Act 1989. **(3)**

4. How and why is a child made a ward of court? **(4, 7)**

5. In wardship cases to what extent is the minor's welfare secondary to other considerations? **(5)**

6. Outline the extent of wardship jurisdiction. **(6)**

7. When may local authorities avail themselves of the wardship jurisdiction? **(8)**

8. What does the phrase 'section 8 order' mean? **(9)**

9. When may a s. 8 order be made and when does such an order end? **(9)**

10. Explain the effects of the following s. 8 orders: contact, prohibited steps, residence and specific issue. **(10–13)**

11. What is a 'family assistance order'? **(13)**

12. Who has a *right* to apply for a s. 8 order? **(14)**

13. In what circumstances must an applicant for a s.8 order first obtain leave? **(14)**

14. What powers does the divorce court have to make a s. 8 order? **(15)**

15. What powers does the family proceedings court have to make a s. 8 order? **(16)**

16. Miss A and Mr B lived together for three years, during which time they had two children, a boy and a girl. A year ago Mr B left Miss A and married Miss C. He has persistently and unsuccessfully requested Miss A to let his son live with him and his wife. Recently Mr B came to Miss A's flat and forcibly took the boy away. Miss A tells you that, though she is living in cramped accommodation and is in receipt of social security, she would be able to give the child proper care and attention, whereas Mr B and his wife both go out to work and the child spends a great deal of time with Mr B's parents, who are both old age pensioners. Advise Miss A: (*a*) what proceedings she may initiate to recover the child, (*b*) the factors the court will take into account, and (*c*) about her chances of success.

17. When Mr and Mrs X married seven years ago, she already had a three year old boy by her former husband. Mr and Mrs X have two other children, a girl aged five and a boy aged three. Mrs X recently left her husband to live with Y but had to leave the children behind because Y had insufficient accommodation. As she missed the children badly Mrs X returned to her husband. Mr X now wishes to terminate the marriage but Mrs X, who intends to go and live with Y who has moved into a large house, says she will fight any application Mr X makes for the children to live with him. Mr X seeks your advice as to (*a*) whether he has grounds for terminating the marriage, (*b*) the powers of the court in relation to the children, and (*c*) his chances of successfully obtaining a s. 8 order.

13
Adoption

Introduction

1. Introduction

Adoption originated in the Adoption of Children Act 1926. Substantial amendments were made to the law of adoption by the Children Act 1975 but this has been repealed by the Adoption Act 1976 (as amended by the Children Act 1989) which now governs adoption.

Adoption has the effect of severing the legal relationship between a child and his natural parent(s) and replacing it with a similar relationship between the child and his adopter(s). The court has power to insert into an adoption order 'such terms and conditions as the court thinks fit': s. 12(6). In appropriate circumstances an adoption order may contain a condition whereby contact between the adopted child and his natural parent(s) is maintained. In *Re C (a Minor) (Adoption: Conditions)* (1988) H.L. the agreement of the adopters to contact was regarded as crucial. It should also be remembered that adoption proceedings are 'family proceedings' within the Children Act 1989 (*see* 12:1 above). Consequently, a court hearing an application for an adoption order may make an order under s. 8 of the 1989 Act instead of an adoption order.

The legal effects of an adoption order

2. The effect of adoption on parental responsibility

The Adoption Act 1976, s. 12, provides that an adoption order gives parental responsibility for a child to the adopters and extinguishes such responsibility vested in others. The order also extinguishes any duty under an agreement or court order to make payments in respect of the child's maintenance or upbringing after the making of the order, but this does not apply if the agreement constitutes a trust or expressly so provides: ss. 12(3)(b), 12(4).

An adoption order has no effect on parental responsibility which existed prior to the making of the order.

NOTE: an adoption order automatically terminates *any* order made under the C.A. 1989: s. 12(3)(aa).

3. The effect of adoption on the child's status

Section 39 of the 1976 Act provides that where the adopters are a married couple the adopted child shall be treated in law as if he had been born as a child of the marriage, whether or not he was born after the marriage was solemnised. In any other case, the child shall be treated as if born to the adopter in wedlock, but not as a child of any actual marriage of the adopter.

Section 39(4) specifically declares that adoption prevents a child from being illegitimate.

4. The effect of adoption on rights of succession

In the case of instruments made on or after January 1, 1976 and wills of testators dying on or after that date, an adopted child may claim, subject to any contrary indication, as the adopter's child, whenever the gift takes effect as regards the adoption.

Where a gift depends upon the date of birth of an adopted child, e.g. a testamentary gift to 'the eldest child of A living at my death', it is to be construed as though the adopted child had been born on the date of his adoption and two or more children adopted on the same date rank in the order of the dates of their actual birth: s. 42(2). This does not affect a gift which depends upon the child reaching an actual age, e.g. a testamentary gift to 'A's children aged 21', in which case the child will take when he actually attains the age of 21, whenever his adoption.

Notwithstanding these rules, an illegitimate child adopted by one of his natural parents *as sole adoptive parent* is not consequently deprived of property, entitlement to which depends on his relationship to that parent. This is also the case where a disposition depends on the illegitimate child's date of birth: s. 39(3).

Adoption does not affect the descent of any peerage or dignity or title of honour: s. 44(1), or, subject to any contrary intent, the devolution of any property limited to devolve along with the same: s. 44(2).

5.   Some miscellaneous effects of adoption

(a) *The prohibited degrees of relationship.* For the purposes of marriage and the crime of incest, adoption does not affect the prohibited degrees of relationship which result from a child's birth to his natural parents: s. 47(1). Moreover, an adopted child, even if subsequently adopted by someone else, cannot marry his adoptive parent: Marriage Act 1949, as amended by the Children Act 1975. Somewhat anomalously, an adopted child may marry its adoptive brother or sister.

(b) *Entitlement to pensions.* An adopted child is still entitled to any pension actually paid to him or for his benefit at the time of his adoption: s. 48.

(c) *Insurance of funeral expenses.* Any insurance policy for the payment of funeral expenses on the child's death effected by the natural parents with a friendly society, collecting society or industrial insurance company, will be regarded as having been effected by the adoptive parents: s. 49.

(d) *Nationality.* The adoption of a foreign minor by a British citizen confers British citizenship on that minor from the date of the adoption order. If the principal motive of an adoption application is to confer British citizenship on a foreign child rather than to promote his welfare during the remainder of his childhood as required by s. 6 (*see* 6), the application should be refused: *Re W (a Minor) (Adoption: Non-patrial)* (1985) C.A. This case stressed that in applications to adopt a foreign child the following matters applied:

(i)   the applicant should notify the Home Office of the application to see if the Home Secretary wishes to be added as a party;

(ii) the weight to be applied to s. 6 decreased the nearer the child was to attaining his majority;

(iii) the court should consider whether the child's welfare might be equally or as well advanced by some other order which did not affect nationality or immigration; and (*iv*) the court should strike a balance between the child's welfare and considerations of public policy in relation to nationality and immigration.

(e) *Access to birth records.* On an application (plus payment of the prescribed fee) any adopted person aged at least 18 whose birth record is kept by the Registrar General must be supplied with information necessary to enable the applicant to obtain a certified copy of his birth certificate: s. 51(1) and sched. 10, para. 20 C.A. 1989. Persons adopted before 12th November 1975 must be counselled before being able to obtain such information, whereas those adopted on or after that date merely have to be offered the opportunity of counselling. Under s. 51A the Registrar General must maintain an Adoption Contact Register which enables both adopted persons and relatives (i.e. those related to the adopted person by blood (including half-blood) or marriage) aged at least 18 to provide a contact address. This means that both adopted persons and their relatives may indicate a willingness to maintain contact with each other after the adoption.

The welfare principle

6. The first consideration

By s. 6 of the 1976 Act, in reaching any decision relating to the adoption of a child, a court (i.e. the High Court, county court or magistrates' court) or adoption agency must have regard to all the circumstances, first consideration being given to the need to safeguard and promote the welfare of the child throughout his childhood. Section 6 also provides that the child's wishes and feelings regarding the decision must be ascertained and due consideration given to them as far as is practicable and having regard to his age and understanding. Section 6 does not require the court to find that, as a condition precedent to the making of an adoption order, such order is necessary so as to safeguard and promote the child's welfare while a minor: *In re D (a Minor)* (1991) C.A. (adoption order made in respect of a severely mentally handicapped child).

The precise formulation of this welfare principle was the subject of a lengthy parliamentary debate. The aim was to find a form of words which would preserve the parental right to withhold agreement to the adoption but would at the same time emphasise that the child's welfare should be given greater weight than other considerations. It was thought that to make the child's welfare the 'first and paramount' consideration, as under the then guardianship legislation, would make such welfare prevail over all other considerations including the above parental right. At the Report stage of the 1975 Children Bill in the House of Lords, Lord Simon said that 'first consideration' directed the court to consider specifically the child's welfare and to give that welfare greater weight than other considerations, but it did not mean that that welfare must prevail over other considerations. Though this interpretation was commended to the House of Commons by the then Minister of State, its meaning is by no means clear. Even though the child's welfare is clearly a weighted factor, the amount of weight to be given to it remains unspecified and is, presumably, a matter for the court.

Notwithstanding the specific reference in s. 6 to 'any decision' relating to a child's adoption, there has been judicial controversy over whether the section applies to the court's decision whether to dispense with parental agreement to adoption (*see* **9**).

Who may be adopted?

7. Criteria to be satisfied
The person to be adopted must:

(a) be under 18: s. 72(1) (in *In re D (a Minor)*, above, the child was adopted six days before his eighteenth birthday);
(b) be at least 19 weeks old and have had his home with the applicant(s) at all times during the preceding 13 weeks, if either applicant is the child's parent, step-parent or relative, or the child was placed with the applicant(s) by an adoption agency or by order of the High Court: s. 13(1). If the applicant is not a parent, step-parent etc., the child must be at least 12 months old and must have had his home with the applicant(s) at all times during the preceding 12 months: s. 13(2);

> NOTE: the applicant(s) must have a home in England or Wales: *In re Adoption Application (121 of 1984)* (1985) (a step-father domiciled here but living abroad was unable to

adopt jointly with his wife her children by a former marriage because the applicants had no home in England or Wales).

(c) never have been married: s. 12(5); and

(d) have parental agreement to his adoption: s. 16, or be free for adoption: s. 18.

8. Parental agreement to adoption

Each parent or guardian of the child must freely, and with full understanding of what is involved, agree unconditionally to the making of the adoption order (whether or not he knows the identity of the applicants): s. 16(1)(b). As this agreement must be unconditional, it is no longer possible for a parent to impose conditions regarding the child's religious education when giving agreement, although the court may impose such a condition under the powers conferred by s. 12(6). When placing a child for adoption an adoption agency must have regard, as far as is practicable, to any wishes of the child's parents and guardians as to the child's religious upbringing: s. 7.

'Guardian' has the same meaning as in the Children Act 1989 (*see* 11:4 above). The father of an illegitimate child is not a 'parent' for the purposes of the 1976 Act (*In re L (a Minor) (Adoption)* (1990) C.A.) unless he has been given parental responsibility for the child: s. 72.

A mother's agreement is ineffective if given less than six weeks after the child's birth: s. 16(4).

The court has a discretion to dispense with a parent's or guardian's agreement on specified grounds which will be considered in **9**.

9. Grounds for dispensing with parental agreement

By s. 16(2) the court may dispense with the agreement of a parent of guardian to the adoption of a child on the ground that the parent or guardian:

(a) *Cannot be found or is incapable of giving agreement.* 'Cannot be found' means cannot be found by taking reasonable steps: *Re F (R)* (1969) C.A. Even though a person's address is known, the court will hold that he cannot be found if there are no practicable means of communicating with him. Thus in *Re R* (1966) the child's parents lived in a totalitarian country, from which the child had

escaped illegally, and any attempt to communicate with them would endanger them. This case also illustrates the meaning of incapacity to give agreement because the parents could not be made aware of the need for their agreement and, even if they could, it was unlikely that the regime would allow them to agree.
(b) *Is withholding his agreement unreasonably*. It has been consistently stated that the mere fact that adoption would advance the child's welfare does not of itself make the withholding of agreement to that adoption unreasonable, as it is eminently reasonable for a parent to want to preserve the legal relationship between himself and his child. However, as this provision clearly envisages that in some circumstances a withholding of agreement will be unreasonable, it is necessary to determine what circumstances amount to unreasonableness.

> *Re W* (1971) H.L.: an unmarried mother placed her third illegitimate child with foster-parents with whom it had lived for some 18 months when the mother withdrew her agreement to its adoption by them. HELD: the test of unreasonableness is the objective test of what a reasonable parent, placed in the situation of the actual parent, would do in all the circumstances of the case. Thus, the welfare of the child is not *per se* the test but, since a reasonable parent would have regard to his child's welfare, that welfare must be a relevant factor in determining reasonableness.

> *Re D* (1977) H.L.: a wife divorced her husband because of his homosexuality and she had custody of their eight year old son. The wife had remarried and she and her husband wanted to adopt the boy. The boy's father refused his agreement because he wanted to continue to see his son but he was prepared to give an undertaking not to bring the boy into contact with his homosexual friends. HELD: the father's refusal of agreement was to be judged by what a father in the actual father's circumstances, but hypothetically endowed with a mind and temperament capable of making objectively reasonable decisions, would do. Thus, despite modern tolerance of homosexuality, the reasonable parent in these circumstances would inevitably want to protect his son from the risk of exposure to

homosexuality. Accordingly the father's agreement was dispensed with because it had been unreasonably withheld.

NOTE: (1) *Re S* (1976) C.A. held that s. 6 of the 1976 Act was inapplicable to decisions regarding the reasonableness of withholding agreement to adoption. On the other hand both Ormrod LJ in *Re P* (1977) C.A. and Lord Simon in *Re D* (1977) H.L. thought it did not apply. On the assumption that the reasonable parent gives first consideration to his child's welfare, this judicial controversy would seem to be of little practical importance.

(2) The 'reasonable parent' test refers to the reasonably mature parent, regardless of age: *Re V (Adoption: Parental Consent)* (1985) C.A. (the fact that the mother was 14 did not affect the operation of the test).

(c) *Has persistently failed without reasonable cause to discharge the parental duties in relation to the child.* 'Persistently', under the corresponding provision in the 1958 Act, was held to mean permanently and this involved such a complete abrogation of parental duties that the parent should be deprived of his child against his wishes.

'Parental duties', by analogy with parental 'obligations' under the 1958 Act, includes a parent's natural and moral duty to show his child affection, care and interest, and his common law or statutory duty to maintain the child financially: *Re P* (1962).

(d) *Has abandoned or neglected the child.* 'Abandoned' connotes conduct which will render a parent criminally liable, e.g. leaving a child by the roadside: *Watson* v. *Nikolaisen* (1955). A similarly restrictive interpretation was placed upon 'neglected' in *Re P* (1962).

(e) *Has persistently ill-treated the child.* There is no authority on the interpretation of this provision. As the ill-treatment must be 'persistent' one act will be insufficient but it is debatable whether the ill-treatment must be permanent, by analogy with (c) above, or whether two acts on the same day might suffice, by analogy with persistent cruelty under the Matrimonial Proceedings (Magistrates' Courts) Act 1960 (now repealed).

(f) *Has seriously ill-treated the child.* This new ground was introduced because of the limitations of (e) caused by the need for the ill-treatment to be persistent. This ground does not apply unless the rehabilitation of the child within the parent's or guardian's household is unlikely because of the ill-treatment or for other reasons: s. 16(5).

10. Freeing for adoption

An alternative method of satisfying the requirement of parental agreement to adoption is a declaration by the court that the child is free for adoption. As such parental agreement may be withdrawn at any time before the adoption order is made, the anxiety of potential adopters may be increased by the awareness of this possibility. In order to obviate this difficulty the Children Act 1975 introduced a new procedure, now to be found in s. 18 of the 1976 Act, whereby a child may be declared free for adoption before adoption proceedings are initiated and even before a child has been placed for adoption. Once a child has been freed for adoption parental agreement is no longer necessary. The freeing procedure is available only on the application of an adoption agency, which may apply for no other type of order.

Under s. 18 the court must be satisfied that either each parent or guardian of the child freely, and with full understanding of what is involved, agrees generally and unconditionally to the making of an adoption order, or that such agreement should be dispensed with on one of the grounds dealt with in 9. A mother's agreement is ineffective if given less than six weeks after her child's birth. Agreement cannot be dispensed with unless the child is already placed for adoption or the court is satisfied that the child is likely to be so placed.

An application for freeing cannot be made unless either at least one parent or guardian consents to the making of the application, or the adoption agency is applying for the agreement of each parent or guardian to be dispensed with and the child is in the agency's care. For these purposes a child is in an adoption agency's care if the agency is a local authority and the child is in its care: s. 18(2A).

If the application relates to an illegitimate child, the agreement of its father is not required unless he has obtained parental responsibility under ss. 4 or 10 of the C.A. 1989. So as to give some protection to such a father who has not obtained parental responsibility by the time of the application to free the child for adoption, s. 18(7) provides that the court must be satisfied, before freeing the child, that he has no intention of applying under ss. 4 or 10 or, if he did make any such application, he would be likely to fail.

Before making an order under s. 18 the court must satisfy itself that each parent or guardian who can be found has been given the option of declaring his preference for not being involved in future questions concerning the child's adoption. Only if such a declaration is not made, does such parent or guardian have the right both to be informed by the adoption agency whether an adoption order has been made within 12 months of the freeing order (s. 19) and to apply for the revocation of a s. 18 order (s. 20) (*see* **11** below).

The effect of a freeing order is that no further evidence of parental agreement is necessary and parental responsibility for the child vests in the adoption agency until the adoption order is made or the freeing order revoked.

> NOTE: a freeing order automatically terminates any order made under the C.A. 1989: ss. 18(5) and 12(3)(aa).

11. Revocation of a s. 18 order

Under s. 20 the natural parent may apply to the court which made the freeing order for that order to be revoked on the ground that he wishes to resume parental responsibility. Such an application can be made only if more than 12 months have elapsed since the making of the freeing order and the child does not have his home with a person with whom he has been placed for adoption: s. 20(1).

The revocation of the freeing order:

(a) *extinguishes* the parental responsibility given by that order to the adoption agency: s. 20(3)(a);
(b) *gives* parental responsibility for the child to its mother and to the father provided he was married to the mother when the child was born: s. 20(3)(b); and
(c) *revives* any parental responsibility agreement, any order under s. 4(1), C.A. 1989 and any court or other appointment of a guardian to the child: s. 20(3)(c).

Section 20(3A) specifically states that revocation does not revive other orders under the C.A. 1989 or duties to maintain the child extinguished under s. 12(3)(b) (*see* **2** above) or affect any person's parental responsibility during the subsistence of the freeing order.

Who may adopt?

12. Criteria to be satisfied by the potential adopters

(a) *A married couple*: s. 14(1). At least one of the applicants must be domiciled in a part of the U.K., or in the Channel Islands or Isle of Man: s. 14(2). It is only in the case of a married couple that an adoption order may be made on the application of more than one person. In *Re S and A F (Infants)* (1976) C.A. Mr and Mrs S adopted the children of Mrs S's first marriage at a time when their marriage was void for bigamy. Mrs S later obtained a nullity decree in respect of this marriage and validly married S. There was then an application to the court to determine the validity of the adoption orders. HELD: as the application did not involve an appeal by an aggrieved person against the adoptions, when justice might require them to be set aside, the adoptions were valid, i.e. the orders were merely violable, not void.

If the applicants consist of a parent and a step-parent, the parent must be at least 18 and his or her spouse must be 21 or over: s. 14(1B).

(b) *Any unmarried person aged 21 or over*: s. 15(1), provided the domiciliary requirements in (a) above are satisfied.

(c) *One married person aged 21 or over*: s. 15(1), provided the domiciliary requirements above are complied with and the court is satisfied that:

    (*i*) his spouse cannot be found or, by virtue of s. 28, Human Fertilisation and Embryology Act 1990, there is no other parent (*see* 11:**5**), or

    (*ii*) the spouses have separated and are living apart, and the separation is likely to be permanent, or

    (*iii*) his spouse is by reason of ill health, physical or mental, incapable of applying for an adoption order.

NOTE: (1) If the application is made by the child's mother or father alone, an adoption order cannot be made unless the court is satisfied that the other natural parent is dead, cannot be found or should be excluded for some other reason: s. 15(3).

(2) Even though the domiciliary requirement is satisfied, the applicant(s) must also have a home in England or Wales (*see* **7** above).

13. Suitability of the applicants for an adoption order

An adoption order cannot be made unless the court is satisfied that sufficient opportunities to see the child with the applicant, or both applicants in the case of a married couple, in the home environment have been afforded to the adoption agency which placed the child for adoption, or, in any other case, the local authority within whose area that home is: s. 13(3).

Where a child has not been placed with the applicant by an adoption agency, an adoption order cannot be made unless the applicant, at least three months before the date of the order, gave notice of his intention to apply for an order to the local authority within whose area he has his home: s. 22(1). The applicant for such an order must give notice of his intention to apply within the two years preceding the making of the application. On receiving such notice the local authority must investigate, *inter alia*, and so far as is practicable, the applicant's suitability and any other matters relevant to the operation of s. 6 (*see* **6**) and report the outcome of such investigation to the court.

14. Convention adoption orders

Under s. 17 adoption orders may be applied for by persons who are not domiciled in a part of the U.K. (cf **12** above). These adoption orders are known as 'convention adoption orders' as the section embodies the jurisdictional rules laid down by the 1965 Hague Convention on the adoption of children.

The person to be adopted must be unmarried, under 18, a national of the U.K. or a Convention country and habitually resident in British territory or a Convention country. A Convention country is a country outside British territory so designated by an order of the Secretary of State: s. 72(1).

If the applicants are a married couple, either (*a*) each of them must be a U.K. national or a national of a Convention country habitually resident in Great Britain, or (*b*) both must be U.K.

nationals habitually resident in British territory or a Convention country: s. 17(4).

A sole applicant must be either (*a*) a national of a Convention country habitually resident in Great Britain, or (*b*) a U.K. national habitually resident in British territory or a Convention country: s. 17(5).

An order cannot be made (*a*) if the applicant(s) and the child are all U.K. nationals living in British territory: s. 17(3), or (*b*) if the applicant(s) are nationals of the same Convention country and the adoption is prevented by the internal law of that country: s. 17(4), (5).

Where the child is a U.K. national, the rules regarding parental agreement are those which apply under s. 16 (*see* above).

Progress test 13

1. Summarise the legal effects of an adoption order. **(2–5)**

2. Discuss critically the overriding principle which guides the court in deciding whether to make an adoption order. **(6)**

3. What criteria must be satisfied by the person to be adopted? **(7)**

4. What kind of agreement is necessary before a child may be adopted? **(8)**

5. On what grounds may the court dispense with agreement to adoption? **(9)**

6. What do your understand by 'freeing for adoption'? **(10)**

7. What are the effects of revoking a freeing order? **(13)**

8. What criteria must be satisfied by applicants for an adoption order? **(11)**

9. How does the court decide whether an applicant is suitable? **(12)**

10. What is a convention adoption order and who may apply for such an order? **(14)**

11. H and W had been married for several years when W began an adulterous relationship with X, as a result of which she gave birth to James. H, though unaware that he was not James' father, discovered W's adultery and divorced her. W found that she was unable to look after James properly because she had to go out to work and she gave him to foster-parents, Mr and Mrs Y, who already had a boy the same age as James. Subsequently W consented to Mr and Mrs Y's proposed adoption because James had settled down so well in his new home. Recently, however, W has renewed her relationship with X and has withdrawn her consent because she is contemplating marrying him. Advise Mr and Mrs Y as to their chances of adopting James who is now aged 5 and has been with Mr and Mrs Y for some four years.

12. 'It seems anomalous that under the Children Act 1989 the child's welfare is the paramount consideration whereas in adoption it is merely the first consideration'. Discuss this statement.

14
Financial orders for children

1. Introduction

The Children Act 1989 repealed the Guardianship of Minors Act 1971, the Guardianship Act 1973 and the Children Act 1975 and has brought together the courts' powers to make financial provision and property adjustment orders in respect of all children in s. 15. The detailed provisions are to be found in schedule 1 to the 1989 Act and references in this Chapter to paragraphs refer to those under this schedule.

An application for a financial order is a 'family proceeding' (*see* 12:1 above) and a court may make any s. 8 order which it considers should be made: s. 10(1).

2. Who may apply for a financial order?

The following may apply to the court (i.e. magistrates', county court or High Court) for a financial order:

(a) a parent, guardian or person in whose favour a residence order is in force with respect to the child: sched. 1, para.1(1).

'Parent' is wide enough to encompass adoptive parents (*see* s. 39, A.A. 1976), unmarried parents (s. 1, F.L.R.A. 1987) and any party to a marriage to whom the child is a child of the family (*see* 8:**10**); and

(b) a person aged 18 or over provided that:

(1) his parents are not living together in the same household at the time of the application: para. 2(4);

(2) immediately before he was 16 there was no periodical payments order (as defined in para. 2(6)) in force in respect of him: para, 2(3); and *either*:

(*i*) he is (or will be if the payments are ordered) receiving instruction at an educational establishment or undergoing training for a trade, profession or vocation, whether or not while in gainful employment: para. 2(1)(a); *or*

(*ii*) there are special circumstances justifying the order: para. 2(1)(b).

NOTE: (1) The only financial orders which may be made in respect of a person aged 18 or over are periodical payments or lump sum orders: para. 2(2). A lump sum may be paid in instalments: para. 5(5).

(2) A financial order may be made, even though not applied for, whenever the court makes, varies or discharges a residence order: para. 1(6).

(3) Where a parent of a child lives in England or Wales and the child lives outside England and Wales with the other parent, a guardian or a person with a residence order in respect of him, these may apply for a secured or unsecured periodical payments order against the parent living in England and Wales: para. 14(1).

(4) Where an application is made under paras. 1 or 2, the court may, at any time prior to the disposal thereof, make an interim order requiring either or both of the parents to make periodical payments at such time and for such term as the court thinks fit: para. 9(1).

3. The range of orders available

The court may order either or both of the child's parents to:

(a) make periodical payments, secured or unsecured, either to the applicant for the child's benefit, or to the child himself: para. 1(2)(a), (b).

(b) pay a lump sum (which may be paid so as to meet liabilities or expenses reasonably incurred prior to the order in respect of the birth or maintenance of the child: para. 5(1)) either to the applicant for the child's benefit, or to the child himself: para. 1(2)(c). A lump sum may be paid in instalments: para. 5(5).

(c) settle property, to which either parent is entitled in possession or in reversion, for the child's benefit: para. 1(2)(d).

(d) transfer such property either to the applicant for the child's benefit, or to the child himself: para. 1(2)(e).

NOTE: A magistrates' court may order only periodical payments and lump sum payments (which must not currently exceed £1,000): paras. 1(1)(b), 5(2).

4. Matters to be considered by the court

In exercising its discretion to make a financial order the court must have regard to the matters set out in para. 4. These are similar to the matters which apply in matrimonial proceedings under the D.P.M.C.A. 1978 and the M.C.A. 1973 (*see* 8:**12** and 9:**20** above).

Para. 4(1) provides that in deciding whether to exercise its powers to make a financial order the court shall have regard to *all* the circumstances including:

(a) the income, earning capacity, property and other financial resources which any parent, the applicant and any other person in whose favour the court proposes to make the order has or is likely to have in the foreseeable future;
(b) the financial needs, obligations and responsibilities which each of those persons has or is likely to have in the foreseeable future;
(c) the child's financial needs;
(d) the child's income, earning capacity (if any), property and other financial resources;
(e) any physical or mental disability of the child; and
(f) the manner in which the child was being, or was expected to be, educated or trained.

Where a court is deciding whether and how to exercise its powers against a person who is not the child's mother or father, it must also have regard to:

(a) whether that person had assumed responsibility for the child's maintenance and, if so, the extent to which and the basis on which he assumed that responsibility and the length of the period during which he met that responsibility;
(b) whether he did so knowing that the child was not his; and
(c) any other person's liability to maintain the child: para. 4(2).

Where an order is made against a person who is not the child's father, that fact must be recorded in the order: para. 4(3).

5. Duration of financial orders

Orders for secured or unsecured periodical payments, which may commence with the making of the application for the order or later, must not initially extend beyond the child's 17th birthday unless the court thinks it right so to order: para. 3(1). In any event, payments must not extend beyond the child's 18th birthday unless it appears to the court that:

(a) the child is, or will be or (if payment were ordered) would be receiving instruction at an educational establishment or undergoing training for a trade, profession or vocation, whether or not while in gainful employment; or
(b) there are special circumstances justifying the order: para. 3(2).

An order for unsecured periodical payments ends on the death of the payer: para. 3(3).

6. Variation and discharge of financial orders

Periodical payment orders and the instalments whereby a lump sum is to be paid may be varied on the application of the payer or payee: paras. 1(4), 5(6). Property adjustment orders *cannot* be varied.

In deciding whether to vary or discharge an order for secured or unsecured periodical payments the court must have regard to all the circumstances of the case, including any change in any of the matters to which the court was required to have regard when making the order: para. 6(1). Variation of such orders includes the power to suspend temporarily, and to revive, any provision in the order: para. 6(2). A lump sum may be ordered on an application to vary or discharge an order for secured or unsecured periodical payments (para. 5(3)) but the lump sum cannot exceed £1,000 in a magistrates' court: para. 5(2).

A child aged 16 may apply to vary a secured or unsecured periodical payments order: para. 6(4). Where such an order ends on the child's 16th birthday, or at any time thereafter before his 18th birthday, the child may apply to the court which made the order for it to be revived: para. 6(5). Revival may be ordered if it appears to the court that:

(a) the child is, will be or (if revival were ordered) would be receiving instruction at an educational establishment or

undergoing training for a trade, profession or vocation, whether or not while in gainful employment; or
(b) there are special circumstances justifying the order: para. 6(6).

If revival is ordered, the payer or payee under the revived order may apply to vary or discharge it: para. 6(7).

Where a parent liable to make secured periodical payments has died, the persons who may apply for variation or discharge include the deceased's personal representatives (P.Rs.): para. 7(1). Unless the court allows otherwise, application must be made within six months of the date on which representation in relation to the deceased's estate was first taken out: para. 7(2). In deciding whether to vary, the circumstances to be taken into account by the court under para. 6(1) above include the changed circumstances resulting from the parent's death: para. 7(5). Should the P.Rs. distribute any part of the estate after the six months' period, they will not be liable on the ground that they ought to have taken into account the possibility that the court might allow an application for variation by the payee under the order: para. 7(3). Para. 7(3) does not prejudice any power that might exist to recover any part of the estate so distributed: para. 7(4).

Progress test 14

1. Who may apply for a financial order in respect of a child and in what circumstances? **(1–2)**

2. What types of financial order may be made? **(3)**

3. What matters must the court take into account when deciding whether to make an order? **(4)**

4. When do financial orders for children end? **(5)**

5. In what circumstances may periodical payment and lump sum orders be varied? **(6)**

6. How may a financial order be revived? **(6)**

7. Sheena has recently given birth to Jason, whose father, Tom, refuses to have anything to do with her or the child. Sheena wishes to know:

    (a) how she may obtain financial provision for Jason;

    (b) what orders the court may make; and

    (c) how long they will last.

Advise her.

15
Local authorities and the family

Introduction

1. The role of the local authority

Section 17(1) of the Children Act 1989 imposes a general duty on every local authority :

(a) to safeguard and promote the welfare of children within their area who are in need; and
(b) so far as is consistent with that duty, to promote the upbringing of such children by their families, by providing a range and level of services appropriate to those children's needs.

A child is 'in need' if he is unlikely to achieve or maintain a reasonable standard of physical or mental health, or physical, intellectual, emotional, social or behavioural development without local authority services; if such health or development is likely to be significantly or further impaired without such services or he is disabled: s. 17(10), (11).

So as to enable this general duty to be discharged, every local authority is given specific duties and powers set out in Part I of Schedule 2 to the Act. For example, steps should be taken to identify children in need within the authority's area, alternative accommodation (e.g. with foster parents) should be provided for children at risk of ill-treatment or neglect, reasonable steps should be taken to reduce the need for care or supervision orders and reasonably practicable steps should be taken to maintain the family home of children in need or contact between such children and their families.

Accommodation

2. Provision of accommodation for children in need

'Voluntary care' under the Child Care Act 1980 was less than satisfactory because, e.g. parents feared they would fail to recover their child and voluntary care carried the stigma of parental failure. Under s. 20(1) of the Act a local authority *must* provide accommodation for any child in need under 18 who requires it because:

(a) there is no person with parental responsibility for him;
(b) he is lost or has been abandoned (presumably to be interpreted in accordance with its meaning in adoption, *see* 13:9); or
(c) the person who has been caring for him is prevented (permanently or not and for whatever reason) from providing him with suitable accommodation or care.

In the case of a child aged 16 or over accommodation must be provided if his welfare is otherwise likely to be 'seriously prejudiced': s. 20(3).

The local authority *may* provide accommodation for *any* child under 18 within its area if it considers that this would safeguard or promote the child's welfare. This power exists notwithstanding that a person with parental responsibility for the child is able to provide him with accommodation: s. 20(4).

3. Removal from local authority accommodation

The voluntary nature of the provision of such accommodation is emphasised by the fact that any person who has parental responsibility for a child may remove that child at any time (s. 20(8)) unless a person with a residence order objects: s. 20(9). Section 20 (8) appears to give a drunken or violent parent an absolute right to the return of his child, despite possible danger to the child. On the other hand, s. 3(5) provides that anyone who has care of a child but no parental responsibility for it (e.g. a foster parent) 'may (subject to the provisions of this Act) do what is reasonable in all the circumstances of the case for the purpose of safeguarding or promoting the child's welfare.' This would, therefore, justify a refusal to hand the child over to the parent. However, is s. 3(5) subject to the provisions of s. 20(8)? If s. 20(8) overrides s. 3(5), a local authority may seek an emergency protection order (*see* **14**), apply for a care order (*see* **5**) or the foster parent may make the child a ward of court (*see* **12:4** *et seq.*).

A child aged 16 or over cannot be removed from local authority accommodation against his will, even by a person with parental responsibility: s. 20(11).

4. The local authority's duty in respect of accommodation

The duty is the same whether the child is accommodated voluntarily or as a result of a care order (*see* **5**). This duty is

(a) to safeguard and promote the child's welfare; and
(b) to make such use of services available for children cared for by their own parents as appears to the authority reasonable: s. 22(3).

This duty is not imposed where it is necessary to protect members of the public from serious injury. In such cases the Secretary of State may give directions to the authority regarding the exercise of its powers: s. 20(6)–(8).

Before making any decision the authority must, as far as is reasonably practicable, ascertain the wishes and feelings of the child, his parents and any other person with parental responsibility for him, and any other person whose wishes and feelings the authority considers relevant: s. 22(4). When making a decision, the authority, in addition to giving consideration to the above, must have regard to the child's religious persuasion, racial origin and cultural and linguistic background: s. 22(5).

Where a local authority looks after a child, the authority must provide him with accommodation and maintain him: s. 23(1). This may be done by placing him with a family, a relative of his or any other suitable person (all such persons are termed 'local authority foster parents'). The policy of the 1989 Act is to maintain contact between the child and his family. To this end s. 20(6) requires the authority to make arrangements to enable the child to live with a parent or other person with parental responsibility for the child, a person in whose favour a residence order was made immediately before a care order was made in respect of the child, or a relative, friend or other person connected with the child, unless it would not be reasonably practicable or consistent with the child's welfare. However, where the child is subject to a care order, accommodation must be provided in accordance with regulations made by the Secretary of State. Where the authority does provide accommodation it should, so far as is reasonably practicable and consistent with the child's welfare, ensure that the accommodation is near his home and with any brother or sister for whom the authority is also providing accommodation: s. 20(7).

Parents remain liable to contribute financially towards their child who is being looked after by a local authority: sched. 2, para. 21.

Care and supervision orders

5. Care and supervision orders

Children may arrive in local authority care without parental consent. Such 'involuntary' care may arise as a result of care proceedings initiated by any local authority or authorised person: s. 31(1).The only other authorised body is the National Society for the Prevention of Cruelty to Children (NSPCC), though a person may be authorised by the Secretary of State: s. 31(9).

Before an application for a care order is made by an authorised person the local authority in whose area the child is ordinarily resident should be consulted if this is reasonably practicable: s. 31(6). An application by an authorised person will not be considered by the court if the child is subject to either an existing care or supervision order or application for the same, an order under s. 7(7)(b) of the Children and Young Persons Act 1969 (a care order made in criminal proceedings in a juvenile court) or a supervision requirement within the meaning of the Social Work (Scotland) Act 1968.

A care order can be made only in respect of a child under the age of 17. If a child aged 16 is married, a care order cannot be made: s. 31(3). Seemingly, there can be a care order in respect of a child under 16 who was validly married overseas.

> NOTE: (1) The court may make an interim care/supervision order if it is satisfied there are reasonable grounds for believing that the circumstances specified in s. 31(2) exist (*see* 6 below): s. 38(2). Interim orders initially last for up to 8 weeks but an order may be extended for one or more periods of 4 weeks: s. 38(4), (5).

(2) All orders under the Children Act 1989 end on the making of an adoption order: s. 12(3)(aa), Adoption Act 1976.

6. Criteria for care/supervision orders

If a local authority is informed that a child in its area is the subject of an emergency protection order or is in police protection, or it has reasonable cause to suspect that the child is suffering, or is likely to suffer, significant harm, the authority must make such enquiries as it considers necessary to enable it to decide whether it should take any action to safeguard the child's welfare: s. 47(1). Where, after having made enquiries, the authority concludes that it should take action to safeguard the child's welfare (e.g. by applying for a care order), it must take such action so far as it is both within its power and reasonably practicable for it to do so: s. 47(8).

A care or supervision order may be made only if the court is satisfied that:

(a) the child is suffering, or is likely to suffer, significant harm; *and*

(b) the harm, or likelihood of harm is attributable to:
  (*i*) the care given to the child, or likely to be given to him if the order were not made, not being what it would be reasonable to expect a parent to give him; *or*
  (*ii*) the child's being beyond parental control (s. 31(2)).

In addition, the court must also have regard to the general welfare principles contained in s. 1 (*see* 12:**2** *et seq.*).

NOTE: (1) In ground **(a)** the phrase 'is suffering' will presumably be interpreted in the same way as the phrase 'is being' in s. 1(2)(a) of the Children and Young Persons Act 1969. In *Re D (a Minor)* (1986) the House of Lords held that where a child suffering from drug dependency was born prematurely to a drug addict the court was entitled to look back to before the child's birth. Consequently, the mother's behaviour during her pregnancy was relevant when considering whether the baby's proper development was 'being . . . prevented'.

(2) 'Harm' is defined as 'ill-treatment or the impairment of health or development'. 'Development' means 'physical,

intellectual, emotional, social or behavioural development'. 'Health' means 'physical or mental health' and 'ill-treatment' includes 'sexual abuse and forms of ill-treatment which are not physical': s. 31(9).

'Significant' is undefined and this gives the court a wide discretion. It should be noted, however, that the 'harm' must be significant, rather than the way in which it was caused. Thus, e.g. a parent's behaviour towards a baby may have more serious consequences than the same behaviour towards an older child. Where the issue of harm depends upon the child's health or development rather than his ill-treatment, the significance of the harm is to be determined by comparing the child's health or development with that which 'could reasonably be expected of a similar child.': s. 31(10).

(3) There is no indication in the Act as to how the likelihood of harm is to be determined. Presumably the court will err on the side of safety, though a line may have to be drawn between probabilities and mere possibilities.

7. Effects of a care order

A care order vests parental responsibility for the child in the local authority which is under a duty to receive the child into its care and to keep him while the order remains in force: s. 33. The parental responsibility of a non-parent who has a s. 8 order (*see* 12:9 *et seq.*) terminates: s. 91(2).

Any person who had parental responsibility for the child before the making of the care order continues to have such responsibility: s. 2(6). In an attempt to clarify the relationship between the local authority and other person having parental responsibility, s. 33(3)(b) gives the authority power to determine the extent to which a parent or guardian of the child may meet his parental responsibility for the child. This power is to be exercised only if the authority is satisfied its exercise is necessary to safeguard or promote the child's welfare: s. 33(4). Nothing in s. 33(3)(b) prevents the child's parent or guardian who has care of the child from doing what is reasonable in all the circumstances of the case to safeguard or promote the child's welfare: s. 33(5).

Under s. 34 the local authority must allow the child reasonable contact with his parents, guardian and any person who had a residence order in respect of the child immediately before the care order was made: s. 34(1). In addition, the authority must endeavour to promote contact between the child and his parents, non-parent with parental responsibility and any relative, friend or other person connected with the child, provided it is reasonably practicable or consistent with the child's welfare: sched. 2, para. 15. This latter obligation will probably assist persons such as grandparents and brothers and sisters (who fall outside s. 34(1)) to maintain contact with the child.

The child is not obliged to make contact with the persons listed in s. 34(1). Such persons may, however, apply for a contact order under s. 34(3) and the court may make such order as it considers appropriate. The object of the care order may have been to prevent contact between the child and a person falling within s. 34(1). In such a case the authority or the child himself may apply under s. 34(4) for an order authorising the authority to refuse such contact.

If an application for contact has been refused, a further application cannot be made within six months of that refusal, unless leave of the court has been obtained: s. 91(17).

It should be noted that before the care order is made the court must consider the local authority's arrangements or proposals regarding care and invite parties to the proceedings to comment on them: s. 34(11).

Despite having parental responsibility for the child, s. 33(6) provides that the authority cannot:

(a) bring him up in a religion other than that in which he would have been brought up had the order not been made (though the authority is bound to have regard to his feelings and religious background: s. 22(5), above);
(b) consent or refuse to consent to the making of an application to free the child for adoption (*see* 13:**10**);
(c) agree or refuse to agree to the making of an adoption order or an order authorising removal abroad for the purpose of adoption there;
(d) appoint a guardian for the child.

In addition, the authority (and anyone else) cannot change the child's surname or remove him from the U.K. for a month or more without the written consent of every person with parental responsibility for the child or leave of the court: s. 33(7), (8). The child cannot leave England and Wales to live abroad without the court's approval: sched. 2, para. 19.

8. Duration and discharge of care orders
A care order ends when:

(a) a court makes a residence order in respect of the child in care: s. 91(1);
(b) the child attains the age of 18: s. 91(12); and
(c) a court discharges the order on the application of the authority, child or person named in the order: s. 34(9).

A care order may be discharged by the court on the application of any person with parental responsibility for the child, the child himself or the local authority designated by the order: s. 39(1). On such application a supervision order may be substituted for the care order: s. 39(4).

9. Supervision orders
Provided that the court is satisfied that the grounds contained in s. 31(2) exist (*see* **6** above), it may make an order placing a child under the supervision of a local authority or probation officer: s. 31(1). The selection of the authority as supervisor depends upon it agreeing or the child living within its area: sched. 3, para. 9(1). The selection of a probation officer must be requested by the authority and the officer must exercise, or have exercised, his duties in relation to another member of the household to which the child belongs: sched. 3, para. 9(2).

The supervisor does not acquire parental responsibility, his duties being to:

(a) advise, assist and befriend the supervised child;
(b) take such steps as are reasonably necessary to give effect to the order; and
(c) consider an application to the court for the variation or discharge of the order where the order is not wholly complied with or the supervisor considers it may no longer be necessary: s. 35(1).

Schedule 3 contains provisions relating to the requirements which may be included in a supervision order, e.g. the right of the supervisor to direct the child to live at a specified place or participate in specified activities and the submission of the child to psychiatric and medical examination and treatment.

Section 36 allows a local education authority to apply to the court for an order placing a child under the supervision of a designated local education authority. An 'education supervision order' may be made only if the court is satisfied that the child is of compulsory school age, is not being properly educated and is not in the care of a local authority: s. 36(3), (6).

10. Duration and discharge of supervision orders

A supervision order initially lasts for one year but the supervisor may apply for extension(s) to a maximum of three years from the date of the order: sched. 3, para. 6. An education supervision order ends when the child ceases to be of compulsory school age or he is the subject of a care order: sched. 3, para. 15.

A supervision order may be varied or discharged by the court on the application of any person with parental responsibility for the child, the child himself or his supervisor: s. 39(2). A person who is not entitled to apply for the discharge of a supervision order, but with whom the child is living, may apply to the court to vary any requirement which affects that person: s. 39(4).

11. Procedure in care/supervision orders

Initially application will be made to the magistrates' court (now termed the 'family proceedings court' (s. 92)) and the matter will be heard in private: s. 97(1). Proceedings may be transferred to the county court or High Court depending upon the complexity of the issues. Appeal against a decision of the family proceedings court to make or not to make an order lies to the High Court: s. 94(1).

(a) Representation. Protection of the child's interests will be secured by the mandatory appointment of a guardian *ad litem*: s. 41(1). Such appointment need not take place if the court is satisfied that it is unnecessary for the protection of the child's interests (ibid). The guardian has the right of access to information held by the local authority in connection with the application. Any copies of such information made by the guardian are admissible as evidence of any matter contained therein: s. 42(1), (2). If a guardian *ad litem* has not been appointed and the child is not represented by a solicitor, the court may appoint a solicitor, provided the child either has sufficient understanding to instruct a solicitor and wishes to do so or the court feels it would be in the child's best interests for him to be represented: s. 41(3), (4).

> NOTE: these provisions apply to a wide range of proceedings, e.g. applications for emergency protection orders and where the court is considering whether to make a residence order in respect of a child subject to a care order.

The guardian *ad litem* will be selected from a panel of persons governed by the Guardians *ad litem* and Reporting Officers (Panels) Regulations (SI 1991, No. 2051). Frequently, the independence of the guardian *ad litem* seems to be compromised because he is often employed by the same authority seeking the order. The importance of guardians *ad litem* not only being seen to be independent but also being assured of their independence in carrying out their duties was stressed in *R* v. *Cornwall County Council, ex p. Cornwall and Isles of Scilly Guardians ad litem and Reporting Officers Panel* (1991). There a restriction imposed by Cornwall County Council's Director of Social Services on the amount of time to be spent by guardians *ad litem* on cases was quashed for being an abuse of his power. The above criticism may be avoided by the guardian being selected from an authority not involved in the court proceedings in question.

(b) Evidential matters. Section 96(1) provides that a child may give unsworn evidence in any civil proceedings if he does not understand the nature of an oath but understands that it is his duty to speak the truth and he has sufficient understanding to justify his evidence being heard. Hearsay evidence is admissible in family proceedings (wherever heard) concerning the upbringing, maintenance or welfare of a child (Children (Admissibility of Hearsay Evidence) Order 1991), operative as from October 1991.

Persons giving evidence have no privilege against self-incrimination (s. 98(1)) but evidence given in the civil proceedings is not admissible against the maker or his spouse in criminal proceedings other than those for perjury: s. 98(2).

Child assessment orders

12. Child assessment orders

One of the difficulties of the pre-1989 Act law was that, though social workers suspected that a child was being abused or neglected, there was no way of ensuring that evidence of such abuse or neglect was forthcoming. To some extent this defect has been overcome by the child assessment order which lasts for no more than seven days and must specify the date by which the assessment is to begin: s. 43(5).

Such an order may be applied for under s. 43 only by a local authority or the NSPCC. Before the hearing of the application the applicant must take such steps as are reasonably practicable to ensure that notice is given to the child's parents or person with parental responsibility, anyone caring for the child, anyone with a contact order in respect of the child or allowed contact with a child in care and the child himself: s. 43(11).

The court may make an order only if satisfied that:

(a) the applicant has reasonable cause to suspect that the child is suffering, or is likely to suffer, significant harm: s. 43(1)(a);
(b) an assessment of the state of the child's health or development, or of the way in which he has been treated, is required to enable the applicant to determine whether or not the child is suffering, or is likely to suffer, such harm; and
(c) it is unlikely that such an assessment will be made, or be satisfactory, in the absence of an order: s. 43(1)(b), (c).

The court cannot make a child assessment order if satisfied that there are grounds for making an emergency protection order (*see* **14** below) and that it ought to make such an order instead: s. 43(4).

NOTE: rules of court provide for the variation or discharge of child assessment orders: s. 43(12).

13. Effects of a child assessment order

The order imposes a duty on any person who is in a position to produce the child to produce him to the person named in the order and to comply with such directions relating to the child's assessment as are specified in the order: s. 43(6). The person carrying out the assessment, or part of it, is authorised to do so in accordance with the terms of the order: s. 43(7).

If a child is to be kept away from home for the purposes of the assessment, this must be necessary, the order must contain directions to that effect and these must specify the duration of such removal: s. 43(9). If, after assessment, it appears in the child's interests to keep him away from home, this may be done by applying for an emergency protection order or interim care order.

The major difficulty with the child assessment order is that it is unlikely that a proper assessment will be possible in many cases in the short space of time made available. Proper assessment will also be made more difficult owing to the fact that a child is allowed to refuse to submit to a medical or psychiatric examination or other assessment if he is of sufficient understanding to make an informed decision: s. 43(8).

Emergency protection orders

14. Emergency protection orders
These replace the much-criticised 'place of safety' orders granted under s. 28 of the Children and Young Persons Act 1969, which allowed children to be detained for an unchallenged period of up to 28 days. They also fill the gap left by the abolition of the availability of speedy wardship proceedings to local authorities by s. 100. Section 44(1) provides that *any* person may apply to the court (or a single magistrate (sched. 11, para. 3(1)(a)) for an emergency protection order (E.P.O.). These last for up to eight days (one seven-day extension is possible if the court has reasonable cause to believe that the child is otherwise likely to suffer significant harm: s. 45(5)).

The court must be satisfied that there is reasonable cause to believe that the child is likely to suffer significant harm if he is not removed to accommodation provided by or for the applicant, or he does not remain where he is presently being accommodated (e.g. in local authority accommodation under s. 20(1), *see* **2** above). Where the applicant is a local authority or the NSPCC they must be making enquiries as to the child's welfare, these enquiries must be being frustrated by the unreasonable refusal of access to the child and the applicant has reasonable cause to suspect that access is required as a matter of urgency. It should be noted that where the applicant is a local authority or the NSPCC the *applicant* (not the court) must have reasonable cause to suspect that the child is suffering, or likely to suffer, significant harm.

> NOTE: a police constable may remove or prevent the removal of a child if he has reasonable cause to believe that the child would otherwise be likely to suffer significant harm: s. 46(1). The child must not be kept in 'police protection' for more than 72 hours: s. 46(6). If the child is still likely to be at risk after this time, application may be made by the police on behalf of the local authority for an E.P.O. with or without its knowledge or agreement: s. 46(7), (8).

15. Effects of an emergency protection order
An E.P.O. operates so as to:

(a) direct that the child be handed over to the applicant,
(b) authorise the removal of the child to accommodation provided by the applicant, and
(c) prevent the removal of the child from where he was being accommodated immediately prior to the making of the order: s. 44(4).

It is a criminal offence intentionally to obstruct the exercise of the powers in **(b)** and **(c)**: s. 44(15). These powers may be exercised on more than one occasion: s. 44(12).

During the subsistence of the order the applicant obtains parental responsibility for the child s. 44(4) but is allowed to take only such action as is reasonably required to safeguard or promote the child's welfare with particular regard being given to the duration of the order: s. 44(5). As the order is of particularly short duration only minor changes to the child's upbringing would seem appropriate, though consent to surgery, for example, would come within the section.

The court may give such directions as it considers appropriate with regard to the following matters:

(a) the contact which is, or is not, to be allowed between the child and any named person: s. 44(6)(a). Subject to this the court must allow reasonable contact with the child's parents and those with parental responsibility, any person with whom the child was living immediately before the order was made, any person having a contact order (*see* 12:**10**) and any person acting on behalf of any of the above: s. 44(13). This list does not necessarily include brothers, sisters or grandparents;

(b) the medical or psychiatric examination or other assessment of the child: s. 44(6)(b). A child with sufficient understanding to make an informed decision is allowed to refuse to submit to any examination or assessment ordered under this subsection: s. 44(7).

As soon as the applicant considers it safe to do so, he must return the child, or allow him to be removed from where he is: s. 44(10). This duty to return is satisfied by handing the child over either to the person from whose care he was removed or, if this is not reasonably practicable, to a parent or person with parental responsibility or such other person as the applicant and the court consider appropriate: s. 44(11).

NOTE: When making an E.P.O. the court may include in it a direction requiring a person to disclose any information he may have as to the child's whereabouts: s. 48(1). The court may also authorise the applicant to enter premises to search for the child named in the order: s. 48(3). If a person with an E.P.O. is being prevented from exercising powers granted under it, he may apply for a warrant authorising a police constable to assist him, with reasonable force if necessary, in the exercise of those powers: s. 48(9).

16. Discharge of an emergency protection order

Although there is no right of appeal against either the making of or refusal to make, or directions made in connection with, an E.P.O.: s. 45(10), an application for the discharge of an order may be made to be heard within 72 hours of the making of the order: s. 45(9). An application for discharge may be made by the child, his parent or person with parental responsibility, or any person with whom the child was living immediately before the E.P.O. was made: s. 45(8). This right does not, however, apply where the applicant for discharge had been given notice of and had attended the hearing at which the E.P.O. was made: s. 45(11)(a), or where the duration of the E.P.O. has been extended.

Judicial control

17. Control of local authority powers

As statute has entrusted the above powers to the local authority, the scope for judicial control over the exercise of those powers by the authority is very restricted. At one time the wardship jurisdiction of the High Court could be invoked in certain limited circumstances but s. 100 of the Children Act 1989 severely restricts the use of this jurisdiction. Where it is alleged that a local authority has exercised its statutory powers improperly an application for judicial review under s. 31 of the Supreme Court Act 1981 may be made. This application requires leave, it is not as quick as the wardship jurisdiction and the welfare of the child is not the paramount consideration.

Complaint may also be made to the European Commission for Human Rights on the basis that the local authority has conducted itself in contravention of a right contained in the European Convention on Human Rights.

Progress test 15

1. What are the grounds for voluntary reception into local authority care? **(1–2)**

2. In what circumstances may the return of a child in voluntary care be refused? **(3)**

3. What are the duties of a local authority towards children in care? **(4)**

4. In what circumstances may a care order be made? **(5–6)**

5. What are the effects of a care order? **(7)**

6. How do parents maintain contact with their child who has been taken into care? **(7)**

7. When does a care order end? **(8)**

8. What is the effect of a supervision order? **(9)**

9. In what circumstances does a supervision order terminate? **(10)**

10. How are the child's interests protected in care proceedings? **(11)**

11. What is the purpose of a child assessment order and how is this achieved? **(12–13)**

12. Explain the operation of the emergency protection order. **(14–15)**

13. When does an emergency protection order end? **(16)**

14. How may the courts interfere with the exercise by a local authority of its statutory powers in relation to the care of children? **(17)**

15. Gemma, who is unmarried, is a drug addict with a five year old child, Jane. Gemma is pregnant and due to give birth at the end of the month. Gemma's friend, Helen, comes to stay with her to look after her during the last few weeks of Gemma's pregnancy. Helen notices extensive bruising on Jane's arms and legs for which she cannot get a satisfactory explanation from Gemma. Helen seeks your advice as to the steps she may take to protect Jane and the unborn child when born. Advise her.

Appendix 1
An outline of procedure

A. Procedure generally

1. The rules governing procedure

The rules governing the procedure to be applied in matrimonial causes are the Family Proceedings Rules 1991 (SI 1991/1247).

The M.F.P.A. 1984, replacing the M.C.A. 1967, provides that every matrimonial cause must begin in a divorce county court and be tried there unless transferred, either of its own motion or on the application of either party to the proceedings, to the High Court (ss. 33 and 39).

The Divorce Registry, which is the Principal Registry of the Family Division of the High Court, is treated as a divorce county court and proceedings may be commenced there.

2. The petition

Proceedings for divorce, nullity, judicial separation and declarations of legitimacy are begun by the filing of a petition: Rule 2.2.

Petitions must be filed in a divorce county court or the Divorce Registry.

Although there is no prescribed form of petition, Rule 2.3 requires a petition to contain the information specified in Appendix 2 of the Rules, unless otherwise directed under that Rule (*see* **B** below).

The following must be filed with the petition, except in the case of a declaration as to marital status and a declaration of legitimacy:

(a) a marriage certificate (Rule 2.6(2));
(b) a certificate as to reconciliation (Form M3), but only if a person is not suing in person and only in cases of divorce and judicial separation (Rule 2.6(3));
(c) a statement as to the arrangements for children of the family (Form M4) (Rule 2.2(2));
(d) a legal aid certificate where relevant;
(e) as many copies of the petition as there are persons to be served and a copy of **(c)** for service on the respondent (Rule 2.6(5)).

The petition must be signed by the person who prepared it, i.e. counsel, solicitor, or the petitioner himself: Rule 11.

If claims are omitted from, or it becomes necessary to alter details in, the petition, it may be amended. Leave to amend is required only if the petition has been served.

If it is desired to allege fresh matters, a supplemental petition is necessary and leave to file is required.

3. Service of the petition

Once the petition is filed a copy must be served on every respondent and co-respondent. It is accompanied by a Notice of Proceedings (Form M5) and an Acknowledgement of Service (Form M6) (*see* **4** below).

Service is normally effected by post, either by the court itself or the petitioner's solicitor: Rule 2.9, but the court cannot serve a person under disability, i.e. a minor or a person suffering from mental disorder within the meaning of the Mental Health Act 1983.

If service by post is impossible, personal service should be attempted. If this proves ineffective, the district judge may order substituted service, e.g. service on an agent or by advertisement, or he may dispense with service.

4. Notice of proceedings and acknowledgement of service

The former explains to the party served the various courses open to him and their consequences; the latter asks the respondent various questions in relation to the suit, e.g. whether he intends to defend or to apply on his own account for residence or contact.

The acknowledgement of service must be completed and

returned. If no acknowledgement of service is received by the court office, service may be proved either by filing an affidavit of service or by the district judge directing, on sufficient evidence, that service has occurred: Rule 2.9(6), (7). If it is intended to defend, the respondent must file an answer within 21 days of the expiration of the time limited for giving notice of intention to defend (Rule 2.12(1)), together with a copy for service on every other party to the proceedings.

5. Undefended suits and the 'special procedure'

If a divorce or judicial separation is to proceed as an undefended suit, the petitioner makes a written request to the district judge for directions for the trial of the suit: Rule 2.24 This request must be accompanied by an affidavit and a completed questionnaire in which the petitioner verifies the facts set out in his petition. These must be accompanied by any corroborative evidence upon which the petitioner intends to rely, e.g. a confession of adultery in a petition based on s. 1(2)(a) or a medical certificate in a petition based on s. 1(2)(b).

On receipt of these documents the district judge enters the case in the special procedure list: Rule 2.24(3). If he is satisfied that, on the evidence filed by the petitioner, the contents of the petition have been sufficiently proved and the petitioner is entitled to a decree, the *district judge* makes and files a certificate to that effect: Rule 2.36(a). If not satisfied he may either allow the petitioner to file further evidence or remove the case from the special procedure list: Rule 2.36(b). A date is then fixed for the pronouncement by a *judge* of a decree nisi in open court. The parties are given notice of the date and place but they need not attend.

A registrar's decision to grant or refuse a certificate under Rule 2.36 is a judicial determination and an appeal lies therefrom to a judge: *R* v. *Nottingham County Court, ex p. Byers* (1985).

NOTE: legal aid is not available where a divorce or judicial separation is undefended, though it is available for most ancillary proceedings, where a petition is directed to be heard in open court and where physical or mental incapacity makes it impracticable for the applicant to proceed without legal aid.

6. Defended suits

If a suit is to be defended an answer must be filed (*see* 4 above). It is possible to file an answer at any time before directions for trial have been given, though this may result in extra costs. Leave of the court will be required to file an answer after directions have been given for what was originally an undefended case.

The answer may take the form of a bare denial but if it is desired to raise a particular defence, e.g. grave financial hardship, the facts giving rise to that defence must be set out.

NOTE: a respondent who has received a statement under Rule 2.2(2) (*see* 2(c) above) may file in the court office his views on the proposed arrangements for the child(ren). This should be done before the judge considers the arrangements for the child(ren) under s. 41, M.C.A. 1973.

A copy answer is served on each party cited.

The petitioner may, without leave, file a reply to the answer within 14 days after receiving a copy answer: Rule 2.13.

NOTE: one party may give a written request to a person who has served him with a pleading which is vague or lacks detail to give particulars of the allegation or matter pleaded. If the person does not give the particulars within a reasonable time, application may be made to the district judge for an order that they be given: Rule 2.19.

7. Preparation for the trial of a defended case

Order 24 of the Rules of the Supreme Court, which deals with the discovery and inspection of documents, applies to a defended matrimonial cause begun by petition: Rule 2.20.

Discovery of documents is to be made within 14 days after the pleadings are deemed to be closed. Pleadings are deemed to be closed 14 days after service of the reply, or if no reply, after service of the answer.

Discovery takes the form of making and exchanging lists of documents, which must be verified by affidavit. The documents are those which are, or have been, in the possession, custody or power of the parties and which relate to matters in question in the proceedings. A party may claim privilege in respect of documents in his possession.

The other party must be allowed to inspect the documents listed, other than those in respect of which privilege is claimed. As regards the latter, the district judge may make an order for their production for inspection in order to determine the validity of the claim.

8. Interrogatories

These are a list of questions which a party is required to answer by affidavit and their purpose is to obtain admissions of the fact and to elicit more clearly a party's case. The answers do not form part of the pleadings but are admissible in evidence at the hearing.

9. Directions for trial

The petitioner, or any party who is defending the suit, may make a written request to the district judge for directions for trial.

At least eight days before making this request a party must give notice of the desired place of trial to every other party. This notice must state the number of witnesses to be called and the places where he and his witnesses reside: Rule 2.25(3). If a party objects he must, within eight days of receiving the notice, apply to the district judge to re-direct the trial. However, if he consents he must, within the same time, acknowledge receipt of the notice and give the number of his witnesses and the places where he and they reside: Rule 2.25(4).

A party's request for directions must state:

(a) the desired place of trial,
(b) the number of intended witnesses,
(c) if it be the case, that no statement has been received from any party (naming him) to whom notice of the place of trial in a defended cause was given, and
(d) the probable duration of the trial.

If the district judge is satisfied that the suit is in order, he will then give directions for trial by setting the cause down for trial and giving notice of this to every party.

In fixing the place of trial the district judge must have regard to all the circumstances, including the following:

(a) the parties' and witnesses' convenience,
(b) the likely costs,

(c) the date when the trial can take place,
(d) the estimated length of the trial.

10. The decree

In divorce and nullity the decree is in two parts — the decree nisi followed by the decree absolute six weeks later, unless the court fixes a shorter period. In judicial separation there is a single final decree. The proper officer sends a copy of the decree to every party to the case: Rule 2.51.

It is possible for the Queen's Proctor and any other person not a party to the proceedings to show cause why the decree nisi should not be made absolute.

The spouse who obtained the decree nisi should, after the six weeks have elapsed, apply to the district judge to have the decree made absolute. The district judge will make the decree after he has satisfied himself that:

(a) there is no appeal, application for re-hearing or for rescission pending;
(b) the time for appealing or for applying for a re-hearing has not been extended or, if it has, it has expired;
(c) there is no pending application for extending the time for appealing or for applying for a re-hearing;
(d) there is no intervention by the Queen's Proctor or any other person pending;
(e) the judge has made an order as to the welfare of children of the family under s. 41(1), M.C.A. 1973 and has not given any direction under s. 41(2);
(f) where a certificate has been granted under s. 12, Administration of Justice Act 1969 (the 'leap-frog' procedure allowing an appeal direct to the House of Lords from the court of trial):

(*i*) no application for leave to appeal directly to the House of Lords is pending,
(*ii*) no extension of the time to apply for leave to appeal directly to the House of Lords has been granted or, if any such extension has been granted, that the time so extended has expired, and
(*iii*) the time for an appeal to the Court of Appeal has expired; and

(g) the provisions of s. 10(2)–(4) of the 1973 Act as to an application by the respondent for consideration of his financial position after divorce do not apply or have been complied with: Rule 2.49(2).

On being so satisfied the district judge will send the petitioner and respondent a certificate of decree absolute.

If the application for the decree absolute is made more than twelve months after the decree nisi, the district judge may require an explanatory affidavit to be filed. If the party in whose favour the decree nisi was made has not applied to have it made absolute within three months of the earliest date on which it could have been made absolute by him, the party against whom it was obtained may apply and the court may make the decree absolute, rescind it, require further inquiry or otherwise deal with the case as it thinks fit: ss. 9(2) and 15, M.C.A. 1973.

In certain circumstances it may be possible for the party who has obtained the decree nisi to apply to expedite the granting of the decree absolute.

NOTE: a decree absolute granted by the court of competent jurisdiction following the correct procedure is unimpeachable and its validity cannot be questioned: *Callaghan* v. *Hanson Fox and Anor* (1991).

B. The contents of a petition

Appendix 2 of the Family Proceedings Rules 1991 provides that unless otherwise directed under Rule 2.3:

1. Every petition other than a petition for a declaration must state:

(a) the names of the parties to the marriage and the date and place of the marriage;
(b) the last address at which the parties to the marriage have lived together as husband and wife;
(c) where it is alleged that the court has jurisdiction based on domicile:

(*i*)   the country in which the petitioner is domiciled, and

    (*ii*) if that country is not England or Wales, the country in which the respondent is domiciled;

(d) where it is alleged that the court has jurisdiction based on habitual residence:

    (*i*) the country in which the petitioner has been habitually resident throughout the period of one year ending with the date of the presentation of the petition, or

    (*ii*) if the petitioner has not been habitually resident in England or Wales, the country in which the respondent has been habitually resident during that period, with details in either case, including the addresses of the places of residence and the length of residence at each place;

(e) the occupation and residence of the petitioner and the respondent;

(f) whether there are any living children of the family and, if so:

    (*i*) the number of such children and the full names (including surname) of each and his date of birth (if that be the case) that he is over 18, and

    (*ii*) in the case of each minor child over the age of 16, whether he is receiving instruction at an educational establishment or undergoing training for a trade, profession or vocation;

(g) whether (to the knowledge of the petitioner in the case of a husband's petition) any other child now living has been born to the wife during the marriage and, if so, the full names (including surname) of the child and his date of birth, or, if it be the case, that he is over 18;

(h) if it be the case, that there is a dispute whether a living child is a child of the family;

(i) whether or not there are or have been any other proceedings in any court in England or Wales or elsewhere with reference to the marriage or to any children of the family or between the petitioner and the respondent with reference to any property of either or both of them, and if so:

    (*i*) the nature of the proceedings

    (*ii*) the date of any decree or order, and

    (*iii*) in the case of proceedings with reference to the marriage, whether there has been any resumption of cohabitation since the making of the decree or order;

(j) whether there are any proceedings continuing in any county outside England and Wales which relate to the marriage or are capable of affecting its validity or subsistence and, if so:

(*i*) particulars of the proceedings, including the court in or tribunal or authority before which they were begun,

(*ii*) the date when they were begun,

(*iii*) the names of the parties,

(*iv*) the date or expected date of any trial in the proceedings, and

(*v*) such other facts as may be relevant to the question whether the proceedings on the petition should be stayed under Schedule 1 to the Domicile and Matrimonial Proceedings Act 1973;

and such proceedings shall include any which are not instituted in a court of law in that country, if they are instituted before a tribunal or other authority having power under the law having effect there to determine questions of status and shall be treated as continuing if they have begun and have not been finally disposed of;

(k) where the fact on which the petition is based is five years' separation, whether any, and if so what, agreement or arrangements has been made or is proposed to be made between the parties for the support of the respondent or as the case may be, the petitioner or any child of the family;

(l) in the case of a petition for divorce, that the marriage has broken down irretrievably;

(m) the fact alleged by the petitioner for the purposes of section 1(2) of the Act of 1973 or, where the petition is not for divorce or judicial separation, the ground on which relief is sought, together in any case with brief particulars of the individual facts relied on but not the evidence by which they are to be proved;

(n) any further or other information required by such of the following paragraphs and by Rule 3.11 as may be applicable.

2. A petition for a decree of nullity under section 12(e) or (f) of the Act of 1973 must state whether the petitioner was at the time of the marriage ignorant of the facts alleged.

3. A petition for a decree of presumption of death and dissolution of marriage must state:

(a) the last place at which the parties to the marriage cohabited;

(b) the circumstances in which the parties ceased to cohabit;
(c) the date when and the place where the respondent was last seen or heard of; and
(d) the steps which have been taken to trace the respondent.

4. Every petition must conclude with:

(a) a prayer setting out particulars of the relief claimed, including any application for an order, under any provision of Part I or Part II of the Children Act 1989 with respect to a child of the family, any claim for costs and any application for ancillary relief which it is intended to claim;
(b) the names and addresses of the persons who are to be served with the petition, indicating if any of them is a person under disability;
(c) the petitioner's address for service, which, if the petitioner sues by a solicitor, will be the solicitor's name or firm and address. Where the petitioner, though suing in person, is receiving legal advice from a solicitor, the solicitor's name or firm and address may be given as the address for service if he agrees. In any other case, the petitioner's address for service will be the address of any place in England or Wales at or to which documents for him may be delivered or sent.

C. A specimen petition

The following is an example of a divorce petition and the italicised details on the left of the page refer to those details required by Appendix 2 above.

IN THE FLINTCOMBE COUNTY COURT

No. C.6817

Details of the marriage

(1) On the third day of April 1980 the petitioner BLANCHE CART was lawfully married to HARRY CART (hereinafter called 'the respondent') at St. Thomas' Church, Flintcombe in the County of Wessex.

Last joint cohabitation	(2) The petitioner and respondent last lived together at 37 Egdon Road, Flintcombe aforesaid.
Domicile, occupation and residence	(3) The petitioner is domiciled in England and Wales, and is by occupation a physiotherapist and resides at 37 Egdon Road, Flintcombe aforesaid and the respondent is by occupation a sales representative and resides at 12 the Downs, Darrowby in the County of Wessex.
Details of each child of the family	(4) There are no children of the family now living *except* ORSON CART who was born on 30th May 1984.
Other children	(5) No other child, now living, has been born to the petitioner.
Details of previous proceedings in England and Wales	(6) There are or have been no other proceedings in any court in England or Wales or elsewhere with reference to the marriage (or to any child of the family) or between the petitioner and respondent with reference to any property of either or both of them.
Details of proceedings abroad	(7) There are no proceedings continuing outside England or Wales which are in respect of the marriage or are capable of affecting its validity or subsistence.
Details of agreements made or proposed	(8) No agreement or arrangement has been made or is proposed to be made between the parties for the support of the petitioner (and any child of the family) *except* that the respondent pays to the petitioner the sum of £30 per week and it is proposed that this shall continue to be paid.

Irretrievable *breakdown*	(9) The said marriage has broken down irretrievably.
The fact *alleged*	(10) The respondent has committed adultery with TESSA CLARE (the co-respondent) and the petitioner finds it intolerable to live with the respondent.

(1) PARTICULARS

Brief particulars *of the facts* *relied on*	(a) On or about the fourth day of March 1991 at 12 The Downs aforesaid the respondent committed adultery with the co-respondent.
	(b) Subsequently the respondent has lived cohabited and frequently committed adultery with the co-respondent at that address.

PRAYER

Particulars of *the relief* *claimed*	The petitioner therefore prays:

(1) That the said marriage be dissolved.

(2) That the petitioner may be granted a residence order in respect of the said ORSON CART.

(3) That the respondent may be ordered to pay the costs of this suit.

(4) That the petitioner may be granted the following ancillary relief:

    (a) an order for maintenance pending suit;

        a periodical payments order;

        a secured provision order;

        a lump sum order;

    (b) a periodical payments order;   } for the

        a secured provision order;   } child of the

        a lump sum order;   } family.

(*c*) a property adjustment
order.

*Counsel's
signature
(Rule 11)*

Signed Herbert Getliffe

*Names and
addresses of
persons to be served*

The names and addresses of the persons to
be served with this petition are:
Respondent: Harry Cart
    12 The Downs, Darrowby, Wessex

Co-Respondent (adultery case only):
    Tessa Clare
    12 The Downs, Darrowby, Wessex

*Petitioner's
address for
service*

The petitioner's address for service is:
    37 Egdon Road.
    Flintcombe, Wessex.
Dated this sixth day of March 1991
Address all communications for the court
to:
The Registrar, County Court, Flintcombe.
The court office at D'Urberville Hall,
Flintcombe, Wessex is open from 10 a.m. to
4 p.m. (4.30 p.m. at the Divorce Registry)
on Mondays to Fridays.

The following are examples of other facts which may be relied
upon under s. 1(2) of the M.C.A. 1973, together with brief
particulars thereof:

(a) 'Unreasonable behaviour' (s. 1(2)(b))

*The fact
alleged*

The respondent has behaved in such a way
that the petitioner cannot reasonably be
expected to live with the respondent.

Particulars

(*a*) the respondent has frequently been
abusive towards the petitioner in front of
other people.
(*b*) Since January 1990 the respondent
has refused to have sexual intercourse with
the petitioner.

(*c*) Since that time the respondent has refused to give the petitioner any housekeeping allowance.

(b) Desertion (s. 1(2)(c))

The fact alleged	The respondent has deserted the petitioner without just cause for a period of at least two years immediately preceding the presentation of this petition.
Particulars	(*a*) On the first day of January 1989 the respondent left the matrimonial home and said that he never wanted to see the petitioner again. (*b*) Since that date the petitioner and respondent have lived separately and apart.

(c) Two years' separation and consent to a decree (s. 1(2)(d))

The fact alleged	The parties to the marriage have lived apart for a continuous period of at least two years immediately preceding the presentation of this petition and the respondent consents to a decree being granted.
Particulars	(*a*) On the first day of January 1989 the petitioner and respondent agreed to separate. (*b*) In pursuance of this agreement the respondent left the matrimonial home on the twenty-fifth day of January 1989. (*c*) Since that date the petitioner and respondent have lived separately and apart except that the said parties have lived together for one period not exceeding six months, namely from the third day of September 1989 until the second day of October 1989, of which no account should be taken. (*d*) The respondent by a letter dated the

twenty-fourth day of February 1990 has consented to the granting of a decree.

(d) Five years' separation

The fact
alleged

The parties to the marriage have lived apart for a continuous period of at least five years immediately preceding the presentation of this petition.

Particulars

(*a*) On the fourth day of February 1985 the petitioner left the matrimonial home.

(*b*) Since that date the petitioner and respondent have lived separately and apart.

Appendix 2
Examination technique

As a student of family law you will most probably already have some experience of law exams. Consequently, you will have built up a technique which you justifiably think works for your in view of your past exam successes. Although it is not the purpose of this commentary to get you to change a successful system, it may be that you can further improve it, and it is with this aim in mind that the following hints on examination technique are offered. You may also find it helpful to look at exams from the point of view of an examiner.

It is a trite, yet nonetheless true, observation that the only worthwhile preparation for an exam is that contained in that four-letter word, much detested by so many students, 'work'. If you have done sufficient work to a sufficient depth, so as to understand and be able to apply the law covered by this book, the substantive law of most family law exams may be approached with confidence. How you reach this stage is a matter for you, but practice on past examination papers at least as difficult as that to be sat is invaluable. It is for this reason that past examination questions are set out in Appendix 3.

It is quite natural to be nervous about an impending examination. In fact, a degree of nervousness is necessary in order to put you on your mettle and sharpen your wits. However, it is important not to get things out of perspective and you should always remember that the examiner is not out to trick you. He must set questions within the syllabus and a study of, say, papers from the last five years should cover most of the examinable topics. All that is left for the examiner is to find a different way of covering some of these topics. Remember also that, contrary to popular belief, the examiner is human and is merely trying to present a fair and balanced paper. By the same token he is likely to be exasperated by sloppy expression and poor presentation.

As regards the examination itself, there is no one method of answering an examination paper but the following advice may contain something which you may turn to your advantage.

1.   Familiarise yourself with the examination regulations. All the preparation in the world will be to no avail if you find yourself disqualified because, e.g. you took a dictionary into the examination hall.

2.   Read the paper thoroughly. This means that, as well as reading the questions set, you must read the rubric to the paper. This will tell you how many questions to answer (and there are probably few examiners who have not come across candidates who have answered too many questions), the time allowed (and answering too many questions will make a nonsense of this), and any special considerations which apply to the paper, e.g. that candidates should *assume* that a particular statute is operative.

Having thoroughly read the paper and decided upon a particular question, make sure you answer the question actually asked, not the one you would like to have been asked. Examiners give no credit for having their function usurped. In this context please bear in mind that if you are asked, for example, to advise a party how a marriage may be 'terminated', this covers not only the possibility of divorce but also that of nullity.

3.   In many family law examinations it is customary to provide candidates with copies of relevant statutes in the examination hall or allow them to provide their own copies. If this applies to your examination, you will be doing yourself a disservice, at least from the psychological point of view, if you fail to arm yourself with the permitted material. By allowing you to consult statutory material in the examination hall you are relieved from the tedium of having to memorise large chunks of Acts. However, this places the emphasis on the *application* of the Acts and this, in turn, requires familiarity with interpretative case-law. There will, therefore, be no credit given for merely reciting sections of the Acts you are allowed to consult. Examiners are bedevilled by students who not only copy out statutory material provided for them, but do it inaccurately.

4. Examination questions fall into two types: the problem question and the bookwork or essay-type of question. As a matter of examination tactics, if you find yourself in the happy position of being able to answer more than the required number of questions, it is better to attempt the problems, as marks tend to be given more generously for answers to these than for answers to the essay-type of question.

(a) *Problems.* It is essential to grasp the *IDEA* behind answering this type of question, i.e.
   *I*dentify the area(s) of law and point(s) involved;
   *D*efine your terms;
   *E*xplain your points — examiners are looking for your reasoning; and
   *A*pply the law to the facts, remembering always that facts are usually susceptible to more than one *reasonable* interpretation.

If you consistently adopt this kind of approach to answering problems, you will provide yourself with a method which should stand you in good stead.
   Students are often worried about whether they must come to a firm conclusion. Sometimes this is possible, e.g. it is possible, and necessary, to conclude that two men cannot contract a valid marriage. However, in the space available in an examination question it is unlikely that you will be in possession of all the facts necessary to enable you to come to a firm conclusion. In such a case you must take each possible interpretation to its legal conclusion, e.g. if a question on maintenance agreements merely states that 'H and W agreed ...' it will be necessary to consider what the position would be, first, if the agreement was in writing and, secondly, if it was oral. It may also be necessary to consider whether the written agreement was under seal.
(b) *Essay-type* questions. In this type of question students are asked to discuss the validity of a certain principle, or to explain it, or to criticise and suggest possible reforms to the law. Whatever form the question takes, DO NOT WAFFLE. Examiners can spot mere paper-filling waffle at a glance. Unless you can see what the

question is getting at and can provide a structured answer which gives the required answer, you should refrain from tackling this type of question.

5. Allocate your time so that you can answer the required number of questions in the allotted time, with a few minutes left over for reading through your answers. It is of the first importance that you attempt the required number of questions. The examiner can give you marks only if you give him something to go on, and it is relatively easy to score the first few of the available marks. Thus, if time is scarce, do not be afraid to answer in note form. This may gain you these few valuable marks which will make the difference between a fail and a pass.

6. If you cannot remember the name of a case or of a statute, you can always use the formula 'it has been held that . . . ' or 'statute provides that . . . '. Of course, if you can remember the name so much the better as it gives your script a more polished appearance.

The date of a case is seldom important. The date assumes importance if the case is, e.g. the first decision on a piece of legislation or the case is so old that changed conditions warrant a different approach.

Appendix 3
Specimen questions

The following questions are examples of the type of question that you may be faced with in your examination. They have been taken from past papers set by the University of London and Manchester Polytechnic and it is with those bodies' kind permission that they are reproduced here. The year that the question was set is shown as this will be crucial in relation to dates stated therein, e.g. as regards the bars to divorce or nullity petitions, periods of separation, and the operative date of particular legislation.

1. Adam and Belinda began living together in 1985. Belinda, who is of limited intellect, was informed by Adam that she could only be entitled to a share in his property if she married him. Just before they married in December 1986 Adam discovered that he had AIDS. He only told Belinda about his condition on their honeymoon after consummation had taken place. She was extremely shocked, and upon their return from the honeymoon, they agreed that, while they would occupy the same house, they would not sleep together. Belinda had a child, Caroline, by artificial insemination, the donor of the semen being Adam's brother, David. Adam was aware of the arrangement but did not signify his approval.

Adam and Belinda separated in January 1989. She intends to marry David and wants them both to adopt Caroline.

Advise Belinda:

(a) whether she can have her marriage to Adam terminated;
(b) whether she can obtain financial provision for Caroline from Adam;

(c) assuming that she marries David, what procedures must be followed if she and David want to adopt Caroline.

(University of London, 1989)

2. (a) 'Sex, not procreation, is essential to a valid marriage.' Discuss this statement in the context of nullity suits.
(b) H, a Pakistani domiciled in England, married W in polygamous form while on holiday in Pakistan in 1980. W tells you that she married H only because of intolerable pressure from her family and that after her marriage she had sexual intercourse with him only because he threatened to beat her if she refused. She seeks your advice on whether she may successfully petition for nullity. Advise her.

(Manchester Polytechnic, 1983)

3. Last year Henry and some friends were wrecked on a desert island. Whilst there, Wendy became pregnant and claimed that Henry was the child's father. Adam, a theological student, conducted a wedding ceremony on the island, at which Henry and Wendy agreed to marry each other. The next day they were all rescued.

On their arrival in England, Henry was taken to hospital with appendicitis. Recently Wendy had a child, Bertha, but Henry, who is now out of hospital, refuses to live with her or see Bertha, who he claims is not his. Henry wishes to marry Cora, whom he met in hospital.

Advise Henry on the following:

(a) The validity of his marriage to Wendy.
(b) The status of Bertha and how her paternity may be determined.
(c) Whether Wendy will be able to obtain maintenance from Henry in respect of herself and/or Bertha.

(University of London, 1984)

4. Six years ago after having been married for 10 years H and W, who are now both aged 40, agreed to enter a 'spouse swap' arrangement with their neighbours, Mr and Mrs C, whereby Mrs C would live with H in H and W's matrimonial home and W would

live with Mr C in his home. The couples at all times remained on amicable terms, often going out in the evening together until two months ago when W discovered that Mrs C is pregnant and that H is the child's father. Since this discovery W has become extremely jealous of the relationship between H and Mrs C and has been hostile to both H and Mrs C, culminating in an incident one week ago when H violently assaulted W when she called Mrs C 'an old slag'. H has been charged by the police with assault occasioning actual bodily harm.

Advise H and W as to whether they have grounds for a divorce.

(Manchester Polytechnic, 1990)

5. H and W were married in 1950, when H was 28 and W was 23. Their marriage was happy until, in 1972, H was dismissed by reason of redundancy and had to seek employment a hundred miles away. W refused to accompany him because she wished to continue nursing her invalid mother. H returned to W at weekends and for holidays. When W's mother died in 1974, W still refused to join H because she said that contemplating moving made her suffer from nervous depression and that she was too old to do so. Thereupon H visited W less frequently: he only spent an average of thirty days a year with her. He also began having an affair with his secretary, Lucinda, but still had sexual intercourse with W when he visited her. In 1978 H inherited £10,000 and gave it to Lucinda. H now wishes to divorce W and marry Lucinda, who is pregnant. He says that he knew in 1974 that his marriage to W was over and that he had only visited her out of pity. W has never worked and has no capital. The matrimonial home is in H's name and on retirement he would receive a good pension which could continue to be payable to his widow after his death.

(a) Advise H on what basis he might obtain a divorce against W.
(b) Advise W whether she had any grounds for defending divorce proceedings.
(c) Advise W on what basis a financial settlement would be made if a divorce were granted to H.

(University of London, 1979)

6. Jean and Bill were married in 1970. Jean is a teacher and Bill is an electrician. In 1972 Jean joined a militant feminist group. Since then Bill has been unable to have sexual intercourse with Jean owing to psychological difficulties over her changed views. In 1974 Jean was offered the post of headmistress of a school 40 miles from their home. Bill refused to move but Jean accepted the post and was given a school house. In 1978 Bill was electrocuted at work and is now almost completely disabled. Jean has looked after him in her home for 18 months in return for his sickness benefit as 'wages'. She now wishes to divorce Bill and make her home a refuge for battered wives.

Advise Bill,

(a) whether Jean has grounds for a divorce, and
(b) whether he can oppose the granting of a decree, because he knows that Jean will look after him if they are married but will put him into a home if they are divorced.

(Manchester Polytechnic, 1979)

7. Advise H whether he may petition successfully for divorce in the following unrelated circumstances.

(a) W, unknown to H, becomes pregnant as a result of artificial insemination by donor.
(b) W, as the result of a car accident, becomes comatose and is placed on a life-support machine. There is no prospect of recovery.
(c) In May 1989, W decides that her marriage to H is at an end. In May 1989, H reaches the same conclusion. In June 1989, W becomes mentally ill and has not since recovered.
(d) W, who has lived apart from H for five years, belongs to a religious sect which excommunicates its members who have been divorced.

(Manchester Polytechnic, 1990)

8. Claire and David who married in 1978 have two children, Edward and Fiona, aged 8 and 6 respectively. In 1980 David had purchased on a mortgage the matrimonial home, 'The Elms', in his own name. Claire is a staff nurse at the local hospital and frequently works late hours when David looks after the children. David is self-employed and works at home. In 1986 Claire and

David had a series of violent rows and decided that although their marriage is over they will stay together for the sake of the children. In May 1989 on returning home one morning after work, Claire hears the children crying. She found that Edward had bruises on his legs. David told her that the children had been fighting, and neither of the children would tell her what had happened.

Later that month, Claire's niece, Georgina, came to stay with them for a week. During that time, Claire found that Georgina had bruises on her arms. During a blazing row with David, Claire accused him of hurting Georgina, which David vehemently denied. In the course of the row David threatened to throw Claire and the children out of the house. Claire, being frightened for the children's safety, fled from the house and went to stay at a local women's refuge.

Advise Claire,

(a) how, if at all, the law would protect her if she wanted to return to 'The Elms', and

(b) what alternative possibilities of accommodation there are, in the event of her not being able to return to 'The Elms'.

(University of London, 1989)

9. Ted and Gemma were married nine months ago and because of a housing shortage they lived with Ted's parents. Three months ago Gemma gave birth to a son, Ben. Three weeks ago Ted, who works the night shift at a factory, arrived home to find Gemma having breakfast with his best friend; Ted's parents being away on holiday at the time.

Ted concluded that Gemma was having an affair and, despite her denials, he threw her out of the house. He told her not to return if she knew what was good for her and that he was not having his son brought up by a 'slut'. Gemma was afraid to argue because she knew that three years earlier Ted had been convicted of assaulting his girl friend.

Ted gave Gemma £150 for accommodation and she is living in a bed-sitting room. Two weeks ago Gemma met Ted and Ben in the street and, while trying to take Ben from Ted, she was struck by Ted.

Advise Gemma as to the relief she may obtain in a magistrates' court.

(Manchester Polytechnic, 1981)

10. Soon after H met and fell in love with W in 1975, he left Ethel with whom he had been living. H and Ethel had had an informal understanding that one day they might marry and H had given her a valuable necklace and ring which had belonged to his mother. When H left her, Ethel refused to return the jewellery to him. H and W were married in 1975. W had two sons by her first marriage. Charles, then aged 15, and Bernard, then aged 17. H bought a large house in his name to be a home for them all and in 1976 Bernard started a university course and Charles became an apprentice butcher. H and W became quarrelsome and decided to live apart. H agreed to pay W £15 per week maintenance for herself but refused to pay anything for the two boys. Since then H has been living in two rooms at one end of the house but his presence seriously upsets W and Charles.

(a) Advise Ethel whether she must return the jewellery H gave her.

(b) Advise W, who does *not* wish to divorce H:

    (*i*) Whether she can obtain a maintenance order against H in respect of Bernard and/or Charles and in which court to proceed;

    (*ii*) Whether she can force H to leave the matrimonial home.

(University of London, 1977)

11. When Ivan and Jane became engaged in 1980 they exchanged rings. Ivan presented Jane with a ring worn by his late grandmother during her fifty year marriage; Jane gave Ivan a gold signet ring that she had bought for him. Ivan purchased a small bungalow in his name. He paid the deposit, and the mortgage instalments were paid from his earnings as a merchant banker. Jane rewired the house and repaired the roof.

They married in June 1983 shortly after Jane had become pregnant. She gave up her career and was paid an allowance by Ivan which was used to pay for food, clothes and to pay off the fuel bills. Jane was able to save enough from the allowance to buy a second-hand car and a number of expensive dresses and coats. She gave birth to Karen in February 1984.

In January 1988 Jane confessed to Ivan that he was not Karen's father and that the plumber, Len, was the true father. Ivan immediately left her.

Jane does not want a divorce and hopes that she and Ivan may eventually become reconciled.

Advise Jane who wishes to know:

(a) who is entitled to the rings they exchanged at the time of their engagement;

(b) whether she had a property interest in the bungalow purchased by Ivan;

(c) whether the car, dresses and coats bought from savings made from her allowance belong to her; and

(d) how, if at all, she can obtain financial support for herself and Karen.

(University of London, 1988)

12. After his divorce from W in 1986 H was ordered to make periodical payments of £3,000 per annum to W and £1,500 per annum to each of the parties' children, Alan and Barry, then aged 10 and 7 respectively. The former matrimonial home, which is jointly owned and has been occupied by W and the children since the divorce, was ordered to be sold and the net proceeds of sale divided equally between W and H when Barry, the youngest child reaches 18. At the time of the divorce, W was earning £4,000 per annum in part-time employment.

In 1987 H was made redundant and did not manage to find another job until April of this year. Following H's redundancy, W was forced to work part-time after H applied successfully for a reduction in his maintenance payments for the children to £800 per annum for each child and his maintenance for W became nominal.

In December 1989 H, aged 53, married J, an extremely wealthy widow, and went to live in her house. H is now earning £24,000 per year. W earns £8,000 and she has applied to have the 1987 order varied so as to require H to make substantial periodical payments to her and to have his maintenance for the children increased. W is now aged 50 and has recently had the former matrimonial home valued at £120,000 subject to an £11,000 mortgage.

Advise,

(a) W who, in addition to her application for maintenance to be increased, wished the former matrimonial home to be transferred into her name alone; and

(b) H who wishes to terminate his financial obligations towards W.

(Manchester Polytechnic, 1990)

13. H left his wife W three months ago after 23 years of marriage and is now living with his mistress, Sarah. W is now 55 years old and has never been in paid employment during the marriage. She has no property apart from a legacy of £2,000 inherited from her mother. The home, in which W is living, is owned by H and is worth £20,000. H also owns a country cottage worth £9,000. W lent H £1,000 for the purchase of this cottage and he has repaid £200 of this. H earns £10,000 per year. The two children of the marriage are now adults, but one, Charles, aged 21, is partially disabled and only works part-time. He lives with his mother and the house has been adapted so that he can get around easily in his wheelchair.

H proposes to sell both the house and the country cottage so that he can acquire a new home for himself and Sarah. He considers that the house is far too big for his wife and that he has no obligation to support Charles in any way. Although he has promised to pay W £60 per month and all major bills connected with the home, he has only paid one months' maintenance and a rate bill of £150 is still outstanding. W wants (*a*) to prevent the immediate sale of the two homes, (*b*) to know whether the court is likely to allow her to remain in the home, and (*c*) to know what financial arrangements would be made for her if there were to be a divorce.

Advise W.

(University of London, 1976)

14. 'The settlement of cohabitants' disputes by existing legal principles of contract and trust is fair and workable. The creation of special laws for cohabitants or the extension of marital laws to them retards the emancipation of women, degrades the relationship and is too expensive for society in general and men in particular.' (Deech). Do you agree?

(University of London, 1985)

15. 'Parental rights to control a child do not exist for the benefit of the parent. They exist for the benefit of the child and they are justified only in so far as they enable the parent to perform his duties towards the child'. (Lord Fraser of Tullybelton, *Gillick* v. *West Norfolk A.H.A.* (1976)

What impact, if any, has the Gillick decision had on the law relating to parental rights and duties?

(University of London, 1987)

16. (a) In 1976 Maria, who had become pregnant by Steve, married John who had obtained a decree nisi of divorce from his wife. Shortly afterwards Maria gave birth to Sandra whom John rejected because she reminded him of Steve. In 1977 Maria was pregnant by John as a result of which she gave birth to Celia. Just before Celia's birth John went to live in Scotland but he has frequently sent money for Celia. Maria has now learnt that John has returned to live in England.

Advise Maria whether:
 (*i*) she is free to marry David;
 (*ii*) she can claim maintenance for Sandra and Celia and, if so, from whom; and
 (*iii*) whether Steve and John have any rights as regards Sandra and Celia.

(b) Jane divorced Stuart after he was sentenced to life imprisonment for murder. She remarried Dick and they now wish to adopt her three year old son by Stuart.

What matters will the court take into account when deciding on their application?

(Manchester Polytechnic, 1979)

17. Nine years ago Harry, then aged 13, and Wendy, aged 14 had a brief but passionate love affair, conducted mainly in the school cricket pavilion. Wendy became pregnant and gave birth to

Charlie, now aged 8. Harry went to see Wendy when Charlie was born but thereafter had little to do with mother or child. However, Harry's mother, Mrs Boot, has often looked after Charlie and has established a close relationship with him.

Wendy married Alex, a cricket commentator, 4 months ago and Alex now wishes to adopt Charlie and cut off all contact with Harry's family. Harry, now a successful professional footballer, has recently learned that, owing to a soccer injury, he will never again father any children and has therefore decided to apply for a residence order in his favour in respect of Charlie. Wendy, who is horrified at Harry's intentions, now claims that, owing to his age at the time her child was conceived, Harry could not have been Charlie's father. She has also said that she will never allow Harry to see Charlie again. Mrs Boot, Harry's mother, is very upset and wishes to know if there is any way in which she can legally protect her relationship with her grandson.

Discuss the legal position of Wendy, Harry, Alex and Mrs Boot and consider what action they might take.

(Manchester Polytechnic, 1991)

18. Susan and Richard cohabited for three years until Richard left 18 months ago. There is one child of the relationship, Alice, aged four. The separation resulted in Susan suffering a nervous breakdown. Soon after this Alice was received into care under the Child Care Act 1980, s. 2, where she has remained for the last 16 months. During this time she has been fostered by Mr and Mrs Davies. Six months ago, while in an acutely depressed state, Susan consented to the local authority assuming parental rights in respect of Alice in return for a verbal assurance that she would be allowed regular visits to the child. Recently another social worker has taken charge of Alice's case and decided that visits from Susan are not in the child's interests. Access has consequently been stopped. Mr and Mrs Davies now wish to adopt Alice and the social worker appears to be in favour of this. Richard is now married and living in a large house with his wife. He considers that Alice's future would be best secured by living with him.

Consider:

(a) the steps Susan may take to have Alice returned to her;

(b) the likely outcome of an adoption application by Mr and Mrs Davies and the factors the court would take into account; and
(c) how Richard may attempt to gain custody of Alice and the likely outcome of his application.

(Manchester Polytechnic, 1983)

19. Alice is a 7 year old child, the daughter of Diane and Geoffrey Roberts. Two years ago Diane and Geoffrey were divorced and a residence order was made in Diane's favour in respect of Alice. Geoffrey has a contact order in his favour and sees Alice at least once a week.

For the past 18 months Diane has co-habited with Peter and they have a son, Mark, aged 12 months. Geoffrey has remarried and he and his wife have a 3 month old child.

Consider the legal implications arising from the following facts, answering each stage in sequence without taking into account facts which are revealed in the following stage.

(a) The local authority social services department receives a report from a school that Alice is absent and that Alice's 7 year old friend has informed the class teacher that yesterday Alice showed this child bruises on her arm, saying that 'Peter did it'. When two social workers visit Diane's house later that day Diane refuses to let them in, saying that Alice is staying with relatives. She refuses to inform the social worker where the relatives live.
(b) When the social workers return to Diane's house three hours later Diane's attitude has changed and she allows them in. Alice is seen and found to have bruises to her arms and back: Mark appears to be unharmed. Diane informs the social workers that Peter injured Alice and the child confirms Diane's story. Diane accompanies the children and a social worker to hospital: the paediatrician confirms the non-accidental injuries to Alice but finds no other injuries to either child and says that they can return home. Despite the fact that Peter's whereabouts are unknown and he might return to the family home at any time, Diane refuses the social workers' offer of accommodation in a refuge.
(c) Geoffrey has discovered that Alice has been injured. He is now

determined that Alice should come to live with him on a permanent basis.

20. In 1984 Felicity and Eric Harris were divorced, on Eric's petition based upon his wife's adultery. There are two children of the family, twin girls now aged eight. Following a bitter dispute between the parents over the children's futures, residence orders in respect of the twins were made in favour of Felicity with weekly contact for Eric on Saturdays between 10.00 a.m. and 6.00 p.m. and certain periods during the children's school holidays when they stay with Eric.

Two years ago Felicity married the co-respondent in Eric's divorce petition and Felicity has now informed Eric that she intends accompanying her husband to New Zealand where this man is due to start a new job in two months' time. She also informs Eric that it would be better for the children to be adopted by her husband so as to formalise his legal relationship with the children prior to their emigration.

Following an argument between Felicity and Eric over Felicity's proposals Felicity has refused Eric access to his children.

Advise Eric:

(a) What redress he has in respect of Felicity's refusal to see his children;

(b) If Felicity and her husband were to apply to adopt the children how a court would approach Eric's refusal to consent to his children's adoption;

(c) The remedies available to him should Felicity and her husband simply move to New Zealand without Eric's consent or a court's approval.

Index